This book must be renewed or returned
by the latest date shown below. If not, a
fine of 5p a day will be charged.

**Two week
loan**

The book may be called for another
reader after one week, and it must then
be returned to the library at once.

Please return on or before the last
date stamped below.
Charges are made for late return.

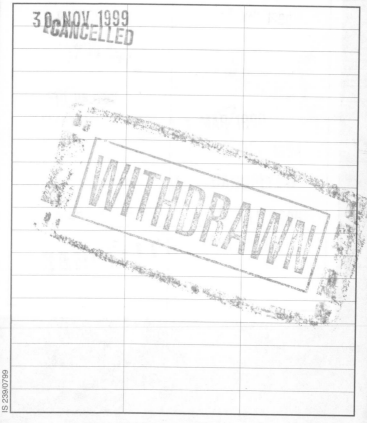

IS 239/0799

INFORMATION SERVICES PO BOX 430, CARDIFF CF10 3XT

Regional Growth Theory

By the same author

ECONOMIC RECOVERY IN BRITAIN, 1932–39

REGIONAL ECONOMICS: LOCATION THEORY, URBAN STRUCTURE
  AND REGIONAL CHANGE

ELEMENTS OF REGIONAL ECONOMICS

URBAN ECONOMICS

INPUT–OUTPUT AND REGIONAL ECONOMICS

BUILDING IN THE BRITISH ECONOMY BETWEEN THE WARS
  (with D. H. Aldcroft)

THE BRITISH ECONOMY, 1870–1939 (with D. H. Aldcroft)

REGIONAL ECONOMICS: A READER (editor)

Regional Growth Theory

Harry W. Richardson

Director, Centre for Research in the Social Sciences
University of Kent, Canterbury

MACMILLAN

First published 1973 by
THE MACMILLAN PRESS LTD
London and Basingstoke
Associated companies in New York Dublin
Melbourne Johannesburg and Madras

SBN 333 14427 9 $\quad$ 15-2-84

Printed in Great Britain by
WESTERN PRINTING SERVICES LTD
Bristol

TO
PAUL, CLARE AND MATTHEW

Contents

Preface

This book contains my ideas on the nature of the regional growth process. It may be puzzling to readers of my 1969 text *Regional Economics* to find so little similarity between the content of this volume and Chapter 13 of that book (there is some overlap with Chapter 2 of this book but the views expressed are very divergent). In comparing the two, it must be remembered that the first draft of the earlier book was written in 1966–7 while the first draft of this volume was not begun until late 1971. My earlier text merely synthesised existing theories of regional growth, and was only mildly critical of the neoclassical models. Yet in my introduction to that text I had already recognised the inconsistencies between the assumptions of neo-classicism and a spatially based regional economics. These views have been reinforced over time and as my understanding of and 'feel' for the subject has increased. The aim of this book is to argue the case for a theoretical approach to regional growth that incorporates space both between and within regions. The theory developed places emphasis on spatial agglomeration economies and locational preferences as opposed to the tradi-tional neoclassical variables of wage and capital yield differen-tials. Also, it is shown that it is essential to take account of urbanisation and the urban structure in regional development and to analyse how the spatial structure influences resource mobility.

Although the book is primarily theoretical, it is not solely concerned with abstract theory. The objective has been throughout to attempt to shed light on the regional growth process in the real world. This has required, *inter alia*, an explanation of the phenomena of concentration and agglomera-tion (and their force relative to dispersion) in the space eco-nomy, and recognition that a satisfactory theory must explain unbalanced growth in the inter-regional system and the spatial unevenness of development within each region. In my view, the doctrine of balanced regional growth both within and between regions does not make good economic sense, though it is easy enough to formulate abstract models that yield predictions of this kind. Another underlying aim of the book is to make regional growth theory more relevant to regional policy-makers, and I discuss the policy implications of the theory at some length.

The book has a serious limitation which I should admit at the outset. Although most chapters contain some reference to empirical work, I do not take the final step of testing my own theory, though I devote considerable efforts into structuring the model in a testable form and discuss the problems of empirical verification. The reasons for adopting this course are fully explained in Chapter 8, but the main reason is that the range and quality of data are at present insufficient to permit an adequate test. I have no doubts at all about the need for empirical testing of any economic theory and I hold an unshakeable prejudice in favour of operational models.

To minimise footnotes, I have referred to authors in the text by name and year of publication. The detailed sources are given in the reference list at the end of the book.

I am very grateful to: Professor O. J. Firestone and the University of Ottawa for permission to use material in Chapters 2 and 8 from a paper I presented at a conference on Regional Development in Ottawa in March 1972 and published in O. J. Firestone (ed.), *Regional Development* (Ottawa U.P., 1973); the Editors of the *Journal of Regional Science* for permission to use material from my article published in April 1973 in Chapter 6; the United Nations for the extracts from 'The Concept of Polarised Development in Regional Planning – A Sociological Interpretation' by T. S. Di Tella and 'Growth Pole Hypothesis Re-examined' by R. P. Misra from *A Review of the Concepts and Theories of Growth Poles and Growth Centres* by T. Hermansen *et al.*; and Wesleyan University Press for use of the extract from *Capital Exports and Growth among U.S. Regions* by J. T. Romans. Finally, I am pleased to acknowledge my debt to Mrs Sandy Sharples for typing my drafts.

HARRY W. RICHARDSON

August 1972

Chapter 1

Introduction

THE PROBLEM OF REGIONAL GROWTH

The growth of nations is a problem that has attracted and perplexed economists over a long period of time, certainly from the days of Adam Smith at the latest. Important contributions were made by Marx in the last century and by Schumpeter in this, while the beginnings of abstract and formal analysis owe much to Harrod's work just before World War II. The avalanche of research came much later, however, falling between the mid-1950s and the mid-1960s. The evolution of the analysis of regional growth has been telescoped into a much shorter period. There was no concern with regional problems until the late 1920s and 1930s, and even then these interests were rather peripheral to the question of regional growth. This early relevant work was on several lines: export base analysis mainly by urban planners; Ohlin's work on interregional trade theory (1933), a study in comparative statics; the analysis of urban-regional relationships by Christaller (1933) and somewhat later by Lösch (1943); and the emergence of pragmatic policy interests in the problems of lagging regions between the late twenties and the mid-thirties as a short-run response to localised heavy unemployment. However, all these themes are disconnected, and there was little direct analysis of regional growth *per se* until the late 1950s.[1] Myrdal's 'cumulative causation' theory (1957), though loosely formulated, has had a pervasive influence on subsequent developments in regional growth theory. Two massive descriptive-analytical volumes on the process of inter-regional growth in the United States were published in 1960 (Perloff, Dunn, Lampard and Muth; Kuznets,

---

[1] Some mention should be made of North's paper (1955) which transformed the much earlier development of the export base concept into a theory of long-term regional growth.

Miller and Easterlin), which provided detailed empirical evidence of convergence tendencies in regional *per capita* incomes. The most dramatic development, however, was the paper by Borts (1960) and the later book by Borts and Stein (1964). This work was significant in two respects: first, they offered a theoretical framework for analysis of the convergence hypothesis that had received empirical support in the books mentioned above; second, they took one of the key strands of aggregate growth theory (neoclassical models) and translated it into a regional growth context.

This bringing together of aggregate (i.e. national) and regional growth theory has had extensive reverberations on the development of the latter in the last decade. It began a habit of borrowing from the literature of growth theory in general rather than working out an independent approach to the specific theoretical problems raised by the regional growth process. In particular, it meant that regional growth economists (at least before Friedmann, 1966) turned their backs on those branches of regional economics that dealt with space, distance, location and urban structure. Although this approach brought new insights to bear upon the problems of regional growth and led to some interesting analysis and results, it nevertheless implied a rejection of the traditional areas of regional economics such as location theory. By treating a region as a mini-nation, by analysing inter-regional factors in a very simplistic fashion, and by introducing abstract assumptions (such as perfect competition, Cobb–Douglas production functions, and constant returns to scale) that in exploring the workings of the space economy mislead rather than clarify, reliance on neoclassicism was detrimental to progress in regional economics. An unwelcome by-product of this line of thinking, though happily not as prevalent as in the growth economics of the national economy, has been a widening rift between theory and policy. This consequence is somewhat paradoxical in view of the fact that a strong policy orientation has been perhaps the greatest spur to research in regional economics.

The evidence on the automatic equilibrating tendencies of inter-regional system growth is very mixed. The experience of developed countries (and this is the focus of the analysis in this book) varies widely both between countries and over time. It is possible for supporters of the cumulative causation thesis, for instance, to match each example of convergence referred to by the neoclassicists with a case of divergence. Moreover, the number of cases of convergence has been increased in recent decades by examples drawn from countries where either explicit regional policies or compensatory fiscal measures (i.e. the inter-regional effects of automatic stabilisers) were in operation. Even so, despite intervention in most advanced economies the economic problems of lagging regions have persisted. Areas suffering from low incomes, high unemployment and sluggish activity rates, a poor growth and productivity performance and high out-migration rates continue to create difficulties for governments committed to full employment, equal opportunities for all citizens and other worthwhile social goals. It is true, of course, that in descending from the national to the regional level we must expect to find a range of regional values for economic indicators around the national mean. There must always be some regions that are above average and others that are below average. The course of trouble, however, has been twofold: first, that the coefficient of variation has in many countries been unacceptably high, with *per capita* income gaps between the poorest and richest region much too wide for social cohesion and stability; second, that the areas at the bottom of the league have remained the same, and at least in the bottom half of regional growth tables rankings have scarcely altered at all over decades.

For these reasons, the need for a regional policy has remained and indeed grown. However, policymakers have been unclear about their objectives, the effectiveness of their instruments, and have only rarely attempted to evaluate the success of their measures. In the United Kingdom, for instance, where experience with regional policy stretches back for forty years, policy evolved prior to any interest in regional economic theory and even today there is very little contact between the policymakers and the theorists. This raises the question of how necessary an understanding of the theoretical framework of regional economics is in order to deal with the problems of lagging areas in a constructive manner. In most cases regional policymakers have given little thought to such a theoretical framework; in the rare circumstances when regional economic analysis has been referred to, the concepts and models used have been static in character (e.g. regional multipliers).

If asked, regional policymakers would no doubt explain their pragmatism on the grounds that both objectives and policy prescriptions are self-evident, and need no theoretical under-pinning. The main aim of regional policy in most mature Western countries is to persuade establishments in the private sector to set up plants or relocate in the lagging regions of the economy rather than in the prosperous areas. To the extent that this aim can be achieved, unemployment and out-migra-tion are reduced and incomes are raised in the depressed areas, while a more equitable balance between labour supply and demand is attained in the various geographical parts of the economy. Since it is recognised that location in these areas is unlikely to be the first choice of firms, various types of induce-ments – usually investment subsidies but occasionally social infrastructure and/or payroll subsidies – are offered. As there are usually severe fiscal constraints on the amount of subsidies that governments can afford to offer, the critical question of how to determine the 'optimal' subsidy never arises. This set of key measures may occasionally be supplemented by other policies – subsidies to migrants to leave depressed regions, rural development measures or a strategy for the spatial concentra-tion of public investment. Though these latter options raise questions of theoretical significance, the inducements to in-dustry approach needs little by way of analytical justification. Thus, so the argument runs, it is unnecessary to give much attention to the underlying nature of the regional growth process.

This type of reasoning is clearly invalid. Our areas of ig-norance are great not only in relation to the causes of regional growth differentials but also as to how policy measures operate. For example, investment incentives are frequently ineffective in persuading firms to locate in backward areas, and this suggests that location decisions are based on criteria other than profitability and costs. To the extent that the macro-economic growth rates of regions reflect the influence of thousands of micro-locational decisions, understanding how location decisions are reached is essential to explanations of regional growth.

Similarly, this understanding is also necessary in order to devise more effective policy measures. Policy is, in effect, one of the major links between the actions of the individual decision takers and their net impact on inter-regional growth differentials that are the very objects of policy. As far as location theory is concerned, evidence is mounting that such factors as access to metropolitan living, social amenities, environmental preferences, and economies of urban agglomeration are important determinants of location, probably more important than rates of return to capital, transport cost advantages, cheap labour costs and the other key elements in traditional location theory. If these arguments have substance the appropriate policy implication is not monetary subsidies but more interventionist planning to influence the spatial distribution of resources, population and economic activities within regions, particularly the intra-regional urban pattern. This further implies that regional economic policy and physical planning are not independent but are intimately inter-connected.

Furthermore, if regional policy-makers are concerned with these broader issues it is no longer possible for them to continue closing their eyes to the nature of the regional growth process. Yet so many of the key questions cannot be answered with the aid of spaceless neoclassical models and other theories borrowed and adapted from economic analysis at the national level. Such questions include: what size of urban agglomeration is necessary to attract outside industry on any scale? what spatial distribution of population within a region is efficient? is distance between regions a relevant factor in explaining regional growth differentials? how important are agglomeration economies as a determinant of regional growth? are the disadvantages of lagging regions remediable, particularly by appropriate injections of public investment? how does the spatial structure of the national economy influence inter-regional factor mobility and diffusion of innovation and hence the dispersion of regional growth? how important are non-economic influences on regional growth rates such as locational preferences, community attitudes and political constraints? what is the role of urbanisation in regional development? These are just a few of the questions that crop up when the spatial dimension is introduced as a relevant element in regional growth. The prime objective of this book is to develop and amplify a spatial theory of regional growth that sheds light on the mysteries of the regional growth process, is operational and, above all, is helpful to regional policymakers in both policy design and evaluation. Since the objectives of regional policy relate, or should relate, to the very long run, it is crucially important that policymakers should improve their understanding of long-term regional development. This very practical reason is probably the strongest justification of all for a work in regional growth theory.

DEFINING REGIONS

A relevant question, though the experienced regional economist knows better than to raise it, is: what is the unit to which the theory of regional growth applies? In other words, how do we define a region? Many hundreds of thousands of words have been written on this topic without coming to a fully satisfactory answer. The only safe statements are: there is no unique definition; we may wish to define a region in different ways as the objectives of inquiry vary; in regional economics a region is understood to be a sub-national areal unit (in international economics, on the other hand, a region might refer to a group of nations) and we frequently define an inter-regional system as the sub-division of the national economy into a limited number (say six to fifteen) of fairly large and contiguous regions. As for methods of delimiting the boundaries of a region, most of them can be grouped under three categories: homogeneity, nodality and programming. According to homogeneity criteria, areas adhere together to form a region if they are considered homogeneous in respect to some key element. This could be economic (e.g. similar *per capita* income levels, a major dominant industry common to all the sub-areas, a relatively uniform unemployment situation) or social and political (delimitation according to regional identity, areas treated together historically, etc.). An implication of homogeneous regions is that their relationship to other parts of the economy counts for more than their internal differences. Consequently, an appropriate methodological approach for the economist dealing with homogeneous regions is to treat them as non-spatial and to handle them within a framework of inter-regional macro-economics. Most current theories of regional growth fall into this category.

The nodal concepts of regions emphasise intra-regional spatial differentiation. They recognise that population and economic activities will not be scattered punctiformly over a region but will be concentrated in or around specific foci of activity, i.e. cities and towns. The urban centres of the region will be inter-dependent, and the degree of inter-dependence can be measured by reference to flows of people, factors, goods and services, or communications. The criterion for including a small area within one region rather than another is based upon whether this area has stronger links of inter-dependence with larger centres within the region than with other large centres outside. Each region will have one or more metropolitan cities, or dominant nodes, and the 'principle of dominance' can be used to establish whether specific peripheral areas fall within the boundary of this region or within another. A special case of the use of this concept is the *functional economic area* (F.E.A.) developed by Karl A. Fox (e.g. see Fox and Kumar, 1965). Although the F.E.A. concept draws upon all kinds of criteria with which to delimit regions, the most universal of these criteria is to define the F.E.A. in terms of a central city (labour market) surrounded by a wider area, the boundaries of which are defined by the outer limits of commuting to work in the central city; this is clearly a nodality approach. It is sometimes argued that a system of F.E.A.s makes the most sensible division of the national economy into an inter-regional system, but this raises many practical problems such as the need to redefine political boundaries (i.e. a need for city-region authorities) and the demand for reorganising the sub-national data base. If a nodal approach is decided upon, there are several techniques and principles available (e.g. graph theory, transitivity) to delimit regions in the space economy.

The third major approach is to define regions in terms of administrative and political areas, where the political delimitation is supposed to give a unity to the area in terms of policy instruments, uniform tax rates, and so on. Such a region is called a programming or planning region. The advantage of this approach is that the analyst can work with available data that conforms to administrative boundaries and can more easily evaluate the effects of any policy instrument that is implemented at the regional level. The disadvantage may be that the administrative boundaries may be inconsistent with regional boundaries derived from economic criteria, and if this is the case policy decisions for the region may be abortive or ineffective. A solution is to attempt to bring about administrative boundary changes and reforms in the political spatial structure that result in closer conformity to meaningful economic regions (e.g. nodal regions or F.E.A.s), but the feasibility of this is in considerable doubt.

It is apparent from this brief discussion that the regional economist must be realistic rather than idealistic, particularly from the point of view of empirical research. It is possible that a system of planning regions based on nodality criteria would provide the most satisfactory framework for analysis, but often he may have to work with existing administrative regions regardless of whether they satisfy economic criteria or not. Another possibility is that the set of regions with which the analyst is concerned may vary according to the objectives of the inquiry; for some problems division of the national economy into less than ten broad regions may be justified, for others a system of 250–300 F.E.A.s may be called for. In terms of regional theory, the latter could be examined in terms of metropolitan rather than regional models. Most existing regional growth theory presupposes the more limited set of broad regions. As far as the positive contribution of this work is concerned, however, it may be possible to avoid the regional delimitation dilemma altogether. This is because our ultimate aim is the development of a theory of spatial growth where, at different levels of disaggregation, the growth process is characterised by agglomeration or some form of dispersion. An underlying hypothesis is that, after a phase of initial concentration associated with the beginnings of the industrialisation process itself, sustained national economic growth is associated with dispersion into different areas of the economy. But this takes the form of spatial concentration within these areas in urban centres, and at a later stage of development associated with transportation improvements and higher income levels metropolitan growth is accompanied by decentralisation. The 'region' as opposed to the 'metropolitan area' may then define itself in the sense that regional boundaries are found, even if they cannot be precisely drawn, in the no-man's land at the spatial limits of the geographical spread of agglomerating forces internal to contiguous regions.

THE DIFFERENCE BETWEEN A REGION AND A NATION

As the preceding discussion on the delimitation of regions suggests, there is no clear-cut and unequivocal approach to the problem of how to define regions. Moreover, since in the context of the international economy we can speak of regions as referring to blocs of contiguous national economies, the question does arise as to whether there is anything distinctive about sub-national as opposed to national and supra-national units. In other words, in the overall hierarchy of spatial units (global, supra-national, national, regional, metropolitan, local) is there any analytical justification for the view that there is a natural break in the hierarchy below the level of the national economy? And, even if this is the case, does it imply that a different type of economic theory is needed for analysing the regional and metropolitan levels from that employed in aggregate growth and international economics?

Answers to this question are made more difficult by the confusion surrounding attempts to define regions. Nevertheless, there are distinctions between regions (sub-national) and nations – some of which are merely matters of degree, though others are matters of kind – and these have serious implications for the type of economic analysis, and in particular for the type of growth theory, required. A first distinction is that a region is much more 'open' than a nation in the sense that a higher proportion of total commodity and factor flows are imported and exported from a region than in the national economy case. Although this is a distinction of degree – the ratio of external to total flows tends to be inversely related to the spatial area and/or the population size of the unit in question, there is nevertheless a sharp break in the value of this ratio when we move from the regional to the national level. This is no doubt connected with the second distinction (this time a distinction of kind), the fact that crossing national borders involves overcoming barriers (customs duties, quotas, import and export licences, immigration controls, exchange controls on monetary and capital flows, differences in currencies, etc.) that do not arise when crossing regional borders. Numerous consequences follow from this. For instance, commuting flows for work are quite common across regional boundaries but rarely occur between nations. Also, market and supply areas with relatively narrow spatial extensions (i.e. excluding cases such as where the relevant supply or market area might be a continent or the whole world) frequently overlap the regional but, again, not national boundaries. Money flows freely from one region to another since the currency used is the same, and most capital transfers, at least in the private sector, go unnoticed; there is not the same freedom of movement for international money and capital flows.

The absence of barriers not only means that inter-regional flows are much heavier but also that many of them go unrecorded. The sparsity of information about inter-regional flows[1] has the important effect that it makes the task of counteracting 'undesirable' movements between regions much more difficult. Thus, it is doubtful whether the concepts of, say, *regional balance of trade* or *regional balance of payments* have any significance. Certainly, despite the fact that regional economists have occasionally written about such concepts, they cannot figure as policy objectives. One inference is that flows between regions have a much greater tendency to be cumulative whereas in an international context it is likely that cumulative flows will be offset by counteracting policy instruments. This applies equally to commodity flows (e.g. spending leakages to pay for imports) and factor flows (continuous immigration). The general conclusion is that growth in a region is much more likely to be a disequilibrating process than in the national economy.[2]

[1] Of course, the extent of information available depends in part upon the political structure of the inter-regional system. In particular, more published information about inter-regional transactions is typically provided in a federal system than in a unitary system. The unfavourable data position in the United Kingdom relative to the United States or Canada is a case in point.

[2] For examples of formal theories that predict or simulate these disequilibrating tendencies see below, pp. 29–34 and pp. 162–71.

A further distinction on similar lines is that regional policy-makers (even within a federal system) do not have the policy instruments that are available to national governments. These include not only the obvious tariffs, immigration controls and exchange controls that primarily influence the balance of payments but also many types of internal measure such as monetary instruments, changes in central government tax rates and levels of expenditure, anti-monopoly controls and policies for industrial reorganisation, and many types of infrastructure investment (the division of responsibility between national, regional and urban governments varies from one society to another). Not only does the range of policy instruments narrow when we descend from the national to the regional level, but the dominant policy objectives change. Controlling inflation, for instance, is not an important regional policy goal because demand changes so easily spill over regional boundaries and because most cost pressures are nationwide. Similarly, stabilisation objectives cannot be handled satisfactorily at the regional level because of the magnitude of uncontrollable external flows. The main preoccupation of regional policy-makers is usually with attaining a satisfactory long-term rate of regional growth and with bringing about an acceptably efficient but equitable spatial distribution of economic activity. Some of the subordinate objectives that may arise out of pursuit of such goals, such as minimising out-migration, may indeed conflict with national goals.

Since part of our argument is that borrowing from traditional economic theory in general and aggregate growth theory in particular is a source of trouble for analysis of regional growth, an important question is what is the burden of these differences between regions and nations for regional economic analysis? The most immediate observation is that we cannot afford to treat a region as a closed system, a procedure which is often acceptable if not precisely accurate at the national level. If regions are open systems, there is a much greater need for specification of the key exogenous variables influencing regional economic activity, to give much closer attention to disequilibrating processes as opposed to determining what constitutes an equilibrium, and to take account of the greater uncertainty and much cruder predictions of regional economic models. Secondly, despite the smaller armoury of policy instruments available to regional policymakers there is a much closer link between economic growth and public policy at the regional than at the national level. Whereas it is widely accepted that it is very difficult, if not impossible, to raise the rate of growth of the national economy, this is clearly not the case for regional economies. The upper and lower ranges of growth rates are much wider for regional than for national economies, and given certain favourable background conditions, the will to implement firm policies, and scope for regional policy expenditures it is quite feasible to raise a region's rate of growth by, perhaps, two or three percentage points.

The most striking distinction between regional economic analysis and the economic theories used to diagnose and prescribe for the national economy is that the former frequently gives considerable attention to the spatial dimension, the latter hardly ever. One reason why it may be crucial to incorporate space and distance in the economic analysis of regions is that such analysis may be improved by defining these regions in functional terms or as 'natural' economic areas. This inevitably implies defining regions in spatial terms. For the national economy, there is no need to refer to space explicitly for definitional purposes since the political boundaries defined by the limits of national sovereignty are the sole relevant boundaries.

Another, perhaps the more important, reason for a spatial content in regional economic theory is that the spatial distribution of economic activity affects overall efficiency. However, if this is the case why does it not apply at the national level? The short answer is that it does, but economic analysis has neglected the fact. The absence of the spatial dimension in aggregate growth theory cannot be used as an argument for ignoring space in regional growth theory; rather, the need for space in regional economics provides a strong case for injecting a spatial content into the economic theories used to analyse the performance of the national economy. There are few branches of economic analysis and policy that would not benefit from explicitly recognising space – growth, control of inflation, fiscal policy, evaluation of public investment projects, labour and industrial policy, and the effectiveness of monetary measures among others. That all economic activity has a locational context, that is, takes place at a point (or more likely over an area) in space as well as at a moment (or more usually an interval) of time, has been neglected too long in the mainstream of economics. Thus, the inclusion of space, distance and location as central characteristics of regional economic analysis is not so much an indication that this is a peripheral and outlandish field as a reminder of the too limited perspective and narrow focus of the economics discipline at large.

Chapter 2

The Current State of Regional Growth Theory

INTRODUCTION

The state of the art of regional growth theorising is very primitive. This partly reflects the limited time and effort put into it compared with the vast literature on growth theory in general. However, it also reflects a need to keep models of regional development fairly simple in order to bridge the gap between theory and empirical testing as quickly as possible (this is an urgency apparently not shared by national growth theorists). The pressure for operationality is largely dictated by the strong policy orientation of regional economics. In some cases the demands of policy have had an unfavourable effect by precipitating the use of ill-prepared and unsatisfactory models, but on the whole the pressures of policy requirements have had a favourable effect.

One of the key points of this chapter[1] is that the development of a satisfactory theory of regional growth has been handicapped by the fact that regional economists have borrowed too freely from growth theory in general. The preoccupation with neo-classical models in the work of Borts (1960), Borts and Stein (1964), Romans (1965) and (to a lesser extent) Siebert (1969) is a good example of this tendency. The effect has been to give too little attention to the special characteristics of regional economies. In particular, this has meant a simplistic approach

[1] Most of the material in this chapter, with the exception of the sections on regional input–output and development planning models, is adapted from the first half of a paper 'A Critique of Regional Growth Theory' presented at a conference on regional development held at the University of Ottawa in March 1972 (Firestone, 1973b). I am very grateful to Professor Firestone and the University of Ottawa for permission to use this material.

to the determinants of inter-regional factor flows, possibly the most distinctive feature of the regional growth process compared with the national. It has also led to the neglect of space, distance and location – factors that may be of critical importance in explaining regional growth. It has in some instances meant a focus of attention on growth in an individual region, treating that region as an analogue to the nation, whereas for many purposes much more light is thrown on regional development by analysing the process of growth in a system of interdependent regions. Moreover, many of the assumptions that are common in growth theory (perfect competition, the use of Cobb–Douglas production functions, constant returns to scale) may be singularly inappropriate to regional economics.

The objective of this chapter is to assess some of the most popular regional growth theories. These have been selected according to frequency of use and importance in the development of regional economics, and are not intended to make up a comprehensive list. The 'theories' to be examined are:

Export Base
Neoclassical
'Cumulative Causation' (Myrdal–Kaldor)
Econometric Models
Input–Output Models
Multisector Development Planning Models

The export base model is much too feeble as a theory of regional growth, but it has played an important role in the history of the subject and frequently recurs as one component in even the most sophisticated models of today. Neoclassical and cumulative causation theories stand together since they yield opposite predictions, convergence in regional *per capita* incomes in the former and divergence in the latter. The neoclassical model is the clearest adaptation of aggregate growth theory to regional economics, and has attracted the bulk of the research effort. Although this work has been very interesting, empirical tests of neoclassical models have been inconclusive and indirect, and more seriously the neoclassicists have refused to consider obvious elements in regional growth that cannot easily be accommodated within the scope of their models. The 'cumulative causation' hypotheses urged so cogently by Myrdal (1957) have also been the object of inconclusive tests, with extreme variations in the results according to place, time, level of development and institutional environment.[1] The theory has, in addition, suffered from being formulated in very loose terms and, especially by Myrdal himself, in emotive language. However, Kaldor (1970) has recently proposed a variant of the cumulative causation model that is translatable into more formal economic terms and yields testable propositions. An advantage of this theory over neoclassical models is that it gives considerable stress to agglomeration economies in rich regions as a cause of divergence, and of course agglomeration economies are a phenomenon of some importance in regional, urban and spatial analysis. Econometric and input–output models fall into a different category in that they are predominantly forecasting models rather than theories of regional growth *per se*. In fact, an econometric model ought strictly to be an empirical formulation of a theory of regional growth but, due to the unsettled nature of regional growth theory and scarcity of data, they have assumed an independent existence as a method of explaining certain relationships in regional growth. Regional input–output models are incomplete in themselves since it remains necessary to make independent forecasts of growth in the components of final demand; nevertheless, they are with appropriate refinements useful for explaining the repercussions of exogenously determined growth on the region. Moreover, both econometric and input–output models are easily reconciled with certain other components of the regional growth process; the export base relationship is an obvious example. The development planning approach is more relevant to regional planning than regional growth, but it is useful for illustrating some of the properties of multisector models.

EXPORT BASE MODELS

Despite their long ancestry, export base models would not be worth attention were it not for the fact that export base notions still crop up repeatedly in other, particularly econometric,

---

[1] See Williamson (1965).

models. Their appeal to the econometricians is understandable since they provide the means of linking regional growth performance to G.N.P., and given the regional data famine it is very useful indeed to be able to find a role for G.N.P. in regional econometric models.[1]

In its simplest form, export base theory states that the regional growth rate is a function of regional export performance, i.e.

$$y_i = f(x_i) \qquad (2.1)$$

where y_i = rate of growth of output in region i, and x_i = rate of growth of regional exports.

The value of the theory is that it emphasises the importance of the 'openness' of regional economies and the role played by changing national (or extra-regional) demand patterns in regional growth. This advantage is more than offset by the neglect of autonomous investment and technical progress and insufficient attention to the part played in regional growth by capital accumulation and immigration. Moreover, export base theory has other objections. First, the X/Y ratio is inversely related to the size of the region; unless size is always constant, i.e. is measured in terms of geographical area, an expanding region will tend to have a falling rate of export growth. The parameter that links the rate of growth in regional output to the rate of export growth will continuously change in value, perhaps unpredictably.

Second, problems arise when we consider the implications of export base theory for the direction of regional capital flows. An expansion in regional gross exports (i.e. its export base) tends to induce more growth. Fast-growing regions will tend to run export surpluses except in two situations:

(*i*) When a region starts from a position of heavy deficit; in this case it might, though *only in the short run*, have an improving balance of payments but remain in deficit.
(*ii*) The more serious exception is when increasing exports might be offset by higher induced imports. However, this

---

[1] The undertone in this sentence that the choice of export base theory has been dictated in many instances by data constraints rather than by satisfaction with the theory is intentional.

requires the marginal propensity to spend to be greater than unity;[1] this is a possibility, but only in conditions of explosive growth.

We would normally expect fast-growing regions to import rather than to export capital, i.e. to run import surpluses. For a fast-growing region to be a net exporter of capital (the typical export base case) it is probably necessary for the region in question to have such a high savings rate that it can both finance fast internal growth and export capital to other regions.

Other objections to export base models (their exclusive pre-occupation with demand considerations, the fact that they are single region rather than inter-regional models, and the severe difficulties involved in defining and measuring exogenous income, i.e. the export base) can be understood more clearly by examining one particular model in some detail.

A good illustration of the use of an export base model is the study by Bolton (1966) which had the ultimate purpose of estimating the impact of defence spending on U.S.A. regions and individual states over the period 1947–62. This example indicates the strengths and weaknesses of the export base approach very well. It incorporates several improvements upon more naïve versions of the export base model. First, it uses income as the growth measure rather than the more common, but less precise, reliance on employment. The study draws upon published data on personal income, but considers only the growth in current dollar income on the grounds that trends in prices differ but slightly from one region to another. Second, it adopts a broad definition of exogenous income and recognises that exports alone form too narrow a base for forecasting regional change. In addition to wages and salaries in export industries, exogenous income includes all property income plus transfer payments.[2]

---

[1] That is, $m+c > 1$ where m = marginal propensity to import and c = marginal propensity to consume. Since $\Delta M = m\Delta X/(1-c)$ for $\Delta M > \Delta X$ then $\Delta M/\Delta X$ which is equal to $m/1-c$ must be greater than 1. Thus, m must be greater than $(1-c)$, therefore $m+c$ must be greater than 1.

[2] Indeed, one finding of the study was that the property income component of exogenous income both grew faster and fluctuated more widely in most states than export wage income.

Third, Bolton shows the relationship between the export base theory as a short-run income model, the most common type of application, and as a long-run growth model. The short-run model can be described as follows:

$$Y_p = Y_n + Y_x \tag{2.2}$$

$$Y_n = a + bY_p \tag{2.3}$$

$$Y_x = P + E \tag{2.4}$$

where Y_p = personal income, Y_n = wages and salaries and proprietors' income in local industries, dependent only on total personal income, Y_x = exogenous income which consists of P, the sum of property income and transfer payments, and E, wages and salaries and proprietors' income in industries (including export industries) for which demand is exogenous. The b function applies to spending after import leakages have been deducted. Endogenous income can be expressed as a function of exogenous income, i.e.

$$Y_n = \frac{a}{1-b} + \frac{b}{1-b} Y_x \tag{2.5}$$

Also

$$Y_p = \frac{a}{1-b} + \frac{Y_x}{1-b} \tag{2.6}$$

When the model is translated into a growth context we obtain:

$$y_n = y_x \frac{bY_x}{a + bY_x} \tag{2.7}$$

and

$$y_p = y_x \frac{Y_x}{a + Y_x} \tag{2.8}$$

where y_n, y_x and y_p represent the growth rates of endogenous, exogenous and total personal income respectively.

Equations (2.7) and (2.8) show that the sign and value of the intercept a in equation (2.3) become especially important when the model is employed as a growth model. If $a = 0$, both Y_p and Y_n grow at the same rate as Y_x; if $a > 0$ and income change is positive, both Y_p and Y_n grow more slowly than Y_x;

if a <0, Y_p > and Y_n grow faster than Y_x. In the tests carried out in the study a usually had a negative sign. This could be explained by such factors as investment in local sectors (e.g. construction), a higher than proportional increase in local government spending in response to rising income, or by import replacement. These, in turn, could reflect population growth, accelerated urbanisation or the growth of new export industries. To throw more light on these forces it might be necessary to disaggregate local and exogenous sectors and to estimate separate parameters for each sector, then to compare regional differences in these parameters with regional differentials in population growth, degree of urbanisation, composition of export sectors, etc. The study also revealed that the value of b was usually higher for regions than for single states. This supports the above-mentioned hypothesis that X/Y varies inversely with the size of the region.

Despite the relative sophistication of the export base model used and its reasonable results,[1] the obvious limitations of the approach were as evident as ever. First, the model is a pure demand model and gives no attention to the growth in capacity. Bolton's explanation (p. 21) is:

> Although constraints on capacity are important, mobility of factors makes capacity in any one region more elastic than national capacity. In any case, since regional data on capacity are not generally available, a pure demand model is far simpler to implement than would be one which also attempts to account for changes in capacity.

The assumption that demand creates its own supply is heroic, especially in the short run or the very long run. The excuse of data constraints is understandable, but does not provide a strong enough justification for mis-specifying the model. Second, the model is applied separately to individual states and

---

[1] Estimates of a, b and correlation coefficients for alternative measures of exogenous income by region and state are given in Bolton (pp. 48–9). The model did not work well for states which experienced substantial fluctuations in exogenous income, usually agricultural states such as the Dakotas, Montana, Iowa and Wyoming, but also Alaska. In these cases, a ratchet model (where the ratio of current to previous peak income was an important explanatory variable) worked much better.

cannot be used for the simultaneous explanation of growth in several regions. The neglect of the sources of exogenous income change, the failure to allow for feedbacks, the excessive aggregation of a system of inter-dependent regions into the trivial dichotomy of 'the region' and the 'rest of the world', these are basic characteristics of the export base approach which account for its inferiority compared with any inter-regional model.

Finally, the Bolton study illustrates very well the problems encountered in attempting to separate exogenous from endogenous income, and the arbitrary classifications of exogenous income to which base analysts are ultimately driven. Three alternative measures of exogenous income were used. All three included property income and transfer payments. E_1 adopted the *ad hoc* classification method, treating all mining, manufacturing, agriculture and the federal government as exogenous. E_2 classified agriculture, the federal government, ordnance and transport equipment as exogenous and certain other sectors (state and local government, construction and most services) as endogenous: all other sectors were assigned to the exogenous or endogenous sector according to whether their location quotient[1] was greater or less than $1 \cdot 2$. If an industry had a location quotient greater than $1 \cdot 2$, *all its wages* were included in E_2. This method allows for the possibility that some service industries may be export-oriented while some manufacturing industries may cater primarily for local markets. However, the cut-off point of $1 \cdot 2$ is quite arbitrary.

The third method, E_3, is the most satisfactory conceptually. Apart from one or two *a priori* assignments, the wage bills of all industries were divided between the exogenous and endogenous sectors using the well-known Mattila and Thompson (1955) assignment technique in all cases where $LQ > 1$. The difficulty with this method is that it yields valid results only if certain assumptions (e.g. identical production functions in each state, homogenous demand patterns) are reasonable. In most cases $E_3 < E_2 < E_1$; as it happened, however, all three measures of exogenous income tended to produce good fits. Of course, goodness of fit is little guide to the predictive value of the model. Even if we can disregard the arbitrary procedures

[1] Location quotients in this study were based on wage bills, not employment.

involved in definitions of exogenous income, it remains very difficult to forecast the future levels of exogenous income in any region, especially in the absence of a fully developed inter-regional model. It should be emphasised that this study was not selected for critical comment because it is a bad study; on the contrary, it is one of the best available and certainly the most comprehensive application of an economic base model at the regional level. The purpose of this analysis has merely been to illustrate some of the *unavoidable limitations* of export base models as theories of regional growth.

NEOCLASSICAL MODELS

Neoclassical models have dominated regional growth theory much as they have dominated growth theory in general. However, it is even more difficult to justify this domination at the regional level. The background assumptions of neoclassical growth theory are inapplicable to the regional economy. For instance, the full employment assumption is not usually relevant to regional economics since to a marked extent regional problems emerge because of substantial inter-regional differences in the degree of resource (and particularly labour) utilisation. Similarly, perfect competition cannot be assumed in regional economic analysis since space itself and the existence of transport costs limits competition; oligopoly, pure monopoly or monopolistic competition are much more appropriate market structures. Indeed, if we were to adopt neoclassical models in their pure unadulterated form there would be no such field as regional economics.

Neoclassical growth models have received a heavy battering in recent years, and they have been attacked much more at the national than the regional level. The reason for this is not that the weaknesses of neoclassical growth theory are more serious for nations than regions but merely that much more work has been undertaken in the national area and more controversy aroused.[1]

Features of the real world that are not easily admitted, if at all, into the neoclassical world such as increasing returns, oli-

[1] For a devastating critique of the neoclassicists see Kaldor (1966, pp. 309–10).

gopolistic competition and uncertainty figure prominently in any analysis of the space economy. Had the spatial dimension been introduced into aggregate growth analysis at an early stage in its development, neoclassical models would not have had such a long survival capacity. Many people would now accept that neoclassical growth theory is dead (though there are still many others trying to revive the corpse), but the death-bed scene has been rather prolonged. One reason for this is that much of the literature has consisted of elegant nit-picking. We can note Sen's comments (1970) on this point: 'the extent of controversy may not be a good guide to the innate importance of an issue' (p. 10) and 'the selection of topics for work in growth economics is guided much more by logical curiosity than by a taste for relevance' (p. 33). The working assumptions and abstractions that the neoclassicist uses as a starting point for his analysis could never be justified in a world which recognises the existence of space as well as time. Space is incompatible with perfect competition, complete certainty, marginal adjustments in prices, outputs and locations, and the other background conditions of the neoclassical world. In other words, although a weak case for neoclassical models can be made in aggregate growth theory there is no case at all in regional analysis. However, introducing the spatial dimension reinforces all the other objections to the notion of a homogeneous capital stock and an aggregate production function. The capital stock is heterogeneous not only because it is created at different periods in time (vintage models) and in different sectors each of which embodies a different level of technology (embodied technical progress) but also because it varies with its location. There is little doubt that neoclassicism is succumbing to the gradual accumulation of elegant and sophisticated, though frequently arid, intellectual criticism. But its ultimate irrelevance and its gross predictive fallibility are exposed not in the intellectually respectable and so-called 'core' realm of capital theory but in the upstart and untamed 'fringe area' of regional and urban economics.

Why have neoclassical models attracted so much attention from regional economists? One reason must be the relative ease with which ideas in aggregate growth theory can be borrowed and adapted for regional economic analysis. Another, and probably the most important, reason is that the neoclassical model contains a theory of factor mobility as well as a theory of growth. Since inter-regional factor mobility is such an important element in understanding regional growth, it is much simpler and more elegant to explain both endogenous growth and net factor flows to and from other regions with a single model. Unfortunately, this notion has had more influence than the commonsense view that the determinants of inter-regional mobility of capital and labour may be very complex and more satisfactorily handled by specific sub-models rather than as one aspect of a comprehensive, consistent single theory.

A third reason for its popularity is that in a pure aggregative formulation the neoclassical model yields neat, precise predictions. For example, if we assume full employment, perfect competition, one homogeneous commodity, zero transport costs, regionally identical production functions exhibiting constant returns to scale, a fixed supply of labour and no technical progress, it can be shown that the wage (marginal product of labour) is a direct and the return to capital (marginal product of capital) an inverse function of the capital-labour ratio (K/L). Given identical production functions in all regions labour will flow from low- to high-wage regions and capital will flow in the opposite direction (since low returns to capital imply high wages, and high returns are obtained in low wage regions). These flows continue until factor returns are equalised in each region. According to this view, the process of regional growth will be associated with a convergence in regional *per capita* incomes.

The trouble is that if we disaggregate the model, drop some of the assumptions (e.g. constant returns, identical production functions) and translate the model from comparative statics (as in the above example) to dynamics, we may derive quite different results. For instance, it is possible to construct a set of assumptions whereby we obtain disequilibrating tendencies in regional growth, capital inflows into the high-wage regions, and regional income divergence. Although the neoclassicist may argue that this merely involves an improvement in his basic model to reflect greater reality (though the assumptions of perfect competition and economies of scale stand uneasily together) the predictions in this case are quite consistent with, and arguably better explained by, alternative theories. Whether it is then desirable to preserve any of the neoclassical assumptions is a matter of judgement.

Perhaps the crucial point in answering this question is whether inter-regional factor mobility can be most satisfactorily explained in terms of a response to differentials in inter-regional rates of return. It is doubtful whether inter-regional migration can be wholly explained in these terms; the possibility of an income gain is a necessary but by no means a sufficient condition for migration. Mobility costs, spatial frictions, non-economic resistances to migration, job opportunities and other considerations may all figure prominently in a satisfactory migration model.[1] Similarly, the information available to location decision-makers about regional differentials in expected rates of return to capital is so scanty and uncertain that it is most unlikely that this provides a satisfactory explanation of inter-regional mobility of capital. Bell (1967) found that manufacturing investment in Massachusetts was much more closely related to national aggregate demand than to inter-regional differences in capital yields. Furthermore, if we accept that plant location decisions largely determine changes in the inter-regional distribution of capital, it is very doubtful whether these decisions can be adequately explained by profit maximisation criteria. Uncertainty about the future movement of costs and revenues over space, and high location costs are two obvious reasons in support of this view.[2] To the extent that location decisions fail to be explicable in terms of profit maximisation, any relationship between inter-regional capital flows and inter-regional differentials in the rate of return to capital will be weakened.[3] The relatively small volume of regional econometric analysis is nevertheless quite sufficient to show that regional growth models need much more complex investment and migration functions than those suggested by a neoclassical model.

[1] For a more extensive discussion of inter-regional migration and its determinants see Chapter 4, pp. 89–103.

[2] For a more detailed analysis of these points see Richardson (1969a, pp. 90–100).

[3] See below (Chapter 4, pp. 103–13) for further elaboration of the determinants of inter-regional capital flows.

A regional neoclassical model might take the following form:

$$y_i = a_i k_i + (1 - a_i) l_i + t_i \qquad (2.9)$$

$$k_i = \frac{s_i}{v_i} \pm \sum_j k_{ji} \qquad (2.10)$$

$$l_i = n_i \pm \sum_j m_{ji} \qquad (2.11)$$

$$k_{ji} = f(R_i - R_j) \qquad (2.12)$$

$$m_{ji} = f(W_i - W_j) \qquad (2.13)$$

where y, k, l and t are the growth rates in output, capital, labour and technical progress, a = capital's share in income, s = savings/income ratio, v = capital/output ratio, k_{ji} = annual net flow of capital from region j to region i divided by the capital stock of region i, n = rate of natural increase in population, m_{ji} = annual net flow of migrants from region j to region i divided by the population of region i, R = rate of return on capital, and W = wage. Equation (2.9) is the standard growth equation, and equations (2.10) and (2.11) are definitional stating that the growth of factor inputs is composed of two elements: local inputs and net imported inputs (equation (2.11) assumes that the labour participation rate remains constant). Equations (2.12) and (2.13) are the critical elements in the model in at least two senses: first, the ability to attract inputs from other regions may be the key force that boosts a region's growth rate higher than that of its neighbours; second, these equations represent specific testable hypotheses at the heart of neoclassical theory – that capital and labour move in response to differentials in factor returns.

It is unfortunate that most of the tests on regional neoclassical models have been indirect tests that have merely investigated whether there is convergence in regional *per capita* incomes. Although such a finding is consistent with naïve versions of the neoclassical model it is also consistent with several alternative models. Moreover, the evidence on convergence is very mixed. In some countries, regional *per capita* income divergence is the general rule, while even in countries where convergence tendencies predominate (such as the United

States) there have been periods when 'perverse' results have been obtained. More direct tests have been confined to analysis of the effects of labour migration. Thus, some studies have shown a tendency for inter-regional wage differentials to narrow over time, while others have attempted to estimate the relationship between inter-regional labour mobility and wage differentials. It would not be true to say that a simplistic migration model of this kind has yielded better results than more complex migration models. The real constraint in an adequate test of neoclassical predictions is the absence of satisfactory regional capital yield data. Thus, it has been impossible to perform a clean test on the hypothesis that the return to capital is inversely related to regional capital/labour ratios (though indirect and casual empirical observation probably indicates that such a relationship is, if anything, direct rather than inverse) and that net capital flows are a function of differentials in the inter-regional rates of return on capital.[1]

However, apart from the inconclusive and incomplete nature of the tests on the neoclassical model, its theoretical objections are quite serious. First, it tells us nothing about the characteristics of regional economies. From other branches of regional economic analysis we know that certain phenomena are of some importance: agglomeration economies in location and urbanisation, transport costs, interdependence of location decisions, metropolitan-regional relationships. But these have no role in the neoclassical system. Second, in view of the finding at the national level that technical progress tends to make a larger contribution to the growth rate than growth in factor inputs, it is surprising if understandable that the neoclassical model has given so much attention to inter-regional factor mobility and so little to the inter-regional diffusion of innovation and technical progress. There is now a growing literature on spatial diffusion models. Whether we yet have a satisfactory explanation of the spatial diffusion of all types of innovation is doubtful, but it is clear that the analytical techniques needed to examine spatial diffusion (social networks analysis, communications theory, diffusion waves, Monte Carlo models, urban hierarchy models, statistical curve fitting for spatial

[1] For negative results on this latter point see Olsen (pp. 131–8). Some reference to these results is made below (Chapter 8, pp. 217–20).

diffusion rates, etc.) have nothing to do with neoclassical theory.[1] In my view, the dogged reliance on neoclassical models of regional growth has retarded understanding of the regional growth process.

Despite these objections to neoclassical theory, the neo-classical growth equation may still be very useful as a matter of definition, i.e.

$$y_i = a_i k_i + (1 - a_i) l_i + t_i \qquad (2.14)$$

However, too many criticisms have been levied against the Cobb–Douglas production function to make this acceptable. Also, the theory of regional growth developed here relies quite heavily on the notion of increasing returns due to agglomeration economies in rich regions. Although in Equation (2.14) it may be possible to include all increasing returns effects in t, especially if embodied technical progress assumptions are made, there may also be increasing returns to factors independent of technical change. Thus, we might alter Equation (2.14) into

$$y_i = a_i k_i + b_i l_i + t_i \qquad (2.15)$$

where $a + b \gtreqless 1$.

However, the substitution of b for $(1 - a)$ and allowing $a + b > 1$ in the increasing returns case is awkward in many respects: (i) it may be impossible to ascribe increasing returns to a single factor, whether labour or capital; (ii) allowing a and b to vary, and their sum to be greater than 1, brings too much indeterminacy into the model; (iii) the empirically verified constant-income-shares assumption is useful for obtaining a direct estimate of the weights for the labour supply and capital stock functions. From this point of view, a better formulation might be:

$$y_i = [a_i k_i + (1 - a_i) l_i]^{a_i} + t_i \qquad (2.16)$$

where a_i may be greater than, equal to or less than 1 according to whether returns are increasing, constant or decreasing, and will vary according to the character of the region in question. Generally speaking, a_i should be greater than 1 in prosperous regions. There may be some tendency, therefore, for a_i and t_i

---

[1] The spatial diffusion of innovations is treated extensively in Chapter 4, pp. 113–32.

to be closely inter-related, and in empirical testing it may be difficult to separate out the two effects. Indeed, it may be preferable not to try. Thus, an alternative formulation of Equation (2.16) would be

$$y_i = [a_i k_i + (1 - a_i) l_i]^{\gamma_i} \qquad (2.17)$$

where γ_i is an exponential parameter which normally has a value greater than 1 and represents increasing returns due to scale factors, agglomeration economies *and* technical progress.

CUMULATIVE CAUSATION MODELS

The prediction of regional *per capita* income divergence owes most to the circular and cumulative causation principles of Myrdal (1957). He argued that 'the play of forces in the market normally tends to increase, rather than to decrease, the inequalities between regions' (p. 26). Market forces lead to the clustering of increasing returns activities in certain areas of the economy. Regardless of the initial location advantage (natural resources, a transport facility, etc.), this build-up becomes self-sustaining because of increasing internal and external economies at these centres of agglomeration. The limited advantages of backward regions (such as cheap labour) are insufficient to offset these agglomeration advantages. The main influence on the rate of growth of lagging regions is the induced effects of growth in the prosperous areas. These are of two kinds: spread (favourable) and backwash (unfavourable) effects. The former include markets for the (typically primary) products of the lagging regions and diffusion of innovation. Normally, however, these are outweighed by backwash effects – particularly by disequilibrating flows of labour, capital, goods and services from poor to rich regions. Thus, the free trade of an inter-regional system operates to the disadvantage of poor regions, inhibits industrialisation and distorts their pattern of production. Hence, regional growth is a disequilibrating process. Myrdal couples his arguments with an attack on the neo-classicists who treat the concept of stable equilibrium as if it had 'teleological significance' rather than 'as a very abstract, almost crude and usually unrealistic theoretical assumption' (p. 144).

The trouble with Myrdal's views is that they are difficult to translate into a formal model. In a recent paper Kaldor (1970) has suggested a variant of the cumulative causation hypothesis which puts flesh on to Myrdal's skeletal structure. Kaldor argues that the principle of cumulative causation is nothing more or less than the existence of increasing returns to scale (in the widest sense, i.e. including external and agglomeration economies) in manufacturing, and quotes (as usual and with approval) Verdoorn's Law. As trade is opened up between industrialising and rural regions in a free trade economy such as a system of regions, neither the principles of comparative advantage nor classical mechanisms of adjustment work. Instead, increasing returns favour the rich regions and inhibit development in the poor; because of scale effects the rich regions gain a virtual monopoly of industrial production. Also, since competition in industry is imperfect while near perfect competition prevails in agriculture, movements in the terms of trade favour the rich regions.

All this in line with Myrdal's own arguments. The second strand in the analysis, however, is Kaldor's. He draws upon the export base concept and argues that the behaviour of a region's production and exports depends upon: (i) an exogenous factor, namely the rate of growth of world demand for the region's products; and (ii) an endogenous or quasi-endogenous factor, the movement of 'efficiency wages' in the region relative to other producing regions. He argues that relative efficiency wages determine whether the region's share in the overall markets is rising or falling; in particular, the lower are efficiency wages the higher the growth rate in output. As Kaldor points out, the movement in efficiency wages is the result of two elements: the change in money wages relative to the change in productivity, i.e. is equal to W/T where W = money wage index and T = an index of productivity. He further argues that money wages, and their rate of increase, will be similar in *all* regions. This is explained by several factors: the institutional environment, the effects of inter-regional labour mobility on the narrowing of wage differentials, and nationwide collective bargaining. Thus, money wages will move in a similar fashion in each region even though regional growth rates in employment may vary widely. On the other hand, because of incresaing returns higher growth rates in productivity will be experienced in regions with the faster growth rates in output. These regions will thus have the lower efficiency wages, since W/T will fall relatively in those regions with above average productivity and output growth rates. This explains why the relatively fast-growing regions tend to acquire cumulative advantages over the slow-growing ones.[1]

The Kaldor model may be expressed in formal terms as follows:

$$t_i = f_i^1(y_i), \text{ where } f_i^1 \text{ is rising and } > 0 \qquad (2.18)$$

$$(W_i/T_i) = f_i^2(t_i), \text{ where } f_i^2 \text{ is falling and } < 0 \quad (2.19)$$

$$y_i = f_i^3(W_i/T_i), \text{ where } f_i^3 \text{ is falling and } < 0 \qquad (2.20)$$

$$W_i = \bar{W} \qquad (2.21)$$

where t = rate of productivity growth and $\bar{W}$ = national money wage.

The diagrammatical representation in Fig. 2.1 illustrates clearly the circular cumulative nature of the regional growth process according to this model. Rising growth rates in output induce higher productivity which reduces efficiency wages, and in turn the fall in efficiency wages leads to a higher growth rate in output, and so on.

Whereas Myrdal's analysis of cumulative causation is difficult to test directly,[2] and its main prediction, divergence in regional *per capita* incomes, is consistent with many alternative theories of regional development, the Kaldor version yields testable hypotheses. These are: (*i*) a region's rate of productivity growth is an increasing function of its rate of growth of

[1] Kalbor recognises the existence of spread effects that hold down the regional growth differentials: (*i*) diffusion of growth and stimulation of the demand for 'complementary' products from poor regions; (*ii*) the possibility of diseconomies associated with high rates of industrial growth (e.g. environmental problems); (*iii*) the impact of inter-regional labour mobility in keeping divergences in real earnings per head in check; and (*iv*) built-in fiscal stabilisers. Also, wage subsidies (such as the Regional Employment Premium) may be given to backward regions as a protective device, since a wage subsidy may be treated as equivalent to a cut in efficiency wages.

[2] For a rudimentary attempt at testing see Salvatore (1972).

output; (*ii*) the rate of increase in money wages is approximately the same in all regions; and (*iii*) if (*ii*) does not hold a weaker hypothesis, though still sufficient to make the model work, is that the regional dispersion in productivity increases is substantially wider than the regional dispersion in money wage increases. Although there have been tests of Verdoorn Law

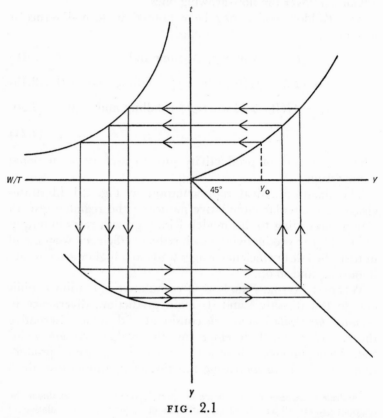

FIG. 2.1

statements at the national and the individual industry level, there have not been to my knowledge any regional tests. However, the data exist for such tests in most industrial countries. The problem of suitable money wage data is more serious in some countries, though not insuperable. I suspect that the possibility of similar regional rates of growth in money wages is much higher in a small, mature and closely integrated economy such as the United Kingdom than in, say, the United States. It is also clear that the likelihood of such uniformity is very much dependent on the nature of the institutional environment. Nevertheless, if we consider the weaker hypothesis (*iii*) it is entirely plausible that productivity growth varies much more widely between regions than rates of change in money wages, and if this is the case efficiency wages will fall in the higher productivity regions.

The circularity of the argument is much more evident in Kaldor's version than in the original Myrdal analysis. This is not a criticism of Kaldor in the sense that his aim was to provide an interpretation of the 'circular and cumulative causation' model. However, a circular model at this level of generality is somewhat unsatisfactory. For instance, it needs a trigger to set the spiral in motion. It does not really explain why some regions enjoy high growth rates but rather given that they have high growth rates why these growth rates persist.[1] Hence Myrdal's analysis stressed initial locational advantages such as natural resource endowment to supply the missing trigger. Moreover, reliance on a simple Verdoorn law relationship is too aggregative for the regional economist since it says very little about the complex role played by agglomeration economies, external scale economies and indivisibilities in the spatial concentration ('polarisation') of economic activity.

Thirdly, the use of the concept of efficiency wages as a mechanism for explaining how productivity performance will induce faster growth raises unsettled questions. In particular, it is possible for money wages in very prosperous fast-growing regions to rise much faster than elsewhere and for this tendency not to be offset by higher productivity growth. The failure of efficiency wages to fall does not necessarily imply that growth in these regions will slacken. The result may be higher prices (which may have negligible effects on the growth rate) rather than slower growth. This is consistent with the argument sometimes advanced that the rich regions in the economy are the prime generators of economy-wide inflation. The assumption that regional growth rates depend upon relative efficiency wages implies that regions are in direct competition with each

---

[1] Kaldor's solution is presumably to subscribe to crude export base theory to explain this.

other. But the sectoral composition of output may differ so widely between regions that this assumption is false. This is particularly the case when the national economy is an open economy and the prosperous regions specialise in foreign export industries. In this example (which may conform to the U.K. pattern) efficiency wages relative to foreigners may be much more relevant than efficiency wages relative to other regions.

ECONOMETRIC MODELS

As yet, relatively little work has been undertaken on econometric models of regional development.[1] Of the studies that have been carried out, several relate to short-run forecasting models not dissimilar (except that they are much simpler) to those developed for the national economy. It is indeed perhaps rather perverse to discuss regional econometric models under the label 'theory of regional growth'. Strictly speaking, such models should be used to test alternative theories of growth and are not linked to any specific theory (unlike, say, the input-output model). However, there are two arguments that can be marshalled to justify some discussion of econometric models here. First, the structure of regional econometric models appears in most cases to have been moulded by the availability of data rather than by the need to test specific hypotheses generated by regional economic theory. To the extent that the equations used have yielded good fits and have been used for predictive purposes, the relationships between the available data variables give the model an implicit theory. In other words, the theory is derived from the data rather than the data used as *a priori* theory.

Second, most regional econometric models have been developed as forecasting models. If there is a high degree of structural stability in the regional growth process and if the

---

[1] However, several studies are worthy of mention. These include H. Thomassen (1957), D. B. Suits (1966), R. E. Bolton (1966), R. Burton and J. W. Dyckman (1967), B. Tuck (1967), F. W. Bell (1967), S. Czamanski (1968 and 1969), J. M. Mattila and W. R. Thompson (1968), R. T. Crow (1969), L. R. Klein (1969), C. C. Harris, Jr. (1970), R. J. Anderson, Jr. (1970), N. J. Glickman (1971) and E. Olsen (1971).

future path of regional development is already visible in present conditions and past trends, then the distinction between a long-run forecasting model and a growth model becomes very blurred. It is doubtful, however, whether there is sufficient structural stability to justify this conclusion.

On the other hand, even if long-run regional growth is characterised by climacterics, breaks and shifts in regional structure which cannot, by their very nature, be derived from a study of past trends in the region under consideration, it does not follow that econometric models have to be abandoned. Instead, belief in this view of the regional growth process suggests the need for a change in emphasis away from single region to inter-regional models. Shifts and breaks in structure can be understood only within the context of inter-regional system growth. Most work on inter-regional growth has been highly theoretical, though Harris (1970) has conceptualised an inter-regional model (as yet without empirical results) that would measure the locational repercussions of investment decisions based on expected regional cost differentials. Similarly, Czamanski (1968) has suggested that in situations where structural breaks in regional development are common inter-regional cross-sectional tests may be more revealing than time series models for a single region. Although the absence of inter-regional econometric models can easily be explained by the short experience with regional econometric analysis, it contrasts unfavourably with major efforts in inter-regional formulations of the input–output model. However, even in the latter it is difficult to allow for breaks in trend with the possible exception of discontinuous shifts in trade coefficients when import substitution immediately follows the establishment of a new plant.

Since the field of regional econometric analysis is so new, it would be unfair to criticise its results too harshly. Nevertheless, there is some value in the argument that resources ought not to be allocated on too large a scale into this area until we have much more progress in two prior fields: the development of regional and urban economic theory, and the collection and construction of data series on key regional variables (among which regional investment deserves a high priority). The unsatisfactory nature of much of the work hitherto reflects these bottlenecks.

The specification problem raises more than its usual crop of difficulties in regional econometric analysis. Several of the models contain odd, unexplained relationships. Some borrow too heavily from macroeconomic research at the national level, and waste valuable time in exploring irrelevant relationships (e.g. tests of the Phillips curve at the regional level).[1] Very often it appears as if the model specification has been trimmed to the variables for which data were available, or to high R^2s, rather than to any feeling for regional economic theory. An extreme case is the use of 'statistical' forecasting models with little or no theoretical content. For example, the Michigan model (see Suits, 1966) forecasted changes in gross state product by reference to three *national* variables: U.S.A. expenditure on automobiles, U.S.A. expenditure on producers' durables and all other privately produced G.N.P. To consider another example, Glickman treated his population forecast by using an equation relating population change to changes in the labour force and to time, where time was used as a proxy for natural increases and *migration*. In view of the fact that his model was for a metropolitan area and considering the importance of migration to urban growth, this approach is incredibly naïve and the regional economist is in no way reconciled to the equation by the high R^2 (0·97).

The inadequate state of regional growth theory, and the contradictions and confusion that have not been sorted out because of limited testing, all mean that each analyst has had a free rein to specify his own models without having to draw upon, or explain why he diverges from, any conventional wisdom. Experimentation is a good thing, but in this field it has prevented comparisons between models. Moreover, in a few cases the analysts have been more experienced in econometrics than in regional economic theory and have specified sub-models that are inconsistent with the operation of the inter-regional system. In other cases, the regional theory behind the models is outdated and inadequate. For instance, virtually all the econometric models that have been published

[1] See Bell (1967) and Glickman (1971). The openness of regional economies (in particular, the greater potential for in-migration) is one reason why we would not expect much of a Phillips curve effect in regional (and local) labour markets.

make explicit use of export base theory. A common form is to make regional manufacturing output a function of G.N.P.

$$Q_M = a + b(\text{G.N.P.}) \qquad (2.22)$$

where manufacturing output is used as a surrogate for regional exports and G.N.P. as a proxy for inter-regional demand. This is a most inadequate treatment of inter-regional trade, making no allowance for the importance of specific regional markets or for shifts in inter-regional competitiveness. Moreover, equating regional exports with manufacturing output is highly danger-ous, since many manufacturing industries sell substantial proportions of their output to local markets while there are frequently important export service sectors in a region, par-ticularly in commerce, banking and finance.[1] The deficiencies of this formulation are frequently compounded, since one or two of the models (the Massachusetts model for example; see Bell, 1967) make G.N.P. the key exogenous variable and are recursive in character where the chain of economic causation runs from exogenous G.N.P. growth→ exports→ service and total income→ demand for capital→ given the production func-tion, demand for labour. Thus, mis-specification at the first stage can ruin the model as a whole.[2] The other consequence of adopting recursive models and treating G.N.P. as exo-genous is that the contribution of the region to national growth is assumed to be negligible, an assumption that may be invalid for either a large or a fast-growing region.[3]

The second major problem in regional econometric growth models is data availability. This is serious in virtually all econometric work, of course, but in few areas are the data constraints as severe as in regional and urban research. Unem-ployment and employment data are frequently the only in-formation available at regular intervals. Population and output can often be estimated with reasonable precision only for

[1] Bell (1967) seems undisturbed by the fact that he obtains an estimate for the regional income multiplier as high as 3·7.

[2] In the Philadelphia model (Glickman, 1971) the forecast for manu-facturing employment (for the period 1964–6) was the weakest element in the whole forecast.

[3] See my distinction between *competitive growth* and *generative growth*, Chapter 3, pp. 86–8.

Census years, and annual regional data have to be collected specifically through surveys, or synthetic series constructed. Investment data are very sparse, yet it is difficult to conceive of a useful regional econometric model which lacks the investment variable. Glickman resolved this dilemma by ignoring non-manufacturing investment altogether, whereas Bell made rough estimates of non-manufacturing investment from national totals. As suggested above, the heavy reliance in many models on unemployment, employment, labour force and wage relationships may be explained more by data availability than by the importance of these variables in the process of regional growth. Data constraints also create statistical problems. For instance, even where data series are available they are almost invariably annual series and go back for only a few years. One result is that regional econometric models often have too many exogenous variables relative to the number of observations. Since omission of some of these variables would aggravate mis-specification, it would then be necessary to use some technique for reducing the number of variables to a compact form, e.g. principal components analysis; see Glickman (1971) and Czamanski (1968).

A further difficulty with the relatively short time span for which annual regional and urban data are available is that the data base may refer to a shorter period than the projection period. This raises a more general problem: that regional econometric forecasting models need to be long-run models. At the national level, more success has been achieved with short-term forecasting models. This is all right since the time horizon for macro-economic stabilisation policies is relatively short. The time horizon for the regional policymaker is much longer. Narrowing inter-regional growth and income differentials is a long-run objective and a planning horizon of ten to twenty-five years is probably the most appropriate. Similarly, in urban analysis when the use of an econometric model will probably be linked to physical planning requirements, a meaningful time horizon for planning will have to be upwards of five years, and very often ten to fifteen years. Thus, both the limited data base and the fact that long-term forecasting is intrinsically more difficult (since the longer the projection period the fewer the parameters that can be treated as constant) make regional econometric research a very long haul, at least if we accept that a strong element in the case for forecasting and growth models is as an aid to economic policymaking.

Another defect of the regional econometric models hitherto developed (though the same criticism applies to most theories of regional growth too) is that not one gives any attention to the dimension of space.[1] Again, one reason for this may be the failure of regional econometricians to break loose from the traditions and habits of national analysts. Yet, it would not be too difficult to accommodate, either implicitly or explicitly, spatial variables in a model. One possibility would be to include them in the sub-models that form part of the overall model: distance and/or migration costs in the migration equation; transport costs in the production function; the use of income potential and population potential concepts; the inclusion of agglomeration economies (as in von Böventer's migration model, 1969); and many other possibilities. An alternative, and one which may give more attention to the urban-regional relationships, would be to use linked models: first, an econometric model to forecast G.R.P. and its constituents; second, a land use or inter-urban allocation model to distribute the forecasted changes in G.R.P. spatially.

Even the most careful of the regional econometric models developed so far have been unsatisfactory in the sense that simulations performed upon them have yielded strange results. The Nova Scotia model (Czamanski, 1968) is a case in point. In many ways, e.g. in terms of comprehensiveness and consistency, this is the best regional model yet developed. It contains fifty-four endogenous variables and fifty-four equations (thirty-one of which are structural equations); in addition, there are fifty predetermined variables. Also, the number of target variables is equal to the number of instrument variables (eight each). The model is reasonably disaggregated into seven sectors, including a welfare sector (referring to standards of education, health and housing). Yet two results of tests on the model are very suspicious. First, despite the inclusion of five national variables (G.N.P., prices, interest rates, total direct taxes, and total personal income) changes in the national economy had a negligible impact on the regional economy,

[1] Olsen (1971) is a partial exception to this statement.

apart from on the exports of mining and manufacturing products. The reason for this could well lie in the construction of the model, e.g. too little weight given to the export sector. However, Czamanski (1968) argues (not altogether convincingly) that this could reflect the real situation in that Nova Scotia is a relatively unproductive regional economy, heavily dependent on government transfer payments and other expenditures, that does not respond to changes in the national economy. Second, the instrument variables had very little effect on the target variables.[1] These aspects of the model are surely worrying.

INPUT–OUTPUT MODELS

Whether a regional input–output model can be treated as a regional growth model is a debatable point. Certainly, it lacks the generality of econometric models and does contain rather precise theoretical implications, i.e. in the form of its linear technical and production relationships. On the other hand, it is incomplete as a theory of regional growth since the input–output model treats regional final demand as exogenous whereas a satisfactory theory would need to determine the growth path of final demand. Projections of final demand may be one of the end products of an econometric forecasting model, yet it is the starting point for an input–output forecast. This means that the input–output model has to be combined with some other theory or model before it is capable of explaining regional growth and development satisfactorily. There are two obvious possibilities. First, many components of final demand can be made endogenous by transferring them into an expanded inter-sectoral matrix – consumption, induced investment and local government spending for example. Similarly, regional exports could be endogenous if an inter-regional model is used with inter-regional trade flow matrices so that each

---

[1] Czamanski's explanation of this, if *not* due to defects in the model, is as follows: 'the values of the instrument variables, during the period under study, have been insignificantly small. This would mean that the tools currently at the disposal of the Government of Nova Scotia are altogether insufficient for influencing the target variables and bringing about a major change' (p. 127).

region's exports can be treated as other regions' imports. A special case of model closure is where, using a single region model, all components of final demand except exports are placed in the matrix; in this case the model becomes synonymous with an export base model. The second alternative is to link the input–output framework to a separate model for predicting future regional final demands. Many studies have used simplified techniques for this, such as ratios of national final demand and shift and share methods. A more useful solution would be to use a regional econometric growth model for forecasting final demand and an input–output model for exploring the inter-industry repercussions of regional growth.

Apart from the assumption of linear production relationships and the large exogenous sector, the input–output model has other weaknesses for regional growth analysis. It is difficult to incorporate factor (and commodity) substitution, there is the related problem of predicting changes in inter-regional trade flows (the input–output model has no comparative advantage in this respect), and the model is unable to take account of agglomeration economies and external scale economies which may be so important in regional and urban growth. On the other hand, an input–output framework has three offsetting advantages. It provides an operational tool, implementable here and now even though data requirements and collection costs may be heavy. It offers a highly disaggregated approach enabling the analyst to explain changes in the sectoral composition of output and to explore the impact of growth sector by sector. In this way, the input–output model is an acceptable compromise between the excessive aggregation of a macroeconomic growth model and the pedestrian description of industrial composition approaches to regional growth. Finally, its framework is extremely flexible; variants of an input–output model can be constructed which look at inter-regional system growth rather than at growth within a single region, or which specifically introduce a transportation sector allowing the analyst to explain production, location and trade simultaneously, or which by extending the inter-regional principle downwards into the region permits an analysis of intra-regional (e.g. urban-regional) relationships that could be important if growth is spatially concentrated within regions.

Further comment on this flexibility is needed since critics of the input–output model frequently choose the simple static model to attack. As a regional growth model, an input–output framework must be dynamic (i.e. it must allow for the investment requirements of expansion in output by including a capital coefficients matrix) and it should preferably be inter-regional.[1] Nor need such a model be bound by its inherent spacelessness. Moses (1960) showed how an input–output model could allow for differential transport costs for each commodity between each pair of regions. Furthermore, provided that productive factors used in transport and in goods production are homogeneous then the minimisation of transport costs as in the linear programming transportation problem will also optimise production and trade. Second, by employing an inter-regional sub-regional framework it is feasible not merely to examine the relationships between the study region and the rest of the world but to look at the spatial aspects of growth within the region. The method is to construct an analogue to an inter-regional model for *intra-regional* analysis. For example, if the region contained a single large S.M.S.A. separate blocks for the central city, suburbs and rural hinterland might be appropriate; alternatively, in a highly urbanised region with several urban centres an inter-urban model containing z cities and n sectors with a $(nz)^2$ matrix could be used.[2] In these ways a regional input–output model would make more allowance for the spatial aspects of growth than most theories of regional development.

The requirements of a satisfactory dynamic regional input-output model are: projections of final demand changes, best provided, as already suggested, with the aid of an econometric forecasting model; several input coefficient matrices throughout the forecasting period; predictions of changes in regional trade coefficients including shifts in imported capital coefficients; an endogenous capital coefficients matrix; and, possibly, changes in the capital coefficients matrix and in the labour coefficients matrix (i.e. to allow for variation in the ratios of primary inputs to output). Another refinement is to

[1] The only empirical dynamic inter-regional models to my knowledge are those of Bargur (1969) and Mathur (1971).

[2] See Richardson (1973), Chapter 12.

make a distinction between *intensive* and *extensive* growth (see Miernyk, 1967, and Tiebout, 1969). Intensive growth refers to growth in *per capita* income of existing residents, and the relevant coefficient in this case in the marginal propensity to consume; extensive growth is increases in income due to the growth of employment (typically associated with immigration) and here use of the average propensity to consume is appropriate.

However, the input–output model provides a forecasting framework rather than a theory of regional development. For example, it offers little for explanations of the tendency for firms and people to migrate between regions in search of higher returns (apart from predicting mechanistic locational shifts in the form of relative changes in regional output as a by-product of minimising transport costs). It is probably for this reason that Harris (1970) primarily uses an input–output table for forecasting intermediate requirements, but introduces linked location and migration sub-models to deal with inter-regional mobility of capital and labour.

Finally, apart from theoretical drawbacks and its incompleteness, a dynamic inter-regional input–output model is not easy to implement empirically. It is difficult to forecast the main source of input coefficient variation, i.e. technological change, though the use of 'best practice' coefficients has been reasonably successful. When it comes to forecasting trade coefficients, however, no satisfactory technique is available other than *ad hoc* prediction methods. Operationalisation of the dynamic components of the model presents awkard practical problems: the measurement of capacity, especially difficult outside manufacturing; separation of net from replacement investment; distribution of capital goods requirements between local supplies and imports; determination of the 'peak' level of capacity beyond which new investment is triggered off; the prediction of *changes* in the capital coefficients themselves. These have not yet been solved satisfactorily, though they have been discussed by Miernyk (1969).

To sum up, regional input–output models do not deserve the bad press they have received in many quarters. They provide a flexible tool of analysis capable of accommodating several of the key dimensions in regional economic analysis. However, they are forecasting rather than growth models and they work best when combined with other economic models, preferably ones containing behavioural relationships. They are certainly not a substitute for a theory of regional growth.

MULTISECTOR MODELS AND REGIONAL DEVELOPMENT PLANNING

The topic of inter-regional multisectoral growth models has been greatly neglected in the regional growth literature. Apart from mechanistic shift-share and other crude industrial sector models and brief and scattered observations on the consequences of introducing more than one sector into neoclassical models, there is very little about multisector growth. The two areas where there has been some work are inter-regional input-output models and development planning models. Neither tells us very much about the natural evolution of the regional growth process. The inter-regional input–output model, as we have seen, is useful for working out the sectoral and regional output consequences of specified changes in final demand or for dealing with simulated growth sequences. Development planning models in an inter-regional context are primarily concerned with working out optimal regional-sectoral distributions for achieving specified regional income targets, i.e. they are relevant to regional planning rather than to analysis of regional growth. Nevertheless, it may throw some light on the complications that arise from introducing multiple sectors into the regional allocation problem to discuss briefly these development planning models here.

The simplest and most clear-cut treatment derives from Tinbergen and his followers.[1] The basic approach is to use a programming model to deal, at least potentially, with three levels of disaggregation – into industries (sectors), locations (regions) and time periods. Usually the model's framework is simplified to achieve a compromise between theoretical acceptability, data availability and computational feasibility. The major simplifications are:

[1] For example, see Tinbergen (1965 and 1967), Tinbergen and Bos (1962) Mennes, Tinbergen and Waardenburg (1969) and Saigal (1965).

(*i*) Compression of the dynamics into a single projection period.[1]

(*ii*) Decomposition of the global planning problem capable of simultaneous solution into three phases (*Planning by Stages*). These are the macrophase (i.e. setting overall targets for G.N.P., investment, government spending, foreign trade, etc.), the middle phase (i.e. sectoral-regional allocation), and the microphase (selection of individual projects). Our concern here is with the middle phase, and the national growth rate is assumed to be a datum for this phase.

(*iii*) Choosing the minimum number of regions and sectors compatible with homogeneity criteria in order to keep the scale of the model down to manageable size.

(*iv*) Most crucial of all, sectors are classified as regional, national and international sectors according to the mobility of their products.[2] This has two important consequences:

(*a*) transport costs can be ignored, since the definition of a regional (national) sector assumes that transport costs can be treated as zero within the region (nation) and considered prohibitive outside;

(*b*) by assuming that the output of regional sectors is a function of regional income (which is determined by the output of national and international sectors in the region) and that the output of national sectors is a function of national income (determined by the output of the international sectors), the national planning problem is reduced to optimising among international sectors. Similarly, the regional planning problem is solved by allocating the given outputs of national and international sectors among regions.

The national planning problem can now be solved. The choice of the 'optimum' sector is limited to the international sectors. Each expansion in an international sector is associated (by a capital coefficients matrix) with capacity expansion in the national sectors, and expansion in each national sector is associated with predetermined capacity increases in regional

---

[1] Tinbergen has developed dynamic models and Saigal (1965) has given some attention to the time shape of investment and production, finding that it did not alter the key properties of the model.

[2] For a suggested regional, national and international sector classification scheme see Mennes, Tinbergen and Waardenburg (1969), pp. 314–19.

sectors.[1] Thus, the economic system displays hierarchical dependence. Assuming only one overall policy aim – the increase in national income – and only one scarce factor – capital – the international sectors may be ranked on the basis of a simple profitability criterion, i.e. minimisation of the *total* (including complementary) investment needed to increase national income by one unit.[2] The international sector with the lowest capital cost per unit increase in national income is the optimum sector. If we further assume that the national economy faces an infinitely elastic world demand for its exports[3] the optimal allocation of investment resources calls for complete specialisation in the optimum sector. In practice, demand limitations, political constraints and other upper bounds may prevent complete specialisation, but nevertheless optimal allocation will still lead to specialisation in a few rather than in many sectors.

The regional allocation problem can now be solved by casting it as a linear programme. The previous solution gives us the target increase in national income and the most efficient allocation in terms of international sectors to achieve it. We now set regional goals in terms of target increases in regional incomes, where the sum of regional income targets adds up to the predetermined national income. Regional equity criteria may be taken into account in fixing these targets. Given the existence of the necessary basic data, the objective function is to minimise the capital costs of achieving the target regional income levels subject only to obvious internal consistency constraints. The optimal solution will be characterised by regional specialisation in national and international sectors;[4] there can be no specialisation in regional sectors since, by definition, their products cannot be traded between regions.

As described here, the above model predetermines the

[1] Except when there is unused capacity in all national and regional sectors.

[2] We assume that these cost data refer to the expansion of output of each international sector *at its most efficient location*. Once the regional dimension is introduced, this may lead to conflicts between efficiency and equity.

[3] In effect, this requires the country's exports to be small in relation to total world demand.

[4] The sole exception is where regional production functions are identical *and* there are no increasing returns to scale.

regional allocation of international sectors (according to overall efficiency criteria) before tackling the overall regional distribution problem. The sequence of decisions (sector first and region second) may affect the solution. It is possible to handle the national-regional-sectoral planning problem simultaneously by including in the data capital cost-output ratios for expanding the international sectors in *each* region, and a planning model of this type can yield an optimal solution.

This pure model can be described as follows. Assume a system of R regions and N sectors. The sectors are classified into regional sectors $(1, 2 \ldots, N_1)$, national sectors $(N_1+1, N_1+2, \ldots, N_1+N_2)$ and international sectors $(N_1+N_2+1, N_1+N_2+2, \ldots, N_1+N_2+N_3)$. The objective function to be minimised is

$$Z = \sum_{r=1}^{R} \sum_{n=1}^{N} v_n^r y_n^r \tag{2.23}$$

subject to

$$y_n^r = a_n^r y^r \qquad (n = 1, \ldots, N_1) \tag{2.24}$$

$$\sum_{r=1}^{R} y_n^r = a_n y = y_n \qquad (n = N_1+1, \ldots, N_1+N_2) \tag{2.25}$$

$$\sum_{n=1}^{N} y_n^r = y^r \tag{2.26}$$

$$y_n^r \geqslant 0 \tag{2.27}$$

where v_n^r = marginal capital/output coefficient of sector n in region r in value added terms, y_n^r = increase in value added of sector n in region r, a_n^r = increase in total demand (value added) for product n in region r per unit increase of region r's income, y^r = increase in income of region r, a_n = increase in total demand (value added) for product n in the country per unit increase of national income, y = increase in national income, y_n = increase in value added of sector n in the nation as a whole.

Equations (2.24) are the regional sector supply and demand balance equations, while equations (2.25) are the balance equations for national sectors. There are no balance equations for international sectors, and exports and imports for these sectors may be calculated once the optimal solution has been found. Equations (2.26) state that the sum of sectoral income expansions must equal the income target in each region, while the Inequalities (2.27) reflect the assumption that it is inefficient in a growing economy for any sector in any region to reduce its output.[1]

The trouble with the 'pure' model is that its solution may involve either the inefficient location of international sectors or even specialisation in sectors that is inefficient from the national economy point of view. Since most countries give primacy to national over regional planning, a solution of this kind – though optimal, given the goals – may be unacceptable. It is likely that in such a case the regional income targets would be revised and that policy-makers would revert to a sequential planning approach (Reiner, 1965).

Additional refinements to the model include allowing for transport costs (Saigal, 1965) and for indivisibilities and increasing returns to scale. There are several methods of handling the latter problem,[2] but the most satisfactory approach theoretically is by introducing an urban hierarchy model (Tinbergen, 1961; Bos, 1965). This extends the optimisation approach into the space economy by permitting indivisibilities in production and acknowledging the existence of urban centres of different size. The difficulties in the way of implementing such a model are, however, tremendous.

The Tinbergen model represents an interesting approach to dealing with the double problem of allocating resources among sectors and regions. But most of the work on the model has been highly theoretical[3] and mathematical, its data requirements are heavy, and it is doubtful whether the solutions of the model can provide more than very crude and broad guidelines for planning decisions. Also, the model can give absurd results unless upper and lower bounds are introduced into it. These constraints have to be introduced very carefully since the model

[1] This is a useful simplification for computational purposes, though it may conflict with reality.

[2] For instance, minimum levels of output increases for each sector could be predetermined above which constant marginal (= average) costs may be assumed but below which output increases are not feasible. This approach requires mixed integer linear programming models which are difficult to solve. Alternatively, non-linear decreasing cost functions could be approximated by introducing a fixed cost component as part of total costs.

[3] An exception is Carrillo Arronte's (1969) application to Mexico.

has the unfortunate property that its optimal solutions are very sensitive to the levels and types of constraint imposed.

Apart from this, the model is unsatisfactory in many respects:

(*i*) It is applicable only to a centrally planned economy. In effect, it assumes a single decision-making centre whereas the typical situation in a modern mixed economy is an interplay between several partially independent but hierarchically structured decision-making units (central government departments, regional authorities, public or semi-public development agencies and municipalities).

(*ii*) The spectrum of regional policy goals is too broad to be reflected in a set of regional income targets. In particular, the satisfaction of locational preferences and other social goals cannot easily be converted into such targets.

(*iii*) The classification of sectors is arbitrary, and the definition of regional sectors depends heavily upon how regions are selected and on the assumption that market areas do not overlap regional boundaries.

(*iv*) The usefulness of the model depends upon the constancy of its main coefficients.[1] It is doubtful whether these coefficients are stable, and in any event most countries lack the relevant data.

(*v*) Interdependencies are treated in a very superficial way, namely the hierarchical dependence between sectors (international → national → regional). The treatment of space is merely implicit. In my view, a satisfactory regional planning model needs to take account of both spatial agglomeration effects and long-run inter-dependencies between investment (e.g. the inter-relationships between transport investment, urban infrastructure and private sector investment).[2] Neither of these considerations can be accommodated in a short-run spaceless model of the development planning type.[3]

(*vi*) The development planning approach glosses over rather

---

[1] In terms of the model described above, these coefficients are v_n^r, a_n^r and a_n.

[2] For attempts to deal with these problems, see Chapter 6, pp. 151–71.

[3] The urban hierarchy approach aims at inclusion of spatial agglomeration effects. See Mennes, Tinbergen and Waardenburg (1969), Chapter 8, particularly the reporting of empirical analysis by J. E. Parker; Bos (1965); and Tinbergen (1964).

than eradicates the inevitable conflicts that arise in regional development policy and planning. The only conflict that it deals with is that between economic efficiency (optimisation by sectors) and equity (regional income targets). It ignores conflicts between national and regional goals, between economic and social, spatial and political objectives, between the short and the long run, between the individual and the needs of the economy and society, between the relative contributions of the public and private sectors, and conflicts among the different hierarchical levels of government.

(*vii*) Most important of all, to aim for regional income targets by planning expansions in individual sectors on the basis of minimum cost is a misplaced approach to regional planning. Attempts to optimise the regional distribution of each industry are either impossible or ineffective in a mixed economy. The most direct and useful approach to the regionalisation of national plans is through the distribution of public investment and social infrastructure rather than industrial output. Of course, regional policies do, and should, attempt to influence the regional distribution of industry, but the spatial allocation of public investment is under much firmer control.[1]

---

[1] These issues are discussed in more depth in Chapter 9, pp. 226–36.

Chapter 3

Space and Regional Growth Analysis

INTRODUCTION

The appraisal of the current state of regional growth analysis in Chapter 2 cannot, and should not, be interpreted as a demolition job on previous work. There is still scope for future research in these areas, for instance, on more specific cumulative causation models and on econometric and dynamic regional input-output models. Only in regard to export base and neoclassical theories is it arguable that diminishing returns to research effort have set in. Nevertheless, there is a strong case for striking out in a new direction. No regional growth theory hitherto developed has stood up well to empirical tests. All the theories have been too general in character to be of much practical value to the regional policymaker, and since the development of this branch of economics owes almost everything to its policy orientation this is a consideration that we cannot afford to neglect.

My basic premise is that any revision of regional growth theory must start from the explicit introduction of space and distance into the analysis, both in the sense of distance separating regions in the inter-regional system and of spatial differentiation within regions. If this premise is accepted, most conventional economic theories – and certainly all aggregate growth theory – have to be laid aside as irrelevant.

Of course, a minority of regional economists has urged the importance of spatial elements in the analysis of regional growth. Examples worth noting are Friedmann's stress on centre-periphery models and development corridors (1966), the attempts to give a spatial dimension to the theory of *pôles de croissance* as found in Boudeville's work (1966), von Böventer's analysis of agglomeration economies and hinterland effects as offsetting forces influencing the size and spacing of cities and hence of regions (1970), Siebert's generalisations on the role of the transport sector, polarisation forces and the spatial diffusion of technical knowledge in regional growth (1969) and Olsen's inclusion of income potential and degree of urbanisation among the determinants of regional growth (1971). However, with the possible exception of Friedmann's theory which is very loosely formulated and primarily applicable to countries that are just beginning to industrialise, these comments are very general in nature, partial in their coverage of the aspects of the space economy, and fall far short of becoming theories of regional development. The ultimate aim of this book is to develop a theory of regional growth accommodating the spatial dimension. At this stage, however, I wish to discuss some alternative approaches to the problem of how to introduce space into the analysis of regional growth.

The justification for the inclusion of spatial variables in regional growth analysis is so clear-cut that it is scarcely necessary to argue the case. Location theory is an important branch of regional economics, rightly so, yet it is scarcely referred to in discussions of regional growth. Until the two branches of location economics and inter-regional macro-economics are successfully integrated, there is little hope that we shall be able to understand the regional growth process. Of course, the difficulties of achieving this integration are immense. First, there is no widely accepted dynamic theory of location. Second, the reconciliation of a behavioural theory of location based on the actions of the individual decision-maker with the impersonal process of change in regional growth and structure presents severe problems.

Although regional growth theory almost invariably treats the inter-regional system as a set of spaceless points separated by unspecified distances, this is at odds with our methods of regional delimitation. Although for practical reasons regional economists often work with the regions marked out by existing political boundaries, there has been increasing stress on the need to define regions in terms of meaningful economic criteria. One of the most approved concepts of a region, i.e. the *functional economic area* associated with the work of Fox and Kumar

(1965), is itself described in spatial terms (usually the boundary of the commuting area for labour around a central city), and it would be impossible to analyse growth in a F.E.A. by abstracting from space.

In evaluating the relative growth performance of the regions that make up the national economy, we invariably find that the most isolated areas of the country cluster near the bottom of the league. Similarly, within regions (though not within urban areas) the least prosperous areas tend to be those that are furthest away from the main centres of development. There is a marked tendency for levels of prosperity to decline with increasing distance from the richest regions and from the wealthiest metropolitan areas. This is, of course, merely the centre-periphery model once again. The point in this context is that it is difficult to see how to analyse the growth potential of isolated regions (or isolated areas within regions) without considering the effects of their distance from the most prosperous parts of the economy.

From the point of view of the relevance of regional growth models to regional policy and planning, the case for spatial models is overwhelmingly strong. Although there is some scope for a non-spatial regional policy, e.g. inducing inter-regional transfers of firms by investment incentives or other subsidies, the development of comprehensive regional planning cannot abstract from space. The location and scale of urban infrastructure, the development of inter-regional transport networks, the growth of multi-regional strategies for resource management and recreational facilities, in all problems of this kind the spatial dimension is critical. Similarly, the development in many countries of growth pole strategies and the realisation that regional problems are more often than not surrogates for metropolitan problems, emphasise the interdependence between regional economic policy and physical planning. If this argument is valid, then regional growth theory should be of more service to the regional policy-maker than neo-classical or other currently favoured models.

LOCATION THEORY AND REGIONAL GROWTH

A very recent trend in economic theory is the attempts to reconcile its micro-economic and macro-economic components. In the area of regional economics this reconciliation involves bringing together the theory of industrial location (how the individual firm or household decides where to locate) and the theory of inter-regional macro-economics (and, in a dynamic context, the theory of regional growth). In this particular case the integration is particularly difficult. On the top of the usual aggregation problem, we have two further major obstacles. First, industrial location theory is by definition a *spatial* theory whereas regional growth analysis is usually based upon the assumption that the inter-regional system consists of a set of spaceless regions. Second, the dynamic aspects of industrial location are grossly underdeveloped so that the analyst is faced with how to relate static models of location to the dynamics of the regional growth process. These obstacles have still to be overcome, and here we will do little more than indicate some of the major problems with one or two pointers towards possible solutions.

It is not easy to find an internal consistency between the cost and revenue variables facing the individual location decision-maker in a particular industry and the overall macro-economic variables (G.R.P., regional employment, etc.) with which regional growth differentials are measured. The simplest solution is to adopt a neoclassical framework to deal with both levels of aggregation. This means assuming that location decision-makers have perfect knowledge and attempt to maximise profits while regional growth paths are determined by optimality criteria whereby factors are allocated between regions according to the distribution that maximises national income (i.e. maximisation of the output of the inter-regional system as a whole). Unfortunately, this solution cannot be adopted with any confidence because the location theories it demands contradict how location decision-makers actually behave. Imperfections in knowledge, uncertainties about the future course of costs and revenues at each location, high relocation costs, personal locational preferences and other considerations make a profit-maximising location model unacceptable.[1] Indeed, these factors rule out a determinate location theory, and this indeterminacy makes it virtually impossible to make precise predictions about regional growth differentials that are rooted in the decisions of individual firms and households.

This does not necessarily imply a defeatist conclusion. There are at least two possible lines of development capable of linking location with growth. The first possibility arises in those circumstances where growth is conceived spatially. The 'growth pole' concept, for instance, includes within its scope the notion of 'technical polarisation', locational agglomeration consequent upon the location decisions of firms in propulsive industries, and that of geographical polarisation which implies, *inter alia*, the raising of area growth performance by spatial concentration. Similarly, the Tinbergen-Bos urban hierarchy model provides a framework for reconciling the location decisions of individual plants – based on scale economies – with the structure of the intra-regional urban hierarchy.[2] In both these cases, however, the penalty paid for introducing space into the analysis is an inadequate treatment of time, and consequently a fuzzy and imprecise explanation – or none at all – of how spatial agglomeration affects regional growth.

The second approach is potentially more valuable, primarily because it rests upon a much more satisfactory location theory. In effect, there are two slightly different versions – one based on risk-averting non-maximising locational criteria, the other on the assumption that location decisions are purely random – which yield similar results. Both rest on a probabilistic rather than a deterministic framework. In the first case, risk aversion will reinforce the advantages of already established (central) locations rather than new, untried ones (usually located peripherally). The uncertainty and incomplete information that characterise location decisions discriminate in favour of centralised locations. The need to save time in making location

---

[1] See Richardson (1969a, pp. 90–100) for an elaboration of these arguments. See also Olsson and Gale (1968, pp. 229–32) for a similar point of view.

[2] See Tinbergen (1961) and Bos (1965). The Löschian model lends itself to a similar interpretation. For a recent attempt to reconcile individual locations with urban–regional structure see Greenhut (1970).

decisions also favours core locations. Thus, the preference for the centre is easily explained (see Alonso, 1968, especially pp. 24–5 and p. 39). D. M. Smith (1971) suggests that business firms may locate anywhere within the spatial margins of profitability; some firms (quasi-profit-maximisers) locate as near as possible to the optimal location while others who attach importance to non-pecuniary benefits (e.g. personal locational preferences) are free to locate anywhere within the spatial margins. Each potential location will carry a certain probability of firms being located there, and central locations will usually be favoured both by profit-maximisers and risk-averters.

The evolution of location patterns may, on this view, be treated as a stochastic process where different probabilities are assigned to each location. However, even a purely random locational process (this is the second case) can have a similar result on the reasonable assumption that the central locations are objectively better sites than those on the periphery. In such an event, the process of competition itself will eventually result in a clustering of establishments at the core.[1] This is because as the process of industrial change continues associated with the entry of new firms and the exit of old ones certain areas will develop with a well above average spatial concentration of industry, and economies of agglomeration generated there will attract yet more new firms. The dominance of the core will be reinforced by this cumulative process. In analytical terms, the links between the determinants of individual locations (whether risk-averting or purely random) and the *ex post* pattern of inter-area growth differentials may be explored with the aid of a Markov chain model. Such a model enables us to take account of the fact that the occupation of any site by an industrial plant may alter the probability that other locations may be selected, e.g. close-by locations might become more attractive because of agglomeration economies or, conceivably, less attractive

[1] In Hoover's words (1948, p. 10), 'Competition, insofar as it prevails, will reward the well-located enterprises and shorten the lives of poorly located ones. Even if new establishments were to be located purely by guesswork or whim or by sticking pins into a map at random, and if they were never relocated, some semblance of a reasonable pattern would still emerge as a result of competition.' See also Tiebout (1957, p. 84).

because the new plant competes for local labour or other inputs. The Markov chain approach allows the probability of development at a particular time and located to be related to what has gone before. It is possible, therefore, to simulate a regional development path in terms of the evolutionary sequence of a set of individual location decisions.

If we consider these brief comments on location theory in the context of their relevance to regional growth theory, it is clear that a behavioural approach to location is readily consistent with the concept of the centre-periphery model. There are affinities, of course, between the predictions of the centre-periphery model (Friedmann, 1966) and Myrdal's (1957) theory of cumulative causation. Both approaches stress the cumulative and self-reinforcing advantages of the initially established locations in the process of development, with particular stress on the role of agglomeration and other external economies. At the most general level, there is a direct correspondence between profit-maximising location models and the neoclassical inter-regional equilibrium growth model. Similarly, we can identify a correspondence between behavioural models of location (with their emphasis on 'satisficing', reducing uncertainty and risk aversion and, subsequently, the attractive power of agglomeration economies) and the cumulative causation theory of regional growth. In expressing a preference for one growth theory rather than another (whether on *a priori* grounds or as a result of empirical tests), we are, by implication, also taking a standpoint on the status of the theory of location for the individual firm.

THE TRANSPORTATION SECTOR AND REGIONAL GROWTH

At first sight, the simplest method of introducing space into regional growth analysis is to recognise explicitly the existence of the transportation sector. The relationship between spatial efficiency and the mobility of resources, goods and persons is obvious. Transport costs (interpreted widely) are a barrier to mobility, and efficiency in the transportation sector is an important precondition for maximising a region's growth potential.

Analysis of the role of transport in regional growth is not so easy, however.[1] First, we must distinguish between the inter-regional transport system and the intra-regional. It is unclear whether improved efficiency in inter-regional transport models will promote polarisation or dispersion. For instance, by raising the potential mobility of factors of production lower transport costs can stimulate polarisation towards fixed locations due to immobile resources; similarly, lower transport costs for commodities may expand markets and promote the exploitation of scale economies. On the other hand, lower transport costs may widen locational choice and through their impact on resource mobility reduce the effects of an initially unequal spatial distribution of resources; these factors will promote dispersion. We cannot say *a priori* whether inter-regional transport improvements will tend to raise or lower the growth rate of a particular region. On the other hand, intra-regional transport improvements always raise growth potential unless resources are diverted into transportation from more productive uses.

Second, the transportation sector has two separate effects on growth which act to offset each other. Although the output of the transport industry is counted as part of G.R.P., some expenditures on transport services may be harmful to growth if they result from inefficient location patterns, e.g. a consumer is indifferent whether a homogeneous good is produced in the same area or 500 miles away.[2] Overcoming spatial frictions uses up resources that can then no longer be employed in the

[1] An important reason for this is the fact that transport fulfils several different functions. First, it may be thought of as a factor input necessary to move goods and people between and within production and consumption locations. Second, it may shift production possibilities since transport cost changes alter travel times and change inventory and other capital costs. Third, increasing speed and extension of the transport network has favourable effects on factor mobility, bringing about changes in the spatial distribution of population and economic activity. Finally, transport is an important private and public consumption good. See Fromm (1965, pp. 5-6).

[2] Other transportation services clearly confer substantial benefits, e.g. tourism. Also, if a householder chooses a suburban location that involves a long work-trip it cannot be argued that his expenditures on transport services are in any sense wasteful since they enable him to satisfy his housing preferences and to increase his utility. The implication is that we must be very careful about prescribing transport-cost-minimising strategies as always being consistent with maximising welfare.

production of goods. If inputs into goods production and transport are homogeneous, minimising current expenditures on transport is equivalent to minimising all production costs which is (in conditions of inelastic demand) the same as maximising output. In this sense, a reasonable index of regional welfare is G.R.P. minus the 'excess' output of the transportation sector. Any change which *ceteris paribus* reduces the need to move goods, factors or persons around has a favourable effect upon growth, i.e. transport cost savings are an addition to growth.

The second type of impact relates to transport innovations. These raise regional growth, first by increasing the gap between G.R.P. and the putput of transport services, second and more important by their effects on resource mobility (whether this promotes polarisation and spatial concentration or locational dispersion) and on regional specialisation (a fall in transport costs operates in the same way as a reduction in tariff barriers). These two types of effect are not irreconcilable, since one shows itself in a much shorter run than the other. For instance, from the view of policy there is a distinction but no contradiction between minimising expenditures on current transport services and maximising returns – as measured by growth increments – from investments in transport facilities.

These considerations suggest that there might be scope for a theory of regional growth which recognises the special position of the transport sector for spatial analysis and separates it out from other sectors. There is another major reason supporting this view. The demand for the output of transportation does not depend, like the demand for other goods and services, only on regional incomes or the output of other sectors, but also and more fundamentally on the location of production and consumption. Increasing expenditures on transport may be quite consistent with efficiency if they permit a spatial distribution of economic activity that raises output compared with the transport-cost-minimising distribution by more than the increased transport expenditures.

Two major approaches have dominated the literature hitherto. First, a number of analysts (Lefeber, 1958; Berman, 1959; Moses, 1960; and Mohring and Harwitz, 1962, pp. 92–131) have separated out the transportation sector from other sectors in the economy and explored its role within a linear programming framework. In all cases, however, changing location patterns were handled in a very simplistic fashion. It may be feasible to adapt this approach to dynamic analysis.

For example, Mathur (1971) has developed a dynamic inter-regional programming model which is similar to the static models mentioned above in that it is concerned with minimisation of transport costs and hence of total costs (assuming input homogeneity) in an inter-regional system. Its special contribution is to introduce a capital coefficients matrix and a growth rate. Growth is handled by the use of Leontief trajectories where each trajectory is defined by a vector of final demand and the rate of growth of that final demand. Total output and capital also grow at the same rate, so that the model in effect deals with a special case of balanced growth. For the purposes of computation, growth is treated by adding the growth rate multiplied by the capital coefficients to the input–output coefficients, and then operating with the new augmented coefficients substituted for the original ones. For a particular growth rate, the model can be written as:

$$\text{Min } Z = \sum_m^n \sum_i^z \sum_j^z T_m^{ij} X_m^{ij} \tag{3.1}$$

subject to

$$X_m^i + \sum_{j=1}^z X_m^{ji} - \sum_{j=1}^z X_m^{ij} - \sum_{k=1}^n (a_{mk}^i + y g_{mk}^i) X_k^i \geqslant Y_m^i \tag{3.2}$$

$$\sum_{i=1}^z X_m^i \leqslant X_m \tag{3.3}$$

where T_m^{ij} = transport cost for shipping one unit of commodity m from region i to region j, X_m^{ij} = shipments of m from region i to region j, $\sum_{j=1}^z X_m^{ji}$ = imports of m into region i, $\sum_{j=1}^z X_m^{ji}$ = exports of m from region i, a_{mk}^i = input coefficient of commodity m required per unit of k, y = growth rate in output, g_{mk}^i = capital coefficient, Y_m^i = final demand of m in region i, X_m = national output of industry m obtained by solving the dynamic model for the national economy.

This is a standard transport cost minimisation programme which also implies optimisation of production. The model is made dynamic by amending the production inequality equation (3.2) to allow for growth in the economy, and in particular, for its capital creating effects.[1] It was implemented at a five-region, twenty-seven sector level in India using input-output data for 1959, and solutions were obtained for three growth rates (zero, ten and fifteen per cent). Although certain heavy industries (iron and steel, cement, glass, jute, and wood products) were locationally inelastic, the optimal spatial distribution of many industries changed dramatically with variations in the growth rate. This finding, that the optimal spatial distribution of economic activity is sensitive to changes in the aggregate rate of growth, has obvious general significance for the arguments about the interdependence between spatial and growth dynamics urged in this book. Nevertheless, the restrictions of linear programming models mean that the theoretical implications of this type of approach for regional growth analysis remain very limited.

The second possibility is to combine a macroeconomic transport model allowing for changes in mode, routes, shipments and so forth with an input-output model as developed at Harvard for Colombia (Roberts and Kresge, 1969). The problem with these methods of introducing space into the economy is that we cannot properly examine the interdependence between transportation and other sectors during the process of regional

---

[1] Mathur's model also included two other features not represented in equation (3.1) and constraints (3.2) and (3.3). The first was to assume that the distribution of natural resources industries was determined by current shares in national output. This was primarily a device for economising on data requirements. The second modification was to introduce an inter-regional balance of trade constraint, i.e.

$$\sum_{j=1}^{z} \sum_{m=1}^{n} X_m^{ij} - \sum_{j=1}^{z} \sum_{m=1}^{n} X_m^{ji} = 0.$$

While there is no reason why inter-regional trade should balance since regions do not experience balance of payments problems of the kind occurring in nations, nevertheless a long-run balance of payments deficit may be associated with chronic stagnation and persistent out-migration so that a balance of trade constraint may be a useful equity constraint. As it happened, in Mathur's empirical implementation of the model in India the optimum pattern of production was very sensitive to imposition of a balance of trade constraint since many industries were highly localised in certain areas of the country. Neither of these features is an essential characteristic of a dynamic inter-regional programming model, and consequently both have been excluded from the description of the model in the text.

growth without a dynamic general equilibrium model of the space economy. In particular, we cannot determine the optimal rate of investment and levels of output in the transportation sector without simultaneously determining the optimal spatial distribution of activities and population from the point of view of maximising regional growth. Yet the concept of the optimal spatial structure remains elusive, perhaps Utopian.

INCOME POTENTIAL AND GRAVITY TRADE MODELS

Gravity and income potential models are the most obvious way of allowing for the effects that the friction of distance has on inter-regional analysis. In a growth context the income potential concept is the most relevant, but the bulk of empirical research relates to the much simpler problem of how distance affects inter-regional trade (pure gravity trade models). It is now almost twenty years ago since Isard first suggested (Isard, 1954) the use of *relative income potential* as a measure for registering the simultaneous impact of changes in incomes of several regions upon region i, i.e.

$$\frac{{}_iV_{t+1}}{(1+z){}_iV_t}$$

where ${}_iV = \sum_{j=1}^{n} \frac{{}_iY_j}{d_{ij}^{\alpha}} =$ income potential at region i ($Y =$ income and $d =$ distance) and $z =$ rate of growth of income in the inter-regional system as a whole. The element $(1+z)$ is used to yield a relative income potential of unity in the theoretical limiting case where the incomes of all regions of the system increase at the same rate. When the rise in national income is concentrated in regions relatively close to i, the relative income potential for i is greater than 1; this represents an improvement in i's inter-regional economic position. On the other hand, if income growth is concentrated in regions distant from i, relative income potential is less than 1, and i's position in the inter-regional system deteriorates.

A more recent and more ambitious use of income potential approaches is found in Warntz (1965). Warntz develops a model of inter-regional growth and income differentials from inductive generalisations about the relationships between income potential, income density and *per capita* income differentials. There is a fairly clear relationship between income potential and income density, where $D = KV^3$, where $D =$ income density and $K =$ a constant. There is no close connection, however, between income potential and *per capita* income surfaces. The latter are much more discontinuous. Indeed, the discontinuities in the *per capita* income surface are so marked that Warntz describes them as 'income fronts,' analogous to the term used in meteorology to mark the boundary between masses of air of unlike temperature but where there is no discontinuity of the pressure surface across the boundary. In an analysis of state *per capita* incomes in the United States for 1956, Warntz finds three regions separated by two main fronts. The bulk of the United States forms an average zone (called the 'main sequence'), separated by one front from a high value zone in the Far West and by another from a low value front in the South.[1]

Theoretical predictions arise from Warntz's observation that the major income fronts are dissipating over time, because of convergence of values for the Far West and the South to that of the 'main sequence' of states. At any given moment of time regional income differences and the fronts associated with them can be regarded as functions of the friction of distance. The dissipation of the fronts consequently reflects either a decline in the friction of distance over time due, say, to improvements in inter-regional transportation and communications or the fact that spatial adjustment processes take a considerable period of time. The initial regional income differences are, according to Warntz, explained by exogenous disturbances of a general

---

[1] In view of the argument in this book for a general theory of spatial development, it is interesting to notice that the income potential, density and front analysis can be generalised to any level of spatial disaggregation from the highest level, i.e. the world economy, down to the intraregional and the metropolitan levels. For example, Warntz argues that within cities 'Slum Fronts' can be identified, and that these are analogous to the regional income fronts (p. 29).

inter-regional equilibrium. He cites, not very convincingly, natural resource (especially mineral) discoveries in the Far West as an upwards disturbance and the consequences of the Civil War in the South as a downwards disturbance. However, the disequilibrium created is not cumulative (at least not indefinitely) but leads to several spatial adjustment processes which tend to restore equilibrium. These adjustment processes include: inter-regional trade which narrows price differentials; inter-regional movements of capital and labour tending to equalise factor returns; and the equalising impacts of the Federal tax system and social welfare expenditures.[1] Despite the novelty of the concepts (income fronts and, to a lesser extent, income potential), this analysis has a familiar ring to it. I would argue that it is merely the neoclassical theory in disguise. The neoclassical model is the counterpart in economic theory to the inductive income front model a main feature of which is the dissipation of these fronts over time. Yet the Warntz analysis is not totally derivative. One very interesting observation is that if the peak of income potential moves over time, it does not shift slowly but jumps discontinuously over a long distance. Such a shift will be associated with a major technological change (Warntz, p. 108).

These approaches do not succeed in integrating the income potential concept with a regional economic model. Antecedents to such an integration include Isard and Freutel's (1954) attempt to show the usefulness of the concept for long-term economic projections and Clark's stress on the importance of income potential as an influence on location decisions (Clark (1966) and Clark, Wilson and Bradley (1969)). I suggested (Richardson, 1969a) how income potential might be incorporated into a short-run regional macro-economic model of income determination, though the treatment was highly simplistic and distance variables were included solely as an

[1] The interaction between the disequilibrium and equilibrating forces can most easily be illustrated by reference to inter-regional migration. A transfer of population between regions without any change in regional incomes will tend to adjust the per capita incomes surface so as to remove the fronts and bring the surface into close agreement with the income potential surface. However, it is the existence of the income fronts which provides the initial inducement to migrate.

influence on the regional trade propensities. I have thought for some time that income potential models might satisfy the minimum necessary conditions for integrating space with regional growth analysis. A recent paper by Peaker (1971) outlines an income potential model of regional growth. Although unsatisfactory in some respects, such as its neglect of the role of labour in regional growth analysis and the fact that he addresses his attention to the wrong problems, i.e. the conditions of balanced growth in an inter-regional system, his model is nevertheless the first of its kind.[1]

The model may briefly be described as follows. He assumed: a closed system of two regions; no population growth; identical Cobb–Douglas production functions in each region; and no capital depreciation. Investment consists of two components: *induced investment* that is linked to the level of regional output and *mobile investment*, the distribution of which is determined by the relative income potential of the regions. The model's equations are:

$$Y_1 = AK_1^\alpha \tag{3.4}$$

$$\dot{K}_1 = aY_1 + b(V_1 - V_2) \tag{3.5}$$

$$V_1 = \frac{Y_1}{t_1} + \frac{Y_2}{t_1 + t_2 + t_{12}} \tag{3.6}$$

where Y = output, K = regional capital stock, $\dot{K}$ = differentiation of capital stock with respect to time, V = income potential, t_1, t_2 = intra-regional transport costs for regions 1 and 2 respectively, t_{12} = inter-regional transport costs, a, A a and b are all constants. Substituting equations (3.4) and (3.6) into equation (3.5) yields

$$\dot{K}_1 = \left[a + b \left(\frac{1}{t_1} - \frac{1}{t_1 + t_2 + t_{12}} \right) \right] AK^\alpha$$

$$+ b \left(\frac{1}{t_2} - \frac{1}{t_1 + t_2 + t_{12}} \right) AK_2^\alpha \tag{3.7}$$

[1] It should be noted, however, that relative income potential features as an influence on regional capital stock growth in Olsen's model (1971).

Thus, changes in regional investment can be described in terms of regional capital stocks and transport costs (both intra-regional and inter-regional).

Much more work needs to be done on income potential models. Peaker's version merely regards relative income potential as one determinant of regional investment, if the most important part, i.e. the component that is responsible for regional growth differentials. It may be possible to go further and treat *per capita* income potential as a *measure* of regional growth rather than solely as an influence on the inter-regional mobility of capital. Such a measure would take into account (i) the proximity of high income regions as a factor affecting the growth potential of a region, and (*ii*) the size and spatial distribution of the intra-regional market as a determinant of new location decisions.

A more straightforward approach to subjecting the frictions of distance to test is to examine the degree to which distance limits the mobility of factors (capital, labour) and commodity trade. Since both factor and commodity movements tend to equalise regional price and (in a neoclassical world) income differences, distance between regions will reduce these equalising tendencies compared with predictions in a spaceless world. At the same time, proximity to large fast-growing regions will affect the rate of development experienced in an area. Whether the net impact is favourable or not will depend (to employ Myrdal's terminology) on whether 'spread' or 'backwash' effects predominate in the determination of factor and commodity flows.

The simplest method of measuring the friction of distance would be to use a standard type gravity model to see how far inter-regional flows are influenced by inter-regional distances. In a growth context, it would be more important to study factor flows.[1] Unfortunately, the data are too sparse and imperfect for such an analysis. There are no firm inter-regional capital flow statistics. Inter-regional labour migration data are more plentiful though far from perfect. There have been several studies of inter-regional migration that have used gravity components, but the results of these studies have been far from clear-cut.[2] Most of the empirical research into how

[1] See the subsequent analysis in Chapter 4.
[2] See Chapter 4, pp. 89–103.

distance reduces spatial interaction has been concerned with flows which are easier to measure (i.e. because data are more readily available) and where the relevant distance variable is either mileage or transport costs. Hence, the bulk of the work has been concerned with commodity flows. Though less relevant to an analysis of growth than a study of factor flows, it is useful to refer to this literature for a general assessment of the impact of spatial frictions on one type of interaction and for the conceptual framework of how to measure distance effects within a gravity model context. Even so, there are severe data limitations in regard to inter-regional commodity trade, and although there have been some inter-regional studies (see below) the most detailed research has been on international trade flows.

It is relevant to look at this research, but the differences between international and inter-regional trade flows prevent results from being directly transferable. In particular, what Linnemann (1966) calls *artificial trade impediments* such as tariffs, quotas and exchange agreements have a similar attenuating impact on international trade flows as distance itself. One consequence of this is that in an international trade flows model it is frequently necessary to include a variable that reflects the presence of preferential trade agreements between pairs of countries. Moreover, where mileage distance measures are used it is more difficult to select the appropriate origins and destinations within countries than within regions, in the sense that a higher proportion of inter-regional trade may take place between the major regional metropolises than of international trade between national capitals. In measuring international distances, occasionally the road and sea distance between the capitals is used though a more frequent measure is the sea distances between the main ports plus the road distances from the port to the country's 'economic centre of gravity'.

The list of studies in English on gravity models of international trade is now quite extensive (Isard and Peck, 1954; Beckerman, 1956; Tinbergen, 1962; Pöyhönen, 1963; Linnemann, 1966; Yeates, 1969), and there are several foreign-language studies (Vierteljahrshefte zur Statistik des Deutschen Reichs, 1928; G. J. Aeyelts Averink, 1960 and 1961; K. Pulliainen, 1963). The earlier research merely observed the tendency for the volume of trade flows to be inversely related to distance between trading partners, and illustrated this either with simple graphical techniques (e.g. Isard and Peck) or rank correlation techniques (Beckerman). The research from Tinbergen onwards, however, uses multiple regression analysis to estimate a trade flow equation, variants of which conform to a pure gravity model. For instance, the initial Tinbergen tests carried out on eighteen (mainly developed) countries using 1958 exports were based on a simple gravity model:

$$X_{ij} = a_0 Y_i^{a_1} Y_j^{a_2} d_{ij}^{a_3} \tag{3.8}$$

where X_{ij} = export flow from country i to country j, a_0 = constant, Y_i, Y_j = national income, i.e. a mass variable; d_{ij} = distance, a_1, a_2, a_3 = exponents. The variable d was measured as geographical distance, but this was intended as a surrogate for at least two elements: transport costs and an index of information about export markets. The multiple correlation coefficient (R^2) was about 0.82. In further tests dummy variables were added for (i) preferential trade agreements, and for (ii) neighbouring countries, but this raised the correlation coefficient merely by two per cent. In a more detailed investigation of the trade between forty-two countries (accounting for seventy per cent of total world trade) in 1959, a test of the original gravity model merely with a dummy variable added for neighbouring countries yielded a correlation coefficient of 0.8104. In another series of tests a Gini coefficient of export commodity concentration was used as a measure of the degree of export diversification, but this had little explanatory value. In all the tests, a_3 had the expected negative sign, while the values of a_1 and a_2 were always close to 1 (i.e. export flows were almost proportional to the G.N.P. of the exporting and importing country).

The subsequent work differed in detail rather than substance from the Tinbergen study. In Pöyhönen's analysis (1963), for instance, he measured distance in transport cost terms rather than physical distance and introduced an export parameter for the country of export and an import parameter for the country of import. In a test for ten European countries in 1958, the multiple correlation coefficient was about 0.94. In follow-up studies for thirteen years (1948–60) of trade between sixty-two non-communist countries he introduced two additional variables, one to represent the trading area in which each country belonged, the other to reflect meteorological conditions (the assumption being that the larger the differences between mean temperatures, the greater the need to exchange commodities). However, the explanatory power of the model was only slightly increased.

Linneman's study was even broader, based on an analysis of 6300 commodity trade flows between eighty non-communist countries for 1959. The distinctive feature of Linnemann's work was not so much in the testing of the model but in his attempt to provide stronger theoretical underpinnings. He argued that trade flows can be explained by three sets of variables: factors determining the total potential supply of the exporting country; determinants of total potential demand of the importing country; and the resistances to trade flows. The potential foreign trade ratio is defined as the ratio of exports plus imports to G.N.P., and it is hypothesized that this ratio varies only in relation to differences in population size between countries.[1] This hypothesis tests on two assumptions: economies of scale and the diversification of demand at higher levels of income. The more specific hypotheses are: (i) that there is a negative correlation between the foreign trade ratio and population; (ii) independence between a country's foreign trade and its *per capita* income.

The more important part of the analysis from our point of view lies in his discussion of trade resistances. He argues that these fall into two categories, natural trade obstacles and artificial trade obstacles. Among the natural trade obstacles he singles out transport costs, time and 'psychic distance'[2] as the three main influences, and uses geographical distance to measure the combined effect of all three. At the same time he criticises Beckerman (1956) and Balassa (1962) for arguing that

[1] It is relevant here to note Tinbergen's proposal that the scientific definition of the various 'space units' (continents, countries, regions, cities, villages) should be based on the foreign trade ratios of the areas concerned. Also, we should note the similarity between this hypothesis and the well-known generalisations of regional multiplier and export base analysis, that the marginal propensity to import and the X/Y (export/output) ratio are both inverse functions of regional size.

[2] Beckerman was one of the first to emphasise psychic (or socio-cultural) distance as a determinant of trading ties.

economic distance between countries can be measured by the difference between f.o.b. prices for particular commodities. The defect of such a measure is that it can only be applied to commodities actually traded, neglecting commodities that are not traded between a particular pair of countries because transport costs are too high. In other words, this measure underestimates differences in economic distances. As for the artificial trade impediments (tariffs, quotas, etc.), Linnemann suggests that these are normally distributed, and that variations in artificial trade-resisting forces between pairs of countries are random rather than systematic. However, preferential trade agreements are an exception, and hence his empirical analysis includes a preferential trade variable.

The basic Linnemann equation takes the following form:

$$X_{ij} = a_0 Y_i^{a_1} N_i^{a_2} Y_j^{a_3} N_j^{a_4} d_{ij}^{a_5} P_{ij}^{a_6} \qquad (3.9)$$

where N = population, P = preferential trade factor. The exponents, a_2, a_4 and a_5 are negative. Since d is constant over time, improvements in transportation and communications are reflected in a fall in a_5. The results showed a R^2 of around the 0·80 mark. In other tests, a commodity composition variable was introduced but again had little leverage on the R^2 value. Unlike the Tinbergen result, the G.N.P. exponents seemed to matter. When they were arbitrarily fixed at unity, the R^2 declined from 0·80 to 0·56. However, these restrictions did not affect the estimates of the distance parameter, a fact that helps to confirm its independence.

The distance exponents varied considerably between countries. In general terms, they tended to be high (in the range −1·6 to −2·3) for countries on the geographical periphery of the world economy, while they were very low (−0·15 to −0·55) for other countries. The economic implications of high and low distance parameters are somewhat obscure. For instance, a high value might mean that the relatively unfavourably located countries direct a higher proportion of their exports to their nearest neighbours than the better located countries. A low distance exponent, on the other hand, means that imports come from all parts of the world regardless of long distances. This could be explained by a country's sophisticated import requirements or by its superior international transportation and communications. For instance, European countries clustered around the North Sea tended to have the lowest a_5 values. This reflects the traditional dominance of European shipping companies in the world's freight transport markets and the influence which long-established trade connections have on stimulating diversified and widely-spread trade flows. Despite these observations, Olsen's conclusion (1971, p. 32) on Linneman's work is probably fair. Olsen suggests that Linnemann has not been able to put forward any convincing economic theory behind the concept of trade resistance, and that his analysis is based on 'either an analogy from physics or a combination of a good hope and a tolerable statistical fit'.

The Yeates study (1969) adds little in either methodology or theory to the earlier research. He employs the volume of trade (imports plus exports) as the dependent variable, national income as the mass variable while distance is measured along the arcs of circles connecting the capital of country i with each of the capitals of its n trading partners ($j = 1$). These distances are used to represent the relative location and the average transport costs of goods being shipped to and from country i. Good results are obtained for the trade of Sweden, Canada, Italy and South Africa. Poorer results are obtained for France and the United Kingdom, due to greater trade flows with former colonies and Commonwealth countries. The results were much improved in the latter cases by adding dummy variables to take account of preference blocs.

The case for using an analysis of international trade flows as a means of examining the impact of distance on spatial interaction rests on the greater availability of data. The underlying assumption is to treat the world economy (or rather the parts of the world economy included in each study) as an interregional system. This requires a cavalier attitude to the fundamental differences between nations and regions conceived as sub-national units. There has been some work on inter-regional trade flows within a country, but the quality of data is very imperfect. For example, Isard and Peck (1954) looked at the I.C.C. Class I railroad shipments for all commodities by twenty-five-mile zones, and found a clear-cut inverse relationship between the *tonnage* shipped and distance.

More recently, there have been several studies connected with inter-regional shipments in different countries – for example, the United States (Leontief and Strout, 1963; Polenske, 1966), the United Kingdom (O'Sullivan, 1971; Edwards and Gordon, 1971) and Japan (Polenske, 1970). However, largely because of the patchiness of the data. these have not been directly comparable with the analysis of inter-national trade flows. For instance, the inter-regional studies are often confined to a limited set of commodities[1] and to a single transport mode. While this approach may be quite appropriate to the objectives of the particular study (e.g. an investigation of inter-regional commodity flows) it is less relevant in our context, which is concerned with using inter-regional trade as one illustration of how distance affects inter-regional inter-dependence. Moreover, several of the inter-regional analyses have been directly linked to inter-regional input-output models (e.g. Leontief and Strout, 1963; Polenske, 1970; Wilson, 1968; Edwards and Gordon, 1971), where the main objective has been to apportion regional input requirements between local and imported supplies rather than to estimate the friction of distance *per se*.[2]

Nevertheless, some illuminating observations may be drawn from the inter-regional trade results. First, in cases where total flows have been analysed the differences between areas in the value of the distance parameter are consistent with Linne-mann's conclusions drawn from international trade. Thus, Chisholm and O'Sullivan (1972) found that in Great Britain the distance exponent is highest for the least accessible origins (e.g. Aberdeen) and lowest for the most accessible (e.g. central London). To the extent that exchange of commodities and services with other (especially prosperous, high income) regions helps to raise an area's levels of income and welfare, this finding throws light on the difficulties facing isolated regions. Second, the studies revealed wide differences in the values of distance

[1] Polenske's study (1966) referred to fruit and vegetable shipments, Leontief and Strout examined coal, cement, soya bean oil and steel shapes, O'Sullivan looked at eleven broad commodity groups, and so on.

[2] In this context, the gravity trade model is an alternative to the linear programming models of production and trade. The main difference is that the gravity model, unlike linear programming, is not based upon an assumption of maximising local supplies.

exponents from one commodity to another.[1] One possible explanation might be connected with the tendency for the size of the distance exponent to be an inverse function of the value per ton of the particular commodity. This finding, though not unexpected, has very serious implications for regional economic analysis. It lends support to Leontief's stress on commodity hierarchies, where goods can be classified hierarchically according to the size of the market areas over which they are distributed and exchanged. If distance effects have a marked differential impact on particular commodities and industries, a direct implication is that the theory of regional growth must give some attention to multi-sector models. Spatial units of different size (nations, regions, cities, etc.) will have dissimilar industrial structures, and assuming that income elasticities of demand vary between commodities, dissimilar structures will be associated with differentials in economic performance.

THE ROLE OF CITIES IN REGIONAL DEVELOPMENT

Although the simplest method of introducing space into regional growth may be via the use of distance or transport cost measures, it is not the sole or perhaps the most important approach. Regional economists are not merely concerned with the distances separating points in space (e.g. raw material locations and markets, one market and another, producers and consumers) but with the internal structure of these spatial points. In particular, the spatial agglomerations of population and economic activities may be the main distinctive feature between an analytical framework based upon a set of spaceless regions and one that recognises the existence of space both between and within regions. Since these agglomerations are always (except in very rare cases)[2] urban agglomerations, this

[1] O'Sullivan's estimates ranged from -0.77 to -1.64, while Edwards and Gordon's forty-commodity analysis of flows to and from Severnside revealed estimates from -0.48 to -2.22. However, the latter estimates may be biased since they relate to a single origin/destination and therefore omit attraction and generation constraints.

[2] The exceptions refer to a large-scale industrial complex (e.g. petroleum, mining, chemicals, heavy metals) which is so capital-intensive that it does not require an urban service centre to meet the needs and demands of its labour force.

raises the question of the relevance of the urban dimension to the analysis of regional development.

At the most general of levels, the relationship between urban structures and regional development is obvious. This is particularly so in the great majority of cases when regional development is based upon industrialisation.[1] As Bos (1965) pointed out, urbanisation and industrialisation are two aspects of the same process.[2] The reasons for this inter-relationship are quite clear. Urban centres imply scale, and scale is the key to specialisation in production, efficiency and industrial growth. Urban scale also creates external economies (spatial and non-spatial) which have a cumulative and reinforcing effect upon subsequent growth (Lampard, 1954–5). Perhaps even more important is the fact that the urbanisation process is closely associated with social and cultural change that transforms attitudes to economic progress, capital accumulation and technological advances. This is partly because the large urban centre is the arena where the traditional attitudes endogenous to an area clash with the usually more growth-minded exogenous attitudes injected from outside; this phenomenon has been labelled 'psychological polarisation' by the growth pole theorists. There is little need to emphasise generalities of this kind; their significance can easily be appraised by studying the economic and social history of any developed economy. Their import is that the growth of urban centres *usually* has a generative impact on national and, by extension, on regional development. The caveat is necessary since in certain circumstances – particularly in developing countries – urban growth may have an adverse effect on development of the surrounding hinterland (e.g. Hoselitz's, 1954–5, concept of the 'parasitic' city).

From the viewpoint of regional growth analysis the role of cities is somewhat wider than implied in the 'urban-industrial matrix' relationship. In terms of intra-regional efficiency, for instance, the spatial concentration of people and activities is an efficient way of organising and distributing regional re-

---

[1] Even in agricultural regions, however, the role of large agricultural service centres may be important for generating development.

[2] See also Hodge (1968, p. 101): 'It causes hardly a ripple of interest today when one suggests that modern economic development takes place chiefly within an "urban-industrial" matrix.'

sources. The key agglomeration economies for promoting regional development are probably urbanisation economies rather than technical inter-industry linkages or other narrowly defined technological external economies. However, spatial concentration is not without limits; it is not necessarily more efficient to continue the agglomeration process until all regional activities and population are concentrated in a single urban centre. There are at least two reasons why this is so. First, there may be some level of urban scale at which net agglomeration economies become negative. To accept this does not necessarily imply commitment to the concept of optimal city size,[1] and even the arguments about the non-economic disadvantages of large cities are unconvincing.[2] Nevertheless, the possibility of an inversion point on the urban agglomeration function must be accepted. Second, and rather more important, a region's largest city cannot be considered in isolation. It is merely the major component of a wider system – the regional urban hierarchy. This hierarchy is the natural form for intra-regional spatial differentiation. People and industries cluster into urban centres of different size so as to achieve the best feasible balance between agglomeration benefits and urban service and transport costs for each individual decision-maker. The highest ranking centre is probably the key city from the point of view of performing systemic functions and for the growth of the system as a whole, but its role and functions can only be understood properly in the context of the wider system.[3]

One of the difficulties in understanding the inter-relationships between the size and spatial structure of the regional

[1] I have expressed serious doubts about the usefulness of this concept elsewhere. See Richardson (1972a).

[2] See Alonso (1971b, pp. 10–11): 'Many of our most perceptive writers and sociologists present a picture that does not square with the equation of the big city and alienation, and which makes smaller places appear stifling. It would appear that some people can lead full and rewarding lives in either kind of place, some in one but not in the other, and finally, it must be feared, that some people's lives will be unsatisfactory in either.'

[3] This system also extends upwards to the national level as well as downwards from the regional metropolis to the smaller urban centres within the region. The upward extension can be described in terms of the national urban hierarchy, the structure of which may have some impact on national economic growth and development.

urban hierarchy and regional growth is that there is no satisfactory theory for explaining how the hierarchy evolves *and* its
strategic significance for regional development. There is, of
course, Christaller's central place theory for explaining the
spatial distribution of the supply of urban services, Lösch's
analysis of hierarchical centres based upon market areas for
industrial firms, and the Tinbergen-Bos model which dis-
tributes industries among centres of different size according to
their relative economies of scale,[1] but none of these has a
serious dynamic content and hence has little value for exploring
the regional growth process. For this reason, analysts such as
Hodge (1968) have had to fall back on an inductive approach.
He found that common structural features underlie the development of all centres within a region, but the relative importance
of these structural factors changes during long-term growth.
The key 'independent' structural features revealed by multivariate factor analysis and principal components analysis
included: population size, quality of the physical environment,
age structure of the population, educational level, the economic base, ethnic and/or religious orientation, welfare, and
geographical location. Furthermore, a subsequent multiple
regression analysis suggested that the main structural conditions conducive to high average household incomes in a
region's urban centre are a good quality physical environment,
a youthful age structure, a high educational level of the adult
population and relative population size. Interesting as these
findings are, they do not go much further towards identifying
the strategic links between urban structure and regional
development.

Although the structure of the overall regional urban hierarchy may have more than a negligible impact on regional
growth, it remains true that the size and efficiency of a region's
leading metropolis is probably the major link between urban
structure and the rate of regional development. There are
several reasons for this view. Broadly speaking, the city of
highest rank in a region tends to be more outward-looking than
its other urban centres. It is likely to be the major 'port of
entry' for new migrants, new ideas, new technology and new

---

[1] See Christaller (1966), Lösch (1954), Bos (1965) and Tinbergen (1961).

habits imported into the region from outside. It will usually have the heaviest concentration of professional people, managers, technologists and other high socio-economic status groups. If there are economies of scale in labour markets, the metropolitan labour market is more efficient and more flexible than other labour markets offering more scope for occupational changes, adaptability, specialisation of skills and choices of different journeys to work. Similarly, the provision of capital, given the spatial concentration of banks, finance houses and other financial institutions, is very much a metropolitan function.[1] These latter two factors imply that inter-regional factor movements consist increasingly of inter-*metropolitan* capital and labour flows.

There is evidence, admittedly largely impressionistic, that the range and quality of urban services can be a powerful attractive force for other industries. If this is true, it underlines the importance of the region's leading city since the growth of service industries is highly correlated with city size and with the level of income (which tends to be higher in large cities). Their role has been formalised by Klaassen (1968) in a framework stressing the role of amenities (especially urban amenities such as health, social services and education) in regional economic growth. Klaassen argues that a key characteristic of amenities as a type of activity is that local demand is stimulated by local supply. This is largely because a local supply reduces the distance between the place of supply and the consumer, the lower transport costs are equivalent to a price reduction, and hence they stimulate demand. Second, the supply and demand for amenities are a function of city size. A large stock of amenities (both in terms of 'high-order' services and the scale of each service) has a favourable effect on urban and regional growth in two major respects: amenities have a beneficial impact on worker productivity (the health and educational services are obvious examples); the greater the supply of amenities the more attractive is a city and its region to new industries and activities. If this analysis is correct, the most efficient way of allocating regional infrastructure from

[1] On the other hand, D. M. Smith (1971) refers to some plant location studies in the United States which showed that the financial cost of borrowing capital did not vary systematically with city size.

the point of view of stimulating dynamic growth is to concentrate it on the leading city. A consensus view is that a city having a minimum critical size of 250,000 population may be necessary to exercise a generative function on regional growth performance. Of course, it is not merely a question of absolute size but also of the degree of connectivity with the rest of the national economy.[1] This emphasises the importance of interregional transport and communication networks.

REGIONAL GROWTH THEORY AND GROWTH POLES

There is no doubt that the theory of growth poles, as adapted to a spatial context by Boudeville (1966) and others, has been an important construct in recent years for linking analysis of the growth process with spatial changes and, perhaps even more important, for integrating theory and policy. In addition, there are similarities, analogies and a certain degree of overlap between some versions of growth pole theory and the theoretical framework developed later in this book. Yet I have not absorbed growth pole theory directly into the subsequent analysis. There are many reasons for this: doubts about the value of some of its key ideas, e.g. diffusion of growth and spillover effects from the pole into its surrounding hinterland; the advantages of sidestepping the confusion and controversy that has characterised the growth pole literature;[2] a conscious under-emphasis (but see earlier, pp. 40–50) of the role of particular industrial sectors in regional growth in order to concentrate on regional rather than sectoral disaggregation, whereas as is well known the original theory of growth poles was primarily a framework for analysis of the dynamics of industrial inter-dependence and structural change in economic space rather than in geographical space.

[1] To take a concrete example, the city of Granada in southern Spain is not much below the critical size but is unlikely to have a propulsive role on the growth of its region because of its high degree of isolation and its very poor communications with all other parts of the economy.

[2] There is no attempt here to survey the voluminous literature. Some of the most useful studies include Perroux (1964), Boudeville (1966), Pottier (1963), Hansen (1967 and 1972), Paelinck (1965), Darwent (1969), Lasuen (1969), Cameron (1970), Hirschman (1958) and Hermansen *et al.* (1970).

Nevertheless, it would be a serious omission to let growth pole theory pass with scarcely a mention. Accordingly, it may be useful to do two things: first, to explain in a little more detail the reasons for *not* integrating growth poles into my theory; second, to elaborate on one or two important aspects discussed in the literature that are directly relevant to the subsequent analysis.

One of the most serious difficulties with growth pole theory is that it means very different things to different people. Part of the problem stems from the manner in which later analysts transformed and modified Perroux's original theory, which really refers to the dynamics of unbalanced growth in a context where location was at best secondary, so that it became a concept for explaining the *spatial* polarisation of development. As Hermansen (1970) points out, once the growth pole concept is applied to geographical space it has to rely on traditional theories of location, spatial organisation and external economies of agglomeration since it is not in itself a theory of location in geographical space for firms, industries or cities. Indeed, he argues that it is necessary to complement Boudeville's theory of locational poles of development with central place theory (Christaller–Lösch) in order to explain where the functional growth poles are or where they will be in the future. Apart from the well-known weaknesses of central place theory, this integration presents problems. In particular, it is difficult to reconcile the deductively derived, static equilibrium theory of central places (which refers to firms) with the inductive dynamic theory of localised development poles (which refers to industries and macro-aggregates). Thus, central place theory cannot be treated 'as some sort of static version of the dynamic development pole theory in which all movement has come to an end, but as the mechanism through which development occurring in functional space can be projected into geographical space' (Hermansen *et al.*, 1970, pp. 56–7).

Another quite separate point is that analysts in different countries with dissimilar problems of economic development have used the term 'growth pole' to describe centres of very different size. In some countries a growth pole may imply an urban-industrial centre with a minimum size of 250,000; in other, primarily agrarian, economies it might mean a service centre in a rural region of less than 20,000 population. Misra (1970) has indeed argued that for operational analysis it is necessary to relate the growth pole hypothesis to a hierarchical system of growth foci, namely small service centres, sub-regional growth points, regional growth centres and national growth poles. However, since in each of these cases the function and roles of the centres would be quite different, the general 'theory' becomes rather fuzzy.

Third, it is now apparent that some of the early proponents of growth poles were starry-eyed about the extent to which such poles might revolutionise the structure and growth potential of lagging regions. In many cases localised growth poles have functioned as isolated enclaves with only very slight effects on growth, incomes or social change in their domiciliary region or even in their immediate hinterland.[1] There have also been defects in growth pole strategy stemming largely from the use of linear, and frequently static, input–output techniques as the main operational tool for applying a theory stressing dynamics, non-linearities and cumulative change. For instance it is sometimes assumed that a development pole might be based upon an industrial complex planned so as to achieve the maximum super-multiplier ('internal blocking') and the minimum net outflow of generated income ('external blocking'). However, whether such a complex could form the basis for a growth pole depends not on internal and external blocking but on its capacity for generating and transmitting innovations that stimulate new interdependencies and possibly even the growth of new industries. There is no satisfactory theory of growth dynamics on these lines.

In spite of these and other objections, there are many elements that have been incorporated in growth pole theory and analysis that are useful for our purposes and that stem from a

---

[1] Suppose for instance that the creation of a growth pole leads to in-migration from the surrounding area. Is this a drain on the region or an economically and socially more efficient redistribution of population? This depends, in part, upon whether population and economic activity is polarised towards a single centre or whether the pole itself is merely the dominant node in a hierarchy of regional settlements. Both configurations might occur in the same region but at different time phases of development.

similar view of the regional growth process. It may be helpful to indicate briefly a few of these.

First, with respect to agglomeration economies some of these economies arise from inter-industry linkages, and the industrial complex concept (which recurs frequently in growth pole discussions) is of some relevance in explaining these. An industrial complex is a set of industries in spatial juxtaposition that benefit from technological linkages and common agglomeration economies. A characteristic of such a complex is that expansion in any of the industries would set in motion a development process sustained by a high super-multiplier, i.e. a multiplier incorporating not only indirect and induced inter-industry repercussions but also the investment accelerator effect – in other words, a dynamic input–output multiplier. In addition, however, as implied above, an industrial complex counts as a development pole only if the 'propulsive' industries of its core are also leading industries, i.e. are relatively new and advanced technologically, face rapidly increasing demand and are able to create and transmit innovations to other sectors. The core unit of the complex can be compared to the concept of the dominant firm in growth pole theory, around which develops a set of inter-related production units based on backward and forward linkages. However, the notion of an industrial complex usually implies that the units are directly planned, both in terms of their composition and their time sequence, in order to ensure optimal development in respect to not merely the complex itself but also the economic and socio-cultural infrastructure, auxiliary and servicing plants, and plants working for the local consumer market.

A major problem arising from attempts to operationalise industrial complex analysis is the heavy data requirements of an industrial complex study. Isard, Schooler and Vietorisz's (1959) study of a petroleum refinery–synthetic fibre complex in Puerto Rico revealed the great mass of technical cost and engineering data needed to undertake such an analysis. The crucial question is whether it is possible at a lower level to go some way towards implementing the basic ideas associated with industrial complex analysis with much more limited data. A possible solution may be found in Klaassen's locational attraction model (Klaassen, 1967, 1970, and Klaassen and van

Wickeren, 1971). This model expands the input–output framework which deals with interindustry linkages on the demand side to deal with locational attraction on the supply side as measured by the relative importance of communication costs (including transport costs) between sectors. This is carried out by use of the concept of attraction coefficients where δ_{hi} is defined as *relative* communication costs between consumers and sector i (the demand attraction coefficient) and δ_{ji} is *relative* communication costs between sector j and sector i (the supply attraction coefficient) and where

$$\delta_{hi} + \sum_{j}^{n} \delta_{ji} = 1 \qquad (3.10)$$

The revised input–output matrix equation becomes

$$X = (\hat{d}A + Z)X + \hat{d}Y \qquad (3.11)$$

where X = vector of gross output, Y = vector of final demand, A = the standard matrix of input–output coefficients (a_{ij}), $\hat{d}$ = a diagonal matrix of demand attraction coefficients δ_h, and Z = a matrix of δ_{β}^{a} coefficients where a_{ji} = fraction of gross output of industry j sold to industry i and β_{ij} = fraction of gross output of industry i required from industry j. Thus Z is a matrix of supply-effect coefficients that measures the locational attraction between industries on the basis of forward and backward linkages.

By matrix inversion we obtain

$$X = [I - (\hat{d}A + Z)]^{-1}\hat{d}Y \qquad (3.12)$$

By pre-multiplying equation (3.12) by a diagonal matrix of value added coefficients we can determine the value added of income multipliers for each sector. The relevance of this type of analysis for industrial complex studies and growth pole policy is that it may reveal strong tendencies for industries to cluster with other industries which may in turn be useful for indicating the importance of giving these industries the opportunity to concentrate.

Second, Pottier's (1963) work on development axes has the useful integrative function of linking the effects of the impact of the transportation network with urban hierarchies and spatial growth poles. The essence of his argument is that economic development tends to be propagated along main transportation routes linking the main industrial centres, and therefore shows itself in the form of linear geographical paths. The reasoning is as follows. When traffic increases along a transportation route as a result of inter-regional trade, scale economies can be obtained leading to lower unit transport costs. Since lower costs stimulate trade and generate increased traffic, transportation infrastructure may be improved by capital investment and transport innovations. This generates more traffic and reduces costs still further. Thus, a cumulative process develops which tends to concentrate transportation demand and facilities along the original axes. Industry, commerce and population tend to be attracted towards these axes, creating easily accessible factor and product markets which may themselves attract other industries. This cumulative process is exceptionally strong at the junctions where routes cross tending to induce substantial urban centres there. The relevance of the development axis approach in this context is that it offers a method of integrating analysis of transportation and regional growth that provides an alternative to the more formal linear programming transportation models discussed earlier (see pp. 57–62). This approach has the advantage that it takes explicit account of the structure of the inter-regional (inter-urban) transportation network.

Third, since growth poles in a spatial context imply *inter alia* urban centres, growth pole theory lays much stress on the role of cities in regional development. In developed economies a growth pole strategy often suggests concentrating infrastructure and other resources on the leading cities of lagging regions so that these cities may act as a counterweight to the metropolises of the prosperous areas, may connect the region through the national urban hierarchy to the inter-regional transmission network for innovation, new ideas and social change, and may make the intraregional distribution of resources and population more efficient. Although this is only one interpretation of a growth pole strategy, it is a view that is fully consistent with the ideas developed in this book. Such an approach emphasises minimum critical size (possibly equivalent to a population of 250,000), a very limited number of growth poles – certainly no more than one in each major region,[1] and a stress on development potential rather than a 'worst first' policy. It also emphasises the significance of certain non-industrial characteristics of major cities as locational attractors, such as high-level amenities (Klaassen, 1968 and 1970) and a growth-minded social structure (Di Tella, 1970).

Since the supply of amenities and services such as health, education and recreation may have beneficial effects on productivity, their availability has some repercussions on economic development. One way of stimulating their consumption and production is to reduce the distance between the point of supply and the consumer by concentrating population in the larger centres where amenities are provided. Also, demand thresholds are important for amenities, so that a growing city not only becomes larger but diversifies and enriches its structure as it passes the threshold size for particular amenities. The impact of this on regional growth is twofold: first, the larger the city the higher the supply of, and the demand for, amenities (amenities have the special characteristic that local demand is stimulated by local supply) and the higher the productivity of the city's residents; second, the greater the supply of amenities the more attractive the city is for new activities, not only those that need these amenities directly but also those that value them indirectly because of the demand of their workers.

Di Tella uses the concept of *associationist leaders*, and stresses their role in attracting investments to a city. In effect, he combines an economic model based on market mechanisms with a sociological model stressing local social pulls. The associationist leaders are 'the people most likely to represent the degree of sociological sophistication reached by their community. If what is necessary for getting the investment is a bit of "pull" and organisation, they will provide it. . . . They will also provide the social atmosphere and civic responsibility which give a good appearance to the community and attract investments when economic factors are not actually against it' (Di Tella,

---

[1] In Klaassen's words (1970, p. 134): 'The greater the number of centres selected, the weaker the impact, because only a limited number of industries is in search of a location and because the financial assistance that can be given in the initial period is in inverse proportion to the number of centres selected.'

1970, pp. 179–80). The hypothesis advanced is that investments will be distributed among cities and urban centres in proportion to the size of their associationist groups, and if this is the case it is important for the economic potential of a growing city to have a strong associationist structure, and to have the amenities, services and quality of life that avoids the net out-migration and depletion of its membership. Similarly, in assessing the growth potential of a lagging region, its inter-urban population distribution and the social structure within its towns and cities become important determinants of how fast the region is likely to growth by attracting outside investments. Although these hypotheses are insufficiently tested, they are consistent with other sociological constructs (for instance, Webber's (1964) concept of 'non-place urban realms') and with the arguments stressing the strategic importance of large cities in regional development advanced later in this book. The policy implication that Di Tella draws from his theory is that 'the creation and nursing of a healthy associationist leadership is one of the more strategic components of a development policy', and that in a lagging region a growth centre is the best bet for nurturing and maintaining an associationist leadership capable of attracting new investment and new industry.

The theoretical strands in growth-pole analysis are spun from many sources: Perroux and Boudeville (polarised development), Christaller and Lösch (theory of the distribution of settlements), Pottier (theory of development axes), Hirschman and Myrdal (analysis of spread effects) and Hägerstrand (spatial diffusion of innovation, social and cultural change). However, the resulting conglomerate structure still leaves many points unanswered.

The meaning of a growth pole or a growth centre is still debatable. Does it mean a functional pole or a geographical pole or a combination of the two? The structural outline appears neat but the details are very fuzzy. What are the elements or the combination of elements which go to make a growth pole? Can the same type and size of growth pole or growth centre be successfully planned and developed in all situations? Is there a dynamic model of growth pole applicable to all situations? Do we really have dependable empirical data from the developed and developing countries passing through different stages of economic development to support the current concept of growth pole and related hypotheses? The answers to these questions are largely negative. This is the reason why the growth pole hypothesis has not yet acquired the status of a theory [Misra, p. 235].

Despite the similarities between certain aspects and implications of growth pole analysis and the theory of regional growth developed in this book, I agree with this assessment. The growth pole literature is confused, and there are many features of the growth pole mechanism that are unexplained or not supported by empirical evidence. These are the reasons why this topic is given skimpy treatment here and why I have not pinned my theoretical framework to the growth pole mast.

'COMPETITIVE' VERSUS 'GENERATIVE' GROWTH

One consequence of treating regions as spaceless subsets of the national economy is that regional growth rates are regarded as being decomposed from the national growth rate,[1] and the possibility of growth in any region having any propulsive impact on the national growth rate is ignored. This approach to regional growth emphasises inter-regional competitiveness (hence the term *competitive growth*). A model of competitive growth assumes that the national growth rate is given, and then examines the forces (locational advantages and disadvantages, relative market potential, comparative costs, etc.) that determine how a given increment of growth will be distributed among the regions of the system. In these models the growth of one region is always at the expense of another.[2] Much of the current regional growth theory (e.g. cumulative causation, neoclassical and most econometric models) falls into the category of competitive growth. The national growth rate is

[1] In a formal sense this is correct since the weighted sum of regional growth rates must equal the national growth rate.

[2] The following quotation from Winnick (1966) illustrates the competitive growth philosophy very well: 'The glitter of higher economic growth for declining areas turns out to be a shining coat for the dross of redistribution' (p. 280).

determined exogenously, and the function of regional economic analysis is merely to allocate this growth among regions. There is little need for such models to include spatial variables since each region can be treated as if it were a sector.[1]

A quite different approach, giving much more stress to the regional dimension, is to treat the national growth rate as the resultant of the growth rates of the individual regions. On this view, all growth is 'place-oriented', i.e. growth within any part of the national economy must have a specific locational origin. The growth performance of an individual region can be raised and may have an impact on the national growth rate without necessarily adversely affecting the growth rate of its neighbours. Growth through new technical innovation is a case in point. Agglomeration economies and the spatial proximity of activities in certain cities or regions may induce a rate of innovation above what it might have been in the absence of agglomeration. Similarly, changes in the intra-regional spatial distribution of factors of production facilitated, say, by an efficient intra-regional transport system may also increase productive efficiency and the regional growth rate. The importance of these spatial impacts on regional growth will be overlooked in the competitive spaceless models. This phenomenon, where the intra-regional spatial efficiency of a region may have a feedback on the aggregate growth rate, may be called *generative growth*.[2]

In a sense, this distinction is saying little more than the fact that the spatial allocation of resources in the economy will have an impact on dynamic efficiency. Nevertheless, the distinction is important since the competitive models would predict that if factors were allocated efficiently *between* regions (e.g. equalisation of factor returns) the growth rate would be maximised. From a social planning point of view, the primary aim should be to promote generative rather than competitive growth. This means concentrating on intra-regional efficiency even more

---

[1] The affinity between inter-regional and multisectoral models is particularly noticeable in multiplier analysis.

[2] Of course, since almost all growth involves some use of resources there is usually a slight competitive 'backwash' on other regions from any kind of regional economic expansion. This must be the case if opportunity costs in other regions are positive.

than on inter-regional efficiency. It implies *inter alia* a commitment to stimulating conditions favourable to growth within a
region rather than merely relying on diverting resources from
other, possibly more productive, uses in other regions. Again,
the need for a regional growth theory with a spatial content and
for urban-regional analysis is obvious.

Chapter 4

Resource Mobility in the Space Economy

INTER-REGIONAL MIGRATION

The theory and empirical analysis of inter-regional migration is a field to which economists and other social scientists have devoted lavish attention, though, unfortunately, without producing clear-cut unambiguous results. It is not my intention here to survey these well-worn paths in depth. However, there are several reasons why the subject of inter-regional migration needs consideration. First, it represents an important adjustment process in inter-regional economic growth, more important than income and price changes and commodity flows and at least as important as inter-regional capital flows. Second, following on from this point, the so-called equilibrating effects of inter-regional migration are the most easily measurable component of neoclassical models, and their analysis is at the heart of the hypothesis that links the neoclassical world with *per capita* regional income convergence. From the trivial observation that net migration flows show some tendency to be functionally related to the wage or *per capita* income differential between regions of destination and origin, there is often a jump to the conclusion that this fact substantiates the neoclassical model. Third, the evidence in favour of economic deterministic models and against 'spatial friction' and non-economic models has frequently been distorted, in the first case by assuming that correlation implies causality and in the second by mis-specifying functions, for instance by measuring distance as airline distance. Fourth, and more positively, it can be shown that the analysis of inter-area migration can be improved by placing it in the same context as the regional growth theory developed in this book. This implies *inter alia*: the introduction of space as a resistance to migration, and defining this resistance much more

broadly than in terms of the monetary costs of moving; allowing for heterogeneity within regions and, in particular, for
the urban dimension which has dramatic repercussions on the
interpretation of the determinants of labour migration; the
recognition that non-economic factors may have some influence,
possibly quite a marked influence, on the spatial redistribution
of population.

Because our primary interest is in explanation and understanding rather than in pure forecasting, our analytical focus is
the determinants rather than the effects of inter-regional migration. Indeed, many aspects of the effects of inter-regional
migration are scarcely a source of disagreement among proponents of competing theories. Most people would agree that
inter-area migration is a readjustment process which tends to
reduce disequilibrium within local labour markets. Migrants
tend to move from low-wage to high-wage areas and from areas
of labour surplus to those with labour shortages. Over time
migration flows will affect the state of labour markets in both
sending and receiving areas. Bringing supply and demand
closer in each labour market, however, is not quite the same as
saying that inter-area migration will have equilibrating
effects on regional incomes. Here the unanimity breaks down.
For example, it is possible (though the circumstances in reality
are probably rare) that the qualitative impacts of out-migration
(i.e. the loss of the young, the educated and the skilled) may
have cumulative effects on the demand for labour that are
more severe, at least in a dynamic model, than the effects on
supply. Moreover, the neoclassicists' prediction that net migration flows will narrow wage differentials may not hold in
conditions of increasing returns or where migration involves
occupational up-grading. Moreover, once we allow for the
possibility that non-economic stimuli may be important determinants of migration, labour movements are as likely to be
disequilibrating as equilibrating. A second major unanimous
view is that areas experiencing high net in-migration will tend
to grow (in terms of aggregate rather than *per capita* changes)
much faster than other areas. This is because in-migration adds
to both labour supply and demand, having a favourable effect
on growth even in pure supply or pure demand models.

Although the structure of most migration models is superficially similar, in that many of them include wage or *per capita* income variables, job opportunity, unemployment or labour market variables, some measure of distance and a variety of other factors, ideologically they fall into two main groups. The first can be described as economic models where the role of income or job opportunity variables is regarded as crucial. The second group is more heterogeneous, including gravity models, information flow theories and non-economic (whether sociological, behavioural or psychological) theories, but all share the common characteristic of stressing the influence, direct or indirect, of space and distance. Thus, models based upon strict economic rationality can afford to treat the national economy as spaceless whereas the second group of theories makes sense *only* in the context of the space economy. It is unnecessary to state which ideological school represents the views of this author. However, it is important to point out that the models are not mutually exclusive. The economic models usually include several of the other variables as a means of reducing the size of the residuals, but these are given scant treatment compared with measurement of wage differentials, employment opportunities and unemployment. Similarly, the spatial models all recognise that an income gain is a necessary if not sufficient condition for migration, and a wage or *per capita* income differential variable is normally included. Strictly speaking, of course, which type of model works best ought to emerge from interpretation of the empirical results especially if the variables of both groups of models are similar. Unfortunately, measurement of these variables is rarely standardised from one piece of research to another while the migration data are drawn from different sources or refer to different countries, regions or time periods. Accordingly, the results have been ambiguous and capable of varied interpretations, at least when they are used to throw light on the *general* determinants of inter-regional migration.

A useful starting point is the naïve neoclassical framework. I have summarised this elsewhere (Richardson, 1969a, p. 295) as follows:

Neoclassical general equilibrium theory predicts that in a situation characterised by inter-regional differentials in real wages, labour will migrate from the low-wage to the high-wage regions until real wages are equalised. This conclusion rests upon several critical assumptions: a comparative statics framework; homogeneous labour; constant returns to scale; zero migration costs; perfectly competitive labour markets; workers move in response to wage differentials and for no other reason.

Since the assumptions are clearly invalid, economic analysts have favoured models for testing which are modified versions of this neoclassical framework. However, all these variants rely heavily on the phenomenon of labour market adjustment. Many of them retain the relative wage as the key determinant, drawing upon additional variables only to correct for the violation of perfect competition. Others drop the reliance on relative wages *per se*, but substitute other variables that under certain assumptions about how labour markets operate are correlated with relative wages (e.g. differential employment opportunities, unemployment differentials). Raimon (1962) showed that interstate migration was strongly correlated with *per capita* income differentials and with differences in job vacancies. However, there was evidence of a functional relationship between wage levels and the excess demand for labour. Since the job vacancy model is subsumed in the wage differential model, Raimon argued that the latter was the more useful.

Alternatively, Fabricant (1970) suggested what she calls an expectational model of migration, which has the advantage that it does not have to bear the intolerable strain of the full employment assumption of the pure classical model. Migration from region i to region j is seen as a response to a positive expected excess demand for labour gap between j and i plus a barrier function (distance, kinship ties and other residual variables). The role of the barriers is primarily to slow down the response to the relative expected excess demand gap. This model explained sixty per cent of the variance in inter-regional migration. Blanco (1963 and 1964) stressed the role of unemployment differentials *per se*. Indeed, eighty-six per cent of the variation in the rate of migration between U.S.A. states, 1950–7, could be explained by two factors: changes in the level of unemployment and changes in the number of military personnel in each state (this factor is important because military movements are accompanied by significant numbers of their civilian dependants). However, a formulation of this kind is much more useful as a statistical forecasting than as an explanatory model.

Lowry (1966) also drew upon the Blanco model but combined it with the relative wage *and* a gravity type formulation:

$$M_{ij} = f\left(\frac{U_i}{U_j}; \frac{W_j}{W_i}; \frac{L_i L_j}{D_{ij}}\right) \qquad (4.1)$$

where M = migration, U = unemployment as percentage of the civilian non-agricultural labour force, L = number of persons in the non-agricultural labour force, W = manufacturing wage, D = airline distance.

The rationale of this model is easy to understand. People tend to migrate from low to high wage and from high to low unemployment areas. The migration flows will tend over time to bring regional wage and unemployment ratios towards unity. Thus, the equilibrium condition is where $W_i = W_j$ and $U_i = U_j$. Even in equilibrium, however, there remains a random exchange of migrants between i and j, the volume of which depends on the size of their labour markets and the distance between them. This model yielded quite good results especially when (again in view of Blanco's analysis) civilians were separated from the armed forces; the R^2 was as high as 0·6821 for a test on the flows between ninety S.M.S.A.s for the period 1955–60. All variables were significant with the exception of U_i and W_i, a finding that suggests that labour market chnditions in the S.M.S.A. of origin have no impact on out-migration.

Gallaway *et al.* (1967) adopted a rather similar model to explain interstate migration:

$$M_{ij} = f(Y_j - Y_i; D_{ij}; U_i - U_j; W_j - W_i) \qquad (4.2)$$

However, its explanatory value was much lower, 27·9 per cent of gross migration variance and 28·8 per cent of net migration variance. The authors drew the obvious conclusion that many of the reasons underlying labour migration have to be explained by other, probably *non-economic*, factors.

These results, though mixed, on the whole tend to be un-satisfactory. Too much of the variance in migration rates is left unexplained. Also, there is the danger of a serious identification problem. For instance, wage increases and in-migration could well be jointly dependent variables with other determinants of regional growth the masked independent variable. Moreover, the many variants of a labour market adjustment model make analysis and interpretation confusing. Apart from the models mentioned above, Bell (1967) treated migration as a lagged function of 'tightness' or 'slackness' in the labour market as measured by the divergence between expected labour supply and demand (cf. Fabricant), Suits *et al.* (1966) as a function of the difference between national and regional unemployment, while Czamanski (1968) analysed out-migration as a function of surplus labour. Harris (1970) suggested a more complex model stratifying migrants by race, age, type of area of origin (urban or rural) and distance of move, but the size of the flow was nevertheless determined by expected income gains and job opportunities. These examples could be multiplied several fold. Because several of these economic models include a distance variable, some might argue that they take into account the existence of the space economy and go a long way to meeting the objections to the strict neoclassical theory. But this argu-ment is weak, primarily because distance is treated in such a naïve fashion. This, it is not surprising that the distance variable in Lowry's tests (considering how it was measured) contributed very little by way of explanatory power. Yet there is no inconsistency between Fabricant's conclusion that straight mileage distance 'may be totally irrelevant in the decision-making process of migration' and our view that distance and spatial structure are of crucial significance.

Consequently, it may be a useful introduction to the migra-tion models not firmly rooted in economic theory and/or a spaceless world to comment on the treatment of the complex and elusive concept of distance. It is clear that distance has a much broader influence than implied either by mileage or the transport costs involved in moving. Vanderkamp (1971) follow-ing Sjaastad (1962) has identified at least four separate aspects of distance: monetary costs associated with moving, of which the actual fares for the migrant and his dependants are only a small proportion of the total;[1] the psychic costs of moving (e.g. leaving familiar surroundings, family and friends); differences in psychic incomes between regions of origin and destination (which is a function of *social* distance); uncertainty about income prospects due to lack of information. In Vanderkamp's own work the importance of this last component leads him to divide regional incomes by distance in his migration-income differential equation. The justification for this is that the greater the distance, the more prospective income gains have to be discounted because of uncertainty.

Since distance reflects so many different factors and there is no reason why these should have the same weight for all migrants or for all regions, it is probably difficult in most cases to rely on an aggregate gravity model with a single distance coefficient. Gallaway *et al.* (1967) found that there were systematic differences in the influence of the distance variable between regions, namely a tendency for distance to be more important among migrants in western and southern states. They thought that such differences might be due to the fact that distance is a surrogate for many separate influences. In particular, 'it could be indicative of an asymmetry in the flows of labour market information between areas. It is entirely possible that workers in the east and midwest have better knowledge of economic conditions in the south and west than southern and western workers have about economic conditions in the east and midwest' (Gallaway *et al.*, p. 222).

This possibility draws attention to the significance of information flows in the evaluation of distance effects.[2] If the information element is the key factor in the inverse relationship between migration and distance, this can be handled from a

---

[1] This item also includes an indirect monetary cost, namely opportunity costs in the form of earnings foregone while travelling, searching for and learning a new job.

[2] Consider, for example, the following quotations: 'The susceptibility of communication to sheer distance is an established fact. This explains why the volume of migration falls off with increasing distance: the possibilities for getting information concerning opportunities which warrant migration decrease as distance increases' (H. ter Heide, 1963, p. 61); and 'information decreases, and hence uncertainty increases, with increased distance from a person's home. Thus, distance serves as a proxy for information' (Greenwood, 1970, p. 375).

modelling point of view in at least two different ways. First, we might employ a spatial diffusion model of the type suggested below to explain the *flow of information* about innovations,[1] either with or without an urban hierarchy framework.[2] The preferred type of spatial diffusion model for analysis of innovation diffusion is a gravity model rather than an innovation wave mechanism. The Zipf hypothesis (what is frequently referred to as the P_1P_2/D hypothesis)[3] for analysis of inter-urban migration is, of course, a crude gravity model. This analogy suggests that the P_1P_2/D hypothesis primarily describes the spatial flow of information and refers only indirectly to the pattern of migration. With this interpretation, of course, it is feasible to assign weights to the population variables to represent variations in the propensity to send or receive information.

A second approach is to link the flows of information from possible destination regions with the social contacts (especially friends and relatives) which potential migrants may have there. This suggests the need to develop some method of representing the influence of friends and relatives in the migration function.[4] Nelson (1959) argued that since the spatial distribution of relatives and friends is a function of past migration, it is therefore a function of all the variables determining past migration. Greenwood's solution (1970) to this was to use a migration stock variable (i.e. the number of persons born in state i and living in state j) as an indirect surrogate for the 'friends and relatives effect'. He found that including this variable raised the R^2 on a test for forty-eight contiguous states from $0 \cdot 77$ to $0 \cdot 93$ in a model with income, population, distance and mean yearly temperature terms. An even more interesting finding was that the distance elasticity coefficient was significant in only twenty-three states when the migration stock variable was included compared with forty-six states when excluded. The interpretation of this is obvious but important. 'To the extent that the migration stock variable picks up the

[1] See pp. 113–32.   [2] In particular, see p. 128, n. 1.   [3] See Zipf (1946).
[4] It should be noted in passing that friends and relatives not only send back information but make acclimatisation of migrants in their new surroundings easier and occasionally even provide help and assistance with the move.

effects of the non-economic factors for which distance is a proxy and hence allows the distance elasticity to reflect more clearly the effects associated with the economic factors, the results of this study suggest that transportation expenses may themselves not be a particularly important deterrent to migration' (Greenwood, p. 381).[1] Less convincing though more direct evidence for the 'friends and relatives effect' has been provided in the survey results of Lansing and Mueller (1967). As many as seven out of ten of their respondent migrants moved to communities where they already had friends or relatives, and locational preferences were strongly influenced by kinship and friendship ties. On the other hand, these preferences appeared subordinate to better economic opportunities.

One aspect of incomplete information flows is that knowledge received over long distances is subject to uncertainty. However, we need to distinguish between uncertainty due to imperfections in knowledge about income and job prospects at a distance and uncertainty due to inability to predict the future. Uncertainty over space is potentially remediable, for instance by investment in information agencies. Uncertainty over time is more difficult to handle and, in particular, strikes a blow against macroscopic models. This is because time preference varies from one individual to another, so that people differ in their willingness to sacrifice their present income for a larger but uncertain future income. Allowing for uncertainty over space is relatively easy in a migration model. Wolpert (1965) argued that migration choices which minimise uncertainty tend to be preferred. Also, evidence shows a tendency to postpone decisions and to rely upon information feed-backs. Furthermore, uncertainty can be reduced by imitating the successful moves of others (the friends and relatives effect, once again). The cumulative impact of these tendencies is that migration can be treated as a lagged response to incentives to move.

[1] This conclusion is also supported by Vanderkamp (1971). In the trade-off between dollars and miles, the implicit costs per mile were much too high to be accounted for by moving, settling and opportunity costs. This suggests that the other non-monetary aspects of distance (such as psychic costs, preferences for nearby locations and uncertainty) must have been quantitatively important.

Another feature of distance effects is that 'social distance' may be more important than either economic or geographical distance. Social distance may refer to cultural or linguistic differences, gaps in life styles (particularly noticeable between urban and rural areas or between metropolitan cities and small towns), or differences in economic motivation or traditions of work. It explains why internal migration rates greatly exceed international migration rates even if geographical distance is held constant. An interesting example within a country is Quebec where the different language and culture is associated with a smaller volume of inter-regional migration both into and out of the province compared with other Canadian provinces (Vanderkamp, 1971). Yet another approach to spatial frictions is Stouffer's intervening opportunities concept. This may be expressed as

$$M_{ij} = a\frac{X_j}{X_{ij}} \qquad (4.3)$$

where X_j = number of opportunities at j, X_{ij} = number of intervening opportunities between i and j. Although the intervening opportunities model stood up reasonably well to some early tests (e.g. Isbell, 1944; Strodtbeck, 1949), it was a poor predictor of the migration streams of 1955–60 in the United States (Stouffer, 1960).

The most sophisticated single model of migration drawing upon gravity concepts, social distance and allowing for another important non-economic determinant of migration – the relative attractiveness of areas – is the one suggested by W. H. Somermeijer some years ago (Somermeijer, 1961; for discussions in English see ter Heide, 1963, and Lowry, 1966). He partitioned gross migration into directional flows with the aid of indices of attractiveness (F) of each place as a destination. Thus:

$$M_{i \to j} = [\tfrac{1}{2}k + c(F_j - F_i)]P_i P_j D_{ij}{}^a \qquad (4.4a)$$

and $$M_{j \to i} = [\tfrac{1}{2}k + c(F_i - F_j)]P_i P_j D_{ij}{}^a \qquad (4.4b)$$

By aggregation gross migration is obtained

$$M_{ij} = kP_i P_j D_{ij}{}^a \qquad (4.5)$$

In addition, Somermeijer included a variable to take account of religious composition differences between regions, i.e. a possible social distance variable. However, the most interesting aspect of the model is the indices of attractiveness. In his tests he included factors such as *per capita* income, the unemployment rate, degree of urbanisation, recreational resources and the quality of dwellings. Although the first two variables feature in many of the standard economic models, the others reflect variations in the spatial structure of the economy. Good results with this model were obtained for migration between Dutch provinces, and correlation coefficients for the effects of indices of attractiveness on net migration were in the region of 0·90.

One of Somermeijer's indices of attractiveness, the degree of urbanisation, deserves separate consideration as an influence on migration. A general line of argument in this book, that the urban dimension must be introduced if we are to explain regional growth satisfactorily, is particularly relevant to the analysis of labour migration. Inter-regional migration may be much easier to understand if we decompose the migration streams into rural-urban and inter-urban flows. Also, the spatial distribution of regional growth, and possibly even its overall rate, may be influenced by intra-regional migration flows, which can similarly be broken down into rural-urban and inter-urban components. The role of agglomeration economies as a force behind the spatial concentration of population, either directly in the form of household agglomeration economies or indirectly because business agglomeration economies attract firms and jobs attract migrants, is discussed later.[1] To the extent that regions grow because their urban centres grow (and its corollary, that industrial growth means urban growth) and to the extent that regional growth is associated with changes in the distribution of population that favour metropolitan areas, then agglomeration economies may be a critical variable in the migration function. Such economies may reflect economic tangibles such as the benefits accruing from larger labour markets or higher incomes but also include social attractors such as leisure and cultural facilities, the quality of educational, health and social services, and environmental

[1] See Chapter 7, pp. 175–96.

amenities. It is for these reasons that the migration function used in the regional growth model developed here includes an agglomeration economy variable, which in fact takes the form of a somewhat complex urbanisation variable.[1] Finally, there are strong grounds for thinking that a metropolitan area (or, more specifically, a functional economic area) makes much more sense than a broader region as the appropriate geographical unit for migration analysis. The two most obvious arguments for this view are that a relevant areal unit is one characterised by relatively homogeneous economic conditions and the fact that the optimal size 'region' for migration studies is one with boundaries coinciding with the outer limits of a single labour market. Such a labour market more closely resembles a metropolitan area than the larger regions employed in inter-regional analysis.

The importance of these considerations suggests a switch in emphasis from pure inter-regional migration models towards urban migration models. It is beyond the scope of this survey to analyse urban migration in depth, but it may be useful to refer to a recent study of migration into West German cities by von Böventer (1969). He examined three groups of factors determining migration into cities: city size, location and structure. The influence of size was measured in two ways: first, by dividing the non-linear migration-city size function into five linear sections, each representing a particular population size class; second, by use of a population potential (excluding the population of the city) variable. Similarly, location is dealt with in multivariate terms. Its most important aspect, at least from a theoretical point of view, is von Böventer's argument that proximity to a larger city gains access to spillovers and external economies (the agglomeration economy effect) though at the risk of exposure to a strong competitive pull, whereas location at a considerable distance from other cities ensures an element of monopolistic protection (the hinterland effect). He also suggests that some intermediate distance (the *pessimum distance*), where all agglomeration economies have disappeared but the hinterland effects are still weak, will be the worst of all worlds.

[1] See equation (8.3), Chapter 8, p. 213 and n. 2. This is an urbanisation measure in the sense that it refers to the number, relative size and spacing of urban centres.

As for measuring these influences, he relies on population size and distance variables: $N_i^{a_1} N_j^{a_2}/D_{ij}^{a_3}$ to act as a surrogate for the decline of agglomeration economies, and $D_{ij}^{\beta_1} N_i^{\beta_2}$ to represent hinterland effects.[1] On *a priori* grounds, he suggests parameter values of $1 > a_1$, a_2, $\beta_2 > 0$ and about 1 for a_3 and β_1. Two other types of locational variable were included: a measure of connectivity to the transportation network, as reflected in the weighted number of railroad connections and major inter-city roads; and a measure of access to recreational areas and of climatic factors. Many variables were used to represent city structure: employment in tertiary industries; employment in manufacturing, especially in new or in declining industries; unemployment; the level of *per capita* income; the growth rate in city income; tax receipts; living costs (as measured by housing rents); housing stock deficit or surplus; importance of the city as an administrative centre; and its importance as a cultural centre (the number of university students was adopted as a surrogate). In tests of this model, city size and employment structure (particularly in service sectors) were the most important variables, and there was some support for the agglomeration-hinterland effects hypothesis (at least in the larger city-size classes).

Some other, perhaps relatively minor considerations deserve a brief comment. For instance, it is sometimes helpful to use a wide variety of social, economic and psychological characteristics of the population as potential predictors of migration (see Lansing and Mueller, 1967). This involves prediction of migration rates from the demographic and social structure of the population in areas of origin, a method that requires, analytically, extensive disaggregation of the migration streams. Relevant characteristics might include: age, marital status; number of dependants and stage of family life cycle; race; education; financial status (including the availability of funds for moving expenses); car ownership; ties to the local community (place of birth, length of residence, presence of relations, membership of community organisations, home ownership, wife in employment, children in school, etc); outside contacts (travel experience, relations or friends in other

---

[1] N_i = population of city i and D_{ij} = distance between i and j as before.

communities); vested interests in a particular job (job seniority, pension rights); and, last, but not least, motivational and attitudinal variables related to the desire to move. There are, of course, many strong cross-correlations between these characteristics. For example, the tendency for migration rates to be higher for people in the twenties age group may be partly explained by the linkages between age and education as a determinant to mobility. Opportunities for migration may be an inducement to undertake further education. Also, Becker (1964) argued that migration can be treated as a form of investment in human capital. If young people have an incentive to migrate in order to increase their future earnings, they will have an incentive to do so immediately.

A factor of obvious importance in influencing the distribution of population in the space economy is locational preferences. Such preferences may be related to a host of influences, including many already mentioned such as community ties, socio-cultural traditions, and length of settlement.[1] Their significance for regional growth analysis is that they distort the predictions of economic theory and deprive wage and job opportunity differentials of their leverage effect on mobility. One influence on locational preferences that has occasionally received special emphasis is that of climate. As Sjaastad (1962) pointed out, climate may be considered as a psychic income component and as a form of consumption that has a zero cost of production. Some analysts, Greenwood (1970) and Blanco (1963) for instance, have included climate as a variable in the migration equation, though with conflicting results. Greenwood found that temperature, and/or the variables for which it stands as a surrogate (e.g. lower living costs, its attraction for retired persons who may be in relevant cases a substantial proportion of the migration stream), was an important determinant of inter-state migration. Climate at the destination was also a significant variable in Alonso's study of inter-metropolitan migration flows (Alonso, 1971a, pp. 12–13, 23). In the Blanco model, on the other hand, climate was not statistically

---

[1] For instance, in Canada the west is much more mobile and more recently settled than the east. Mobility and immobility may be matters of tradition, or in other words mobility may be an inverse function of the length of settlement of the region.

significant. However, she recognised that this did not necessarily imply that it was unimportant since its impact could have been exerted indirectly by its influence on employment; certainly, climate was more highly correlated with changes in job opportunities than with changes in migration. However, regardless of whether or not climate shows up in regression analysis of migration flows between, say, fifty regions it can be of critical significance in a few particular cases. Increased migration into California and Arizona are obvious examples that cast doubt on the view that economic factors are of exclusive significance.

In the regional growth model described in Chapter 8 a simplistic migration function is used with only three independent variables: agglomeration economies, locational preferences and regional wage differentials. However, the locational preference function includes several of the factors discussed above such as length of residence in the region (a surrogate for community ties), distance from the nearest (i.e. the regional) metropolis[1] and mobility costs. It is not difficult to construct a much more complex migration model, but the formulation selected has the advantage of facilitating a direct evaluation of key elements in our regional growth model (i.e. agglomeration economies and locational preferences) compared with the crucial variable of neoclassical migration models – the relative wage differential.

THE MOBILITY OF CAPITAL

Whereas most analysts, even those in the neoclassical mould, accept that there are non-economic influences on labour migration that can lead to a wide variety of predictions about the impact of migration on regional growth, there is a broader measure of agreement among economists that the mobility of capital can be explained by strictly economic factors and that the capital market works almost perfectly even in the space economy. The justification for this standpoint is that the costs of transporting capital flows over space are close to zero and

---

[1] The justification for this is that if metropolitan life offers particular kinds of attraction for households, the distance at which households live from the region's leading metropolis may have a marked impact on their propensity to move.

that the capital market in a mature industrial economy is highly developed, knowledge of capital sources and of investment opportunities is freely and readily available, and that the supply of capital is offered on a competitive basis to all parts of a country by predominantly national financial institutions. If these assumptions are correct, then capital should flow from low to high return regions tending towards an equilibrium in which regional rates of return to capital are equalised. Whether these flows will tend to widen or narrow inter-regional income and growth differentials depends upon whether rates of return are relatively higher in the rich or the poor regions. There has been much controversy on this point: the cumulative causation theorists stress the former while the neoclassicists stand on the latter.

The determinants of inter-regional capital flows in the real world are, however, widely at odds with the abstract assumptions of the perfectly mobile capital market. Upon closer examination market imperfections, dynamic considerations and the channels through which capital transfers are made make the idealised neoclassical model as invalid in regard to capital as to labour. If the capital for all existing and new investment opportunities were borrowed on the open capital market, if it took the form of publicly quoted issues either on a national stock exchange (or on regional stock exchanges to which access was freely available) and if these issues were bonds with a guaranteed rate of return the model might have had a high degree of relevance. Unfortunately, only a tiny proportion of inter-regional capital flows are of this type.

A great deal of reliance in the critique of the neoclassical model has to be placed on logic and, on some points, assertion since direct empirical tests are very rare. However, a recent study by Olsen (1971), admittedly with imperfect and incomplete data referring to U.S.A. regions, yielded results that were difficult to explain but were certainly in conflict with neoclassical predictions. His capital stock model took the following form:

$$K_i{}^{t+n} = K_i{}^t e^{n\gamma} \left(\frac{\Upsilon_i^t}{\Upsilon^t}\right)^{n\delta_1} \left(\frac{r_i^t}{r^t}\right)^{n\delta_2} \left(\frac{iV^t}{V^t}\right)^{n\delta_3} \quad (4.6)$$

where K_i = capital stock of region i, n = growth period, γ = extrapolated rate of growth of capital stock, e = Napierian logarithmic base, $\hat{Y}$ = per capita income, r = rate of return to capital, V = income potential, δ_1, δ_2, δ_3 = exponential parameters.

The *a priori* predictions of the model are that the δs would be positive, and the δ_2 parameter is a direct test of the neoclassical position. In fact, although δ_1 turned out to be positive, suggesting as expected that regions with relatively high *per capita* incomes would tend to experience a higher growth rate in their capital stocks, both δ_2 and δ_3 were negative and statistically insignificant. These latter results strike a blow against neoclassical theory. The δ_2 result is difficult to explain, the δ_3 result somewhat easier by resorting to arguments that are fully consistent with our general thesis. Olsen suggests the value of δ_2 may reflect the pull of opposing forces: the Heckscher-Ohlin hypothesis that capital flows towards higher returns; and the friction of distance that limits the inter-regional capital movements so much that the capital stock grows relatively faster in the rich regions despite capital exports. He argues that the latter influence may have more than offset the former. However, even this argument implicitly assumes that rates of return to capital are relatively higher in the poorer regions, a hypothesis that cannot be justified empirically. Olsen's explanation of the negative sign found for δ_3 is more interesting. Investors 'feel more comfortable when their capital is invested in rich regions and they are willing to pay for this comfort' (p. 136). Also, the more information they have about other regions (as measured by the level of inter-regional interaction), the stronger the preference for investing in the rich regions. This emphasis on investors' preference for investing at the centre rather than at the periphery regardless of the real rates of return is of more general significance.[1] It obviously conflicts with profit maximisation criteria, and the link between neoclassicism and profit maximisation is a very strong one.

The neoclassical case can be demolished with the aid of a mix of theoretical arguments and casual real-world observations. The main modifications are allowing for dynamic models,

[1] See also Hirschman (1958, pp. 184–6), Friedmann (1966, p. 15) and Alonso (1968).

uncertainty and the fact that many capital flows are not by way of the open capital market but take the form of intra-firm transfers and/or the movement of physical plants. In a dynamic framework, rates of return may be continuously changing because of technical change and inter-regional variations in demand – both factors that frequently work in favour of high income regions. Perhaps more important are the imperfections in knowledge. These mean, as in the case of migration, that the diffusion of information over space becomes a major determinant of the spatial distribution of capital. Without exploring this point in depth, it is clear that it works to the disadvantage of investment opportunities in isolated areas and favours those created in and near the metropolitan cities of the prosperous regions.

Risks and uncertainty may exert influence in the same direction. Risks may be conceived as higher in poor regions, even if relative marginal rates of return were greater, on the grounds that the average return to capital had been lower in the past. Uncertainty can be explained not only in terms of imperfect knowledge about current investment opportunities but also by doubts about regional tax policies, the course of regional demand and other aspects of the future. Although uncertainty may be treated by discounting future expected returns at a higher rate, a more realistic way of handling risk and uncertainty is to show how they are reflected in inter-area differentials in the cost of obtaining capital. The costs of obtaining capital and the terms on which it is supplied may reveal a tendency to vary directly with distance from major financial centres,[1] perhaps one feature of the spatial capital market that may be analysed with a gravity model. If the costs of obtaining capital vary between regions, then even on neo-classical assumptions the equilibrium condition is no longer equalisation of regional rates of return but the equalisation of capital costs and returns within each region.[2]

There are other restrictions on mobility. Some investment

[1] However, see the evidence referred to above (Chapter 3, p. 77) indicating that costs of borrowing capital do not vary systematically with city size.

[2] See Richardson (1969a, pp. 304–10). There is an analogy here with the conditions of spatial price equilibrium which do not require equal prices between regions but merely that $p_i - p_j = TC_{ij}$.

projects may be so large that due to indivisibilities capital must flow in very large lumps or not at all. In such cases marginal adjustments in response to slight regional differences in rates of return will be impossible. Furthermore, capital for infra-structure projects (a common source of inter-regional capital transfers) very frequently gives rise to external economies. Without subsidies or government capital, capital flows will tend only to equate private not social rates of return.

Another consideration is that the savings-income ratio may be much higher in some regions than in others because of higher incomes, previously high growth rates and/or an above average concentration of property owners, and that this fact could be an important determinant of capital flows working independently of any forces making for an equilibrium allocation of resources. In some circumstances capital may flow out of such regions because it is surplus to requirements, but in others these higher savings may still be invested in the home region (usually the richer regions) because of 'psychic income' benefits and an overestimation of agglomeration economies.

The most important argument of all against the notions of a perfect capital market and equilibrating capital flows in response to differentials in the rate of return is that they are based on a totally false conception of the nature of inter-regional capital flows and of how they take place in the real world. For one thing, most of the existing capital stock is im-mobile, being 'locked' in equipment, machinery and infra-structure and is therefore tied to a particular location (this is in contrast to the existing labour force which is potentially mobile at all times). Thus, physical capital can be shifted only gradually and indirectly by the diversion of replacement in-vestment. This factor not only reduces the potential mobility of capital between regions but also has an impact on the intra-regional spatial distribution of new investment since past and present investment decisions are spatially interdependent.

Second, a substantial proportion of inter-regional capital flows takes place within existing corporations. This reflects the importance of multi-plant firms in a modern industrialised economy. Its significance in this context is that such intra-firm transfers are carried out for reasons other than differentials in relative rates of return, particularly for reasons associated with the policies of the individual firm. For instance, a corporation may transfer capital to a lagging region in order to extend a branch plant because of an inability to expand at, say, the headquarters plant. Third, capital flows on government account – again a substantial share of the total – are totally unrelated to regional rates of return, but are determined by national infrastructure requirements or the demands of regional policy.

Finally, and this is the most crucial factor, the most important inter-regional capital flows are those which are directly associated either with the establishment of a new plant or the relocation of an existing plant (or other business enterprise). In effect, this means that to this extent it is not a question of the spatial mobility of capital but of inter-regional location theory. We must consequently pay some attention to the dynamics of location theory. The finding that in a dynamic setting a profit-maximising model of location does not make good sense reinforces the arguments against a rate of return equalisation model of inter-regional capital flows.

Profit maximisation is an unsatisfactory goal for location decision-makers for several reasons. For most types of establishment a location decision, once taken, must stand for a very long time because of heavy relocation costs. Even the minimum duration for locating on a particular site is far longer than the period over which it is possible to predict future changes in costs and revenues. Technical change, variations in product mix, input costs, demand for final output and changes in the institutional and fiscal environment will all tend to vary over time. Thus, location decisions based on present data and/or on extrapolations into the future will be unlikely to maximise profits in the long run. Moreover, in a dynamic context the optimal location will depend on the time preference of firms which will vary. For instance, whether a firm goes for early profits or for larger later ones may involve a quite different site selection. Similarly, an enterprise may place a great deal of emphasis on security and consequently may prefer to locate at existing industrial centres where costs of error (because of the experience of other firms) may be lower than, say, at an untried, even though theoretically optimal, site. In a largely oligopolistic space economy, maximising can be an ambiguous goal because the optimal course of action for one firm depends upon the somewhat unpredictable actions of other firms (locational interdependence). If future changes in spatial costs and revenues are very unpredictable, we might expect firms not to spend resources and time in seeking out the most profitable site but instead to opt for a location that appears viable in the long run and to rely on increasing efficiency in other respects to raise their profitability.

Apart from theoretical objections, profit maximisation is not consistent with how location decision-makers actually behave. There is increasing evidence, though much of it is impressionistic, that the location decision, more than most managerial decisions, has to take into account 'psychic income' influences and other personal factors which are not easily compatible with narrow definitions of economic rationality. Also, locational attractors may include social amenities, a pleasant and healthy environment, recreational facilities, climate and many other kinds of influences. The impact of these on profits and costs is very indirect, to say the least. Subjective locational preferences that cannot be related in any identifiable manner with objective factors, even non-economic factors, may also be the chief determinant of location in a few cases. However, this particular feature is much less likely when the firm making the site selection is a large corporation than in the now much rarer case of the firm under sole ownership.

If profit-maximising location models are unacceptable, then to the extent that the spatial distribution of capital reflects the establishment and relocation of plants it is clear that such capital does not move in response to differentials in the rate of return. Indeed, because of the long duration of a location decision, high relocation costs and the impossibility of forecasting spatial costs and revenues into the far future, there is no room for a deterministic model. The importance of imperfections in knowledge (particularly the high risks and uncertainty) and of the pursuit of non-material goals by location decision-takers suggests the desirability of quite different locational models. Two obvious alternatives are a 'satisficing' model (see Simon, 1959, and Richardson, 1969a) and a probabilistic behavioural model (see Pred, 1967 and 1969).

The 'satisficing' models attempt to explain how firms in

reality behave. Because of lack of data and uncertainties about the future, the firm will choose more limited objectives than searching for the optimal location. It may set itself some minimal standard of achievement which will ensure its long-run viability at the chosen site and at the same time achieve a reasonable level of profits. The implication of satisficing hypotheses for locational choice is discrimination in favour of core locations in the prosperous regions (in Friedmann's terminology, the 'centre') and against new, untried and isolated locations (the 'periphery'). Firms will tend to choose safe locations at centres of industrial agglomeration in preference to dispersed locations. Although they will try to avoid congested and high rent central city sites, they will nevertheless wish to be located near existing transport routes, raw material sources or labour pools, nodal points and major population centres. The particular site may be chosen on personal or non-economic grounds, such as environmental preferences.

The virtue of a satisficing model is that it is consistent with locational behaviour. It helps to explain, for instance, the tendency for environmental preferences, such as access to a metropolis or to a favoured cultural and social milieu, to influence location decisions even in the face of lower costs and higher potential profitability in other regions. Also, it accounts for why many new entrants, especially small firms, more often than not set up in business in the areas where the founders live rather than at more profitable locations. Moreover, it is consistent with the evidence of considerable locational inertia and with the reluctance of established firms to relocate even when offered large inducements. The satisficing firm is rarely a candidate for inter-regional relocation. The implication of these locational models for the mobility of capital over space is quite obvious. Capital flows, especially from prosperous metropolitan areas to lagging regions, will be much more restricted than expected rate of return differentials might suggest. To the extent that inter-regional capital flows do take place in association with location and relocation decisions, regions with thriving metropolitan centres and with a wide range of social, cultural, recreational and environmental amenities are more likely to attract capital than other areas.

Probabilistic locational models, though somewhat different

in structure, are similar to the satisficing models in their consequences. They, too, stress behavioural factors and cast doubt
on the usefulness of deterministic models, and their predictions
about inter-regional capital mobility are much the same. Pred
(1967) developed the concept of a behavioural matrix measuring the quantity and quality of information available to location decision-makers down the columns (where movement
downwards implies more information) and the ability to use
information along the rows (where a movement to the right
implies greater ability to use the information available). As
knowledge and ability increase, i.e. as we move towards the
bottom right of the matrix, the probability of an optimal or
near-optimal location increases. The idea is that real-world
location patterns deviate from the deterministic optimal spatial
distribution because of differences in the information available
to decision-makers and their ability to use it. Thus, the actual
spatial distribution contains both regular (non-random) and
random elements. The former result from the location decisions
made near the bottom right of the behavioural matrix, whereas
the random elements reflect choices made on the basis of much
more limited information and ability. Occasionally, even the
decision-maker with limited information and poor ability may
make by chance a sound locational choice.

While agreeing with much of the underlying rationale for
Pred's approach, I find his 'model' unsatisfactory in two major
respects. First, it stresses too much the variety, almost the idio-
syncracy, of locational behaviour. The 'herd' instinct is important in explaining the concentration of firms at established
centres of agglomeration (and as a consequence the relative
immobility of capital), and this is more easily accounted for by
the pure satisficing model than by use of the behavioural matrix. Second, the behavioural matrix itself has no locational
co-ordinates and fails to show that the availability of information is constrained by the spatial structure of the economy.
Pred's attempt to link the behavioural matrix to locational
choices in a geographical context is very cumbersome (Pred,
1967, p. 92, Figure 11).

There is considerable scope for other types of probabilistic
model. For instance, dealing with the question of inter-regional
capital flows as a whole rather than merely the proportion

associated with locational shifts, there may be some value in constructing a probability matrix for the system of regions which assigns probabilities to the likelihood of capital flows between each pair of regions. The case for this is even stronger if industry in general is fairly footloose and if inter-regional rate of return differentials are very small. In such circumstances the main influences on inter-regional capital mobility become inter-regional variations in risks and uncertainty associated with investment and differences in psychic income accruing to investors from investing in particular regions. Such costs (risks, uncertainty) and benefits (psychic income) are much better expressed in a probabilistic than in a deterministic model. Each cell in the matrix could contain a probability coefficient, where the coefficient measures the net impact of negative elements (relative risks and uncertainty) and positive elements (relative psychic income benefits). When a vector of capital funds by region (e.g. as represented by a vector of savings by region) is multiplied by the probability matrix it will yield an inter-regional capital flow matrix where the flows are estimated on a probabilistic basis.[1] However, there is a major difficulty in implementing a model of this kind. This arises because the probability matrix will perforce have to be fairly static, with the coefficients adjusted only infrequently. The income elasticity of the supply of capital may be very high and fluctuate markedly with the level of economic activity (and the rate of economic growth). The trouble arises because the elements behind the probability coefficients – risks, uncertainty and psychic incomes – are not constant but are also dependent upon general economic conditions. Thus, as the capital supply vector changes we might expect simultaneous changes in the cells of the probability matrix. This makes prediction difficult. Nevertheless, it is most improbable that such instability will disturb the factors making for higher probability coefficients in core regions, i.e. the lower risks, greater knowledge and higher psychic income associated with investment there.

The analysis above falls short of a fully developed theory of inter-regional capital flows. However, it shows up fairly conclusively the inadequacies of the neoclassical model, both

[1] A formal model using a probabilistic savings flow matrix is presented below; see Chapter 6, pp. 162–71.

theoretically and because of its inconsistency with real world observation. It also suggests reasons why the rate of growth of the capital stock, and hence the rate of growth of output, tends to be higher in the already developed, industrial and urbanised regions of the economy. There is little comfort in this analysis for those who believe that the inter-regional growth process is automatically equilibrating.

SPATIAL DIFFUSION OF INNOVATIONS

We know that technical progress is an important element in economic growth. A region's rate of technical progress depends both on its capacity to generate technical progress internally and on its ability to adopt innovations first introduced elsewhere. Inter-regional differentials in innovation rates would not matter very much if new technical knowledge and techniques diffused rapidly and universally over space. A major weakness of neoclassical and other traditional regional growth theories is their failure to give adequate treatment to the inter-regional diffusion of innovation and technical progress despite devoting considerable, and quite justified, analysis to inter-regional factor mobility. The assumption that new technical knowledge is freely available to all except for the barriers imposed by imperfectly competitive markets runs contrary to empirical observation. Instead, the diffusion of innovation over space occurs according to predictable patterns which fail, at least as far as entrepreneurial as opposed to household innovations are concerned, to penetrate all conceivable locations.

The strands of the theory of innovation diffusion have been drawn together from different disciplines and perspectives. The mathematical geographers, for instance, have developed theories of the diffusion of social and economic phenomena over space that are analogous to the laws of mathematical physics used to explain the diffusion of particles. They have also shown how the mechanics of the innovation waves can be approximated by some statistical function (e.g. a Poisson or gamma function, a binomial probability density function, or a logistic function). Interesting though the work in this field has been, it is doubtful whether it has much practical value. The trouble is that because space has readily identifiable mathematical locational co-ordinates it becomes too easy to adopt mathematical models to explore spatial relationships. The desire for mathematical precision can lead to mechanistic (or at best mathematically probabilistic) models that are devoid of economic content, that deal with spatial frictions in too general a fashion, and that treat the decision to adopt innovations as if such decisions were taken by automatons.

A second type of theory, again developed in geography – though on this occasion by one man in particular, the Swede T. Hägerstrand – is inductive in character, based on careful empirical analysis of the spatial diffusion process with respect to particular innovations, especially agricultural innovations. In these models, the diffusion of innovation is treated as a function of communication so that delimiting the physical and social structure of the communications network provides the key to tracing the spatial spread of innovations. Hägerstrand also showed how the spatial diffusion process could be simulated by various types of Monte Carlo simulation models. Although his work has many unique features, there is some kinship between his ideas and other contributions to the study of communications, particularly those of the mathematical information theorists (Shannon and Weaver, 1949; Cherry, 1957; Schramm, 1966), sociologists (Katz, Levin and Hamilton, 1963; E. M. Rogers, 1962; Meier, 1962) and social psychologists (Rapaport, 1951 and 1956).

A third line of development, though one in which space is the absent dimension or at best treated implicitly as subsumed under time lags, is by economists (Griliches, 1957 and 1962; Mansfield, 1961, 1963a and 1963b; Sutherland, 1959). Although one of the economists' contributions was to confirm the logistic, S-shaped curve of the time path of innovation observed by other social scientists (e.g. Dodd, 1955 and 1956), their main argument was to suggest that the spread of innovation depended upon each potential adopter's appraisal of the profitability and the risks attached to adopting the innovation. It is also very easy to pick out from the general economics literature other obvious constraints on the diffusion of innovation – the shortage of capital, supply inelasticities in the industries producing the innovations, managerial deficiencies, etc. What is striking about the economic analysis of innova-tion diffusion is the failure to allow for spatial frictions and the blinkered attitude to the contributions of other social scientists in this area, though there are a few recent exceptions (Siebert, 1969, pp. 69–76, 78–83; Richardson, 1969a, pp. 310–16; Day, 1970).

Finally, a fourth group of theories relates the spatial diffu-sion of innovations to the spatial distribution of urban centres in the national economy. The major path of diffusion of innovations through the space economy is via the urban hierarchy (Pedersen, 1970; see also L. A. Brown, 1969; Hud-son, 1969; Berry, 1972; Pyle, 1969, and Pred, 1966). This hypothesis stresses the intimate relationship between urban and industrial growth, and also, if valid, suggests how important it is to integrate urban with regional analysis if we are to under-stand how and why regions grow. It will not be surprising to readers of this book, and the approach to regional growth that it expounds, that I find this group of theories the most satisfac-tory. At the same time, it should be pointed out that all these theories are complementary rather than alternatives. Under-standing the mechanics of diffusion waves is helpful in analysis of the spatial diffusion process. Both the communications net-work approach and the 'profit versus risk' criterion are included within models of hierarchical diffusion. An expected net profit yield is an essential prerequisite for adoption to take place while in respect to communications networks the major difference is merely to suggest that these networks (both public and private, formal and informal, social and personal) are predominantly structured as links between urban centres. A satisfactory theory of the spatial diffusion of technical progress, therefore, should be based on a synthesis of the existing body of knowledge, rather than urging one branch of the theory as opposed to another.

INNOVATION WAVES

The abstract analysis of the theory of diffusion waves owes a lot to Morrill (1968), Tobler (1967) and Beckmann (1970). Morrill looks at what he calls the macro-aspects of the diffusion process, and explores the inter-relationships between its space and time patterns. His analysis stresses a number of features. First, he suggests that the degree of acceptance of innovations through time can be described by a logistic function such as

$$p = \frac{k}{1 + ae^{-bt}} \qquad (4.7)$$

where p = proportion of acceptances at any time, k = the ceiling proportion, a = constant and b = an absorption ratio, or friction coefficient. Second, he shows that if we plot the course of the crests of a series of such time-path functions at distance intervals from the centre where the innovation was first introduced then we obtain an exponential final saturation curve. The more general time-space function takes the following form

$$a_i = \frac{a_0 e^{-bd} d^t}{t!} \qquad (4.8)$$

where a_i = the path of the wave, a_0 = the initial crest amplitude, d = distance, t = discrete time periods, and b = the friction coefficient. When applied to innovation diffusion processes, this function describes two empirically based observations: the highest adoption rate in any area occurs very soon after the time of its introduction; close to the innovation centre the diffusion process takes place early in time, while at greater distances the later is the time sequence of diffusion and the lower the total adoption rate.[1]

Beckmann's analysis is, if anything, even more abstract. What he attempts to do is to demonstrate the similarity between the spatial diffusion of innovations and the spatial spread of other economic variables, e.g. migration, spatial price analysis, and the spatial repercussions of expenditure multiplier effects. However, this similarity is achieved by treating a very simplified case of innovation diffusion, i.e. diffusion through a homogeneous (isotropic) region where the process operates through contact between adjacent locations and where the

---

[1] Morrill also introduces two further refinements: (i) varying the probabilities of receiving information inversely with distance from the innovation centre; (ii) allowing for diffusion barriers. These help to make the model less abstract.

same probability is attached to the effectiveness of each contact regardless of its location. The space over which diffusion spreads is, in reality, non-homogeneous and there are channels of transmission which may by-pass nearby potential adopters. Since we know that there are constraints and restrictions on the spatial diffusion of innovations, Beckmann's models simply assume the problem away.

Beckmann shows that the probabilistic forecast of the spread of an innovation over a rectangular grid in the near future can be described by the differential equation

$$\frac{dP}{dt} = k \left(\frac{d^2P}{dx^2} + \frac{d^2P}{dy^2} \right) \qquad (4.9)$$

where $$k = z \lim_{h,m} \frac{h}{m^2}$$

where P = the probable adoption rate, x, y = locational coordinates, z = probability of a contact resulting in acceptance of the innovation, h = unit of time, m = unit of distance. This is merely an extension to two dimensions of the diffusion equation found in the natural sciences. To the extent that it has any value, this could only be for explaining diffusion in the vicinity of the original innovation since there is no mechanism here to account for the 'leap-frogging' which characterises the spread of an innovation inter-regionally.

Tobler's analysis runs on similar lines except that he introduces several useful (though not substantive) modifications: he translates the above type of model into finite difference form; he shows how to modify the classical diffusion model to yield a logistic type function (see also Hudson, 1969[1] and Casetti, 1969[2]); and he explains how the diffusion equation can be

[1] Hudson argues that neither the spatial spread (neighbourhood effect) model nor hierarchical diffusion through the system of central places alone satisfactorily explains the S-curve of the cumulative number of adoptors, whereas combining the two models does.

[2] Casetti borrows from a refined Hägerstrand model, and shows how an S-curve results if, in a model treating direct personal contacts as the key channel of diffusion, potential users vary in their degree of resistance to change and if resistance can be worn down by receiving a large enough number of messages or signals from adopters.

altered to allow for the eventual spatial decay of an innovation, i.e. an innovation may spread through one region at a time when it has ceased diffusion in the region of origin.

HÄGERSTRAND'S INDUCTIVE MODELS

The virtue of Hägerstrand's work (especially 1967, but also see 1952, 1965a, 1965b and 1966) is that he treats the spatial diffusion of innovations as a human and social communications process rather than as determined by quasi-scientific laws. On the other hand, his models have a somewhat restricted value for understanding the role of spatial diffusion of technical progress as a factor in regional economic growth since his empirical examples (which are very important given the inductive character of the theory) refer to agricultural improvements, consumer goods (automobile ownership) or social institutions (Rotary Clubs) rather than to industrial innovations.

Empirical studies revealed three phases of spatial diffusion: initial diffusion with clusterings of early adopters in the area immediately around the innovation centre; a second phase characterised by radial outward dissemination of adoptions, a rise of secondary agglomerations and continued growth at the initial agglomerations (the neighbourhood effect); and a saturation stage which may be reached near the innovation centre even though the density of adoptions is still low in peripheral areas. These three phases may be regarded as spatial parallels to the three sections of the S-shaped time path curve – slow initial adoption, a more rapid intermediate phase of development, and an asymptotic approach to the ceiling (saturation). These empirical generalisations are reinforced by a number of a priori factors. Adoption of an innovation depends upon a conscious decision; awareness of the innovation's existence is a necessary but not sufficient condition for adoption. Information may be public (e.g. mass media, published materials) or private (e.g. word of mouth, social networks). Finally, potential adopters vary in their degree of resistance; resistance is measured by the number of messages from adopters received prior to adoption; and the frequency distribution of potential adopters classified according to degree of resistance is normal and evenly distributed over space.

By varying the assumptions about these phenomena and treating them as rules of a Monte Carlo game the diffusion of innovation may be simulated through a homogeneous plane over which population is evenly distributed. The justification for the use of Monte Carlo simulations is that the diffusion process is probabilistic and that if we are interested in the sequence of the process and not merely in its final result most well known analytical methods are of little use. A Monte Carlo simulation is, in effect, a game of stochastic sampling, i.e. a computer is used to select at random a sequence of interaction consistent with specified probabilistic distributions and to record the joint outcome of the diffusion process. The purpose of the game is to simulate how society operates as a communication system when an innovation enters at some point and is then propagated through the network.

In his major work (1967, originally published in 1953), Hägerstrand developed three simulation models of this type, each successive model incorporating modifications to bring about a closer approximation to empirically observed reality. The rules of Model I are: the entire population is informed from the beginning; the adoption decision of each individual is independent of the decisions of his neighbours (no neighbourhood effect); information is uniformly available and is assumed to spread through public channels. This model produces a random spatial distribution of adopters, which clearly conflicts with the clusterings found in empirical data particularly in the intermediate phases of development. The discrepancy could be due to an uneven spatial distribution of information and/or an uneven spatial distribution of receptivity to innovations.

Model II corrects for the first of these. It is assumed that: knowledge of innovation is obtained only through private channels, and communications (i.e. tellings) take place at constant intervals of time; in the beginning there is only one innovator located in the centre of the plane, and the probability of information being transmitted from one potential adopter to another declines with distance;[1] once again, adoption occurs as

---

[1] The simplest way of handling this is to divide the homogeneous plane into a rectangular grid, and to assign probabilities to each cell of the message being passed from the innovation centre. Probabilities ought to be derived from empirical estimates, but in a simple model it may be possible

soon as information about the innovation is received. The outcome of this model is much closer to reality. It generates clusters
of adoptions in the intermediate phase of diffusion, particularly a growing concentration of adopters around the original
centre accompanied by radial dissemination from subsequent
agglomerations. This is not surprising. The probability assumptions mean that telling over short distances is much more
common, and hence the neighbourhood effect is very strong.
However, occasionally longer jumps at the beginning tend
to create secondary centres of agglomeration at a later stage of
the diffusion process. Even so, Model II does not produce an
adoption rate around the initial innovation centre as high as is
found in some of the empirical data. This result is obtained
because second and third tellings are redundant, and more
repetitive tellings occur in the neighbourhood of the innovation.

Model III allows for varying degrees of resistance by potential adopters, and in this model the repetition of telling plays a
vital role by wearing down resistance. The outcome is a greater
spatial concentration of adoptions, and Hägerstrand shows
that the higher the average degree of resistance the more
spatially concentrated are the distributions of adoptions.

In his later work (1966) Hägerstrand has taken account of
the finding that many innovations follow a route that is,
broadly speaking, down the urban hierarchy (hierarchical diffusion), reflecting the fact that many communication links (both
private and public) are inter-urban and that for many innovations most communication nodes (i.e. the people or institutions
sending and receiving messages) are located in cities and towns.
In the space economy of the nation where diffusion takes place
inter-regionally the number of actors in the diffusion process is
frequently small relative to the scale of the diffusion plane, i.e.
'the small but important part of the population which plays a
leading role in political, industrial, scientific and cultural
affairs; people who to no small degree act as gate-keepers in
relation to innovations' (Hägerstrand, 1966, p. 33). It is much

---

to assume a statistical function with probabilities declining symmetrically
from the peak. The grid with its assigned probabilities is described as the
mean information field.

more difficult to simulate the spatial diffusion process when the number of people involved is small relative to the area over which the innovation may be spread. If a Monte Carlo simulation is to be attempted, it is important to introduce several modifications allowing for the scale of the information field, urban hierarchies and the barriers formed by national boundaries.

From two examples (the location of contributors to a Festschrift and the spread of Rotary Clubs International) Hägerstrand came up with the following provisional hypotheses:

(i) Innovations tend to be made in the capital city or some other major metropolis.

(ii) National borders restrict the innovation diffusion process. The first adoption in a country of an imported innovation is usually in the capital or some other large city. When innovations cross national boundaries, they spread most easily into neighbouring countries.

(iii) The initial spread tends to be by way of the urban hierarchy. Innovation or early adoption takes place in the leading metropolis, and the first information impulses tend to flow to the cities next in rank. Cities of high rank tend to be in close communication with each other through a host of private and personal links and contacts which bypass lower order towns located between them. However, at an early stage the order down the urban hierarchy is soon broken up, and replaced by a situation where neighbourhood effects predominate over city size succession.

(iv) In this latter situation, the friction of distance exerts itself very strongly. The local area (including lower-order urban centres) around the innovation centre almost always contains the majority of contacts and experiences the highest adoption rate. Beyond this zone of high density (of adoptions) the effects of distance are felt throughout the national economy, though friction coefficients tend to be much higher for people living in provincial than in capital cities.

These hypotheses require more empirical testing. A theoretical model of hierarchical diffusion is considered below.

THE ECONOMISTS' CONTRIBUTION

Although economists have discussed the problems of innovation diffusion at some length (see Mansfield, 1961, 1963a,
1963b and 1968; Griliches, 1957[1] and 1962; Sutherland, 1959),
they have given scant attention to the spatial spread of innovations apart from very general statements found in the work of
Siebert (1969) and others. Nevertheless, the economists' contribution has not been insignificant. First, they have given
ample evidence of the logistic function that describes the
diffusion of innovation over time, and as we have seen this
function has a spatial counterpart. Second, they have developed
and tested models that have been concerned with the narrowly
economic conditions for adopting an innovation, such as the
obvious fact that the innovation must be profitable after
allowing for risk and uncertainty. Griliches's analysis of the
diffusion of hybrid seed corn suggested the hypothesis that the
rate of diffusion is a direct function of profitability. His main
findings were: lags in the adoption of hybrids and in the
entry of seed producers into particular areas could be explained
in terms of the varying profitability of entry, where 'profitability' is a function of market density and the costs of innovation and marketing; differences in the saturation rate and in
the slope of the logistic curve were explained to a large extent
by differences in the profitability of the shift from open pollina-
tion to hybrid varieties. In other words, introduction of an
innovation is largely determined by supply factors while the
adoption rate is determined by demand; both are in turn dependent on profitability. Mansfield (1968, p. 105) has expanded the same argument to take account of the fact that
profitability changes over time so that there might be an
optimal moment for the adoption decision.[2]

[1] Griliches examined *interstate* differentials in the rate of adoption oi
hybrid corn, but he did not investigate the *spatial* spread of the innovation
in the sense of taking account of distance and the spatial structure of the
communications network.

[2] An earlier study by Mansfield (1963a) concentrated on determinants
of the *intrafirm* rate of diffusion. but yielded results consistent with the above
more general model. It was postulated that the intrafirm diffusion rate is a
function of the rate of return from the innovation, the degree of risk at the
time of the adoption, scale of the firm and the firm's liquidity position. The

Apart from the profitability model, economists have not developed a comprehensive theory of innovation diffusion. However, from the economics literature and from *a priori* reasoning it is possible to construct a list of *ad hoc* generalisations that have a bearing on the spatial diffusion of innovations.[1] In the absence of detailed testing it is impossible to evaluate these in the sense of assigning relative weights to each factor, and in most cases their quantitative importance is an empirical question. Accordingly, these generalisations will merely be listed here.

1. In spatial diffusion analysis we must make a clear distinction between different types of innovation since the models needed to explain diffusion may vary from case to case. There are at least five major types of innovations: (*i*) innovation in production techniques and new processes; (*ii*) innovations in new products (consumer goods have received most attention); (*iii*) social and cultural innovations; (*iv*) new agricultural improvements; and (*v*) new managerial techniques.

Most of the literature (especially the non-economic literature) has concentrated on types (*ii*), (*iii*) and (*iv*). It is arguable, however, that innovations of the types (*i*) and (*v*) are the critical ones as influences on regional growth performance. A prerequisite for the spread of both these groups of innovation to lagging regions is the presence of high calibre managers, scientists, technologists and centres of decision-making in these areas. Such potential adopters may be heavily concentrated in the core industrial regions of the economy (Ullman, 1958) and

---

coefficients of all four variables had the right signs and, apart from the scale factor, were statistically significant. (Other plausible factors such as the age distribution of old plant and machines, the investment expenditure needed to adopt the innovation fully and the firm's profit level had no significant effect.) Mansfield suggested that these findings point to an economic analogue to the psychological principle that reaction time is related to the intensity of the stimulus. In this case the profitability of the innovation is such a stimulus, and the degree of profitability tends to influence strongly the speed of response.

[1] The comments here are confined to *economic* influences. Siebert has presented an interesting discussion of set theory as an aid to spatial diffusion analysis (pp. 78–83) and of information theory (pp. 55–9, 69–72), but though appearing in an economics book these discussions cannot be treated as economics.

may also be relatively immobile, while the propensity for managers and technologists to be created domestically in the backward regions may be a function of the regions' past economic structure, social system and educational provision. Thus, the diffusion of many types of innovations may be severely constrained by limitations on the available stock and spatial distribution of managerial and technological skills.

2. A related consideration is the importance of the learning process (Mansfield, 1968; Day, 1970). For instance, diffusion may be delayed if innovation requires new kinds of knowledge on the part of the adopter, new modes of behaviour or the co-ordinated efforts of different groups and organisations. Moreover, decisions to adopt an innovation are probably interdependent. An individual potential adopter's decision will be strongly influenced by the presence of and the decisions taken by other potential adopters in the area, irrespective of the information flows received from them. In other words, the neighbourhood effect has an information diffusion component and a learning component, and the latter though given less attention in diffusion analysis may be equally important.

3. A region's industrial structure (both in the sense of the composition of its output and the size distribution of firms and the market structure within each industry) may influence its capacity to absorb and adopt innovations originally made elsewhere.

(*i*) It is possible that the presence of larger firms in an area may make for a higher adoption rate, though the few empirical tests are unclear (Mansfield, 1968). Also, competitive industries may adopt innovations faster than monopolistic industries.

(*ii*) Many innovations are applicable only to an individual industry, and in this case the presence of that industry in a region is obviously a necessary precondition for the innovation to be adopted in the area. On the other hand, inter-industry flows of technological advances (technology transfer) are becoming increasingly important. This raises the interesting possibility that a modern technologically advanced industrial structure in a region may improve the innovation and the adoption rate of *other* industries located there. On the other hand, this depends on the assumption that the transfer of technology is strongly influenced by spatial proximity, and there is at present very little evidence on the validity of this.

(*iii*) Two other considerations that are partly but not wholly connected with the industrial structure are liquidity (or capital supply) constraints and the embodied character of much technical progress.

a. Liquidity depends on a host of factors, most of which (retained earnings, access to outside sources of finance, depreciation, etc.) reflect characteristics of the region's economic structure. Others, such as the savings rate of the region as a whole, are determined, in part at least, by social factors.

b. To the extent that technical progress is embodied, adoption of innovations requires a high rate of investment.

4. Restrictions on the flow of information about innovations (e.g. the existence of a patent system) obviously slow up the diffusion process. Siebert draws a distinction between government-supported research organisations and private industry. As a generalisation, the former are more concerned with promoting the dissemination of research results, whereas private industry frequently may restrict circulation to preserve a competitive edge. However, this tendency may be stronger in consumer goods than in capital goods industries, since producers of capital goods are often willing to publicise the new technical knowledge embodied in their machines especially to their customers. Moreover, transfers of machines embodying innovations can be regarded as a substitute for the mobility of new knowledge itself.

5. The ability of a region to accept innovations made elsewhere may be restricted by inelasticities on the supply side.

(*i*) There may be bottlenecks in the industries producing the innovations, e.g. capacity constraints which can only be overcome after a substantial time lag.

(*ii*) A neglected factor is that in cases where an innovation is diffused through distributors (e.g. new consumer goods but also certain types of capital goods) the spatial spread of the innovation through the national economy depends upon the spatial network of distribution centres (L. A. Brown, 1969). Since expected profitability for the propagator will largely depend upon market potential, and market potential will tend to be governed (except for agricultural innovations) by size of urban centre, distribution networks will show some tendency to be structured down the urban hierarchy. Hence, the spatial pattern of distribution networks may help to explain the hierarchical diffusion path followed by many innovations.

HIERARCHICAL DIFFUSION

Empirical observation in different societies suggests that there are two broad types of diffusion process. The first focusses on the frictional effects of distance itself and lays great stress on general spatial constraints on the diffusion process. It leads to a spatial diffusion pattern that is highly concentrated with adoptions clustering around the original innovation centre. In this model there is very little penetration into smaller urban centres and rural areas, especially when these are isolated from the main innovating centre. The second diffusion model stresses a process by which innovations are transmitted from the larger to the smaller urban centres in the economy, i.e. down the urban hierarchy. The general spatial diffusion model explains the spatial spread of innovations in underdeveloped countries or in the distant past of today's developed countries; the hierarchical diffusion model is more characteristic of developed societies.[1]

If the diffusion process is largely hierarchical in a developed economy, an important policy implication for backward regions is to promote the growth of their largest urban centres in order to boost their rank in the national urban hierarchy. In this manner, the capacity of the region to absorb and adopt innovations introduced elsewhere should be increased. However, the distinction between spatial and hierarchical diffusion may be much more blurred than the above dichotomy suggests. In the upper end of the urban hierarchy diffusion tends to be hierarchical, but lower down a more general and more

[1] In an empirical study of the spread of cholera in the United States in the nineteenth century, Pyle (1969) shows that in the early nineteenth century when access was difficult and the urban system was embryonic, cholera spread largely through spatial diffusion. By 1866, on the other hand, a national urban hierarchy had developed and the railroads already provided a degree of close national integration. Consequently, the cholera epidemic of that year diffused hierarchically.

ill-defined spatial pattern emerges. Urban centres may still tend to adopt innovations before rural areas, but the phasing of diffusion among these centres may appear random rather than being governed by size (L. A. Brown, 1969). Thus, while for many types of innovations the chain of communication and adoption proceeds from the capital city or some other major metropolis down the urban hierarchy at a certain level of city size the chain breaks up in disorder and a more general spatial diffusion is found.

Pedersen (1970) has suggested that the spatial diffusion model may be more applicable to some types of innovation while the hierarchical diffusion model applies to others. In particular, he makes a distinction between household (H) innovations and entrepreneurial (E) innovations.[1] The former can be treated as continuous wave phenomena, since many adopters are involved and adoption diffuses outwards from the centre of innovation, though the strength of the wave declines with distance. E-innovations, on the other hand, may not be adopted at all in small towns and rural areas, and even in larger towns the incidence of adoption may be small. They tend to jump about in a very discontinuous though not necessarily unpredictable manner, and a short-circuiting of distance through the urban hierarchy is a much more appropriate description than the notion of an innovation wave. These differences in the diffusion process stem from variations in the characteristics of H- and E-innovations. The risks are usually higher for the latter. Second, with H-innovations each new adoption tends to accelerate diffusion whereas the first adoption of an E-innovation in a town of close to threshold size will pre-empt further adoptions there. Of course, in larger towns and cities there will tend to be further adoptions. It follows that E-innovations are largely urban innovations.[2] Third, because the number of potential adopters is so large, there is a significant random element in the determination of timing and spatial incidence of an H-innovation.

[1] See also Berry (1972).
[2] Agricultural innovations are an exception. These have characteristics and diffusion patterns closer to those exhibited by H-innovations. Indeed, the theoretical models of the diffusion of agricultural improvements usually assume farm-households.

Pedersen's most important contribution to the analysis of spatial diffusion is to develop a theoretical model of hierarchical diffusion that takes into account several considerations: (i) exposure to the innovation; (ii) general willingness to adopt innovations; (iii) economic and technical feasibility of the innovation in each urban centre; (iv) the presence of a potential entrepreneur in an urban centre.

(i) Exposure to innovation

This is a function of information flows, and information flows are subject to distance decay. The critical level of information necessary for adoption (F) may be represented by a gravity model,[1] e.g.

$$F = \sum_{j=1}^{i-1} [KP_iP_jd_{ij-}^{-b}] \, (t_i - t_j) \qquad (4.10)$$

We can determine the moment of adoption at urban centre i, i.e. t_i, from this equation.

(ii) Willingness to adopt the innovation

Since urban populations and urban social structures are heterogenous there will be inter-urban differences in *per capita* participation in communication flows and the levels of information needed before innovation is adopted. Thus equation (4.10) may be rewritten as

$$F_i = \sum_{j=1}^{i-1} [Kx_iP_ix_jP_jd_{ij}^{-b}](t_i - t_j) \qquad (4.11)$$

[1] The diffusion process as expressed in a gravity model takes a different form from spatial diffusion as represented by a Monte Carlo simulation and from strictly hierarchical diffusion from the largest to the smallest urban centres. However, both these patterns are limiting cases of the general model where the exponent b increases towards ∞ or approaches 0 respectively. If we assume that the city size distribution can be approximated by a rank size function $P_i = P_1N_i^{-r}$ where N_i = the rank of town i, then the gravity function

$$I_{ij} = KP_iP_jd_{ij}^{-b}$$

becomes

$$I_{ij} = KP_1^aN_i^{-r}N_j^{-r}d_{ij}^{-b}$$

The difference between ranks N_i and N_j can be treated as hierarchical distance to be contrasted with physical distance. As $b \to \infty$ physical distance becomes more important, while as $b \to 0$ hierarchical distances become relatively more significant.

where $x_1, x_2 \ldots x_j \ldots x_i$ are the proportions of the population in each urban centre participating in communication about the particular innovation. F_i will vary in size from city to city; for instance, it may be larger in centres with a traditional social structure, or F_i could be an inverse function of population potential suggesting that towns participating freely in the communication process may also be more receptive to the particular innovation.

(iii) Feasibility of innovation in an urban centre

For many innovations, diffusion may depend on scale and agglomeration economies. In such cases there may be a threshold city size ($\bar{P}$) below which the innovation cannot be adopted. $\bar{P}$ itself tends to increase over time; at any given time, its value depends on the production function for the innovation and on the size and distribution of population and income. The role of the threshold in the model is to act as a barrier to diffusion further down the urban hierarchy; further adoptions in new areas are then feasible only as more urban centres expand above the threshold.

(iv) Presence of a potential entrepreneur

Since entrepreneurial ability is scarce, stochastic factors may determine whether or not an entrepreneur is located in a particular urban centre. The Poisson distribution gives the probability $(1 - p_0)$ that at least one entrepreneur is found in a town of population P as

$$1 - p_0 = 1 - e^{-\lambda} = 1 - e^{-P_q} \tag{4.12}$$

where $q = $ the small frequency of entrepreneurs through the population, and $\lambda = $ mean number of entrepreneurs in cities of size P. The frequency of potential entrepreneurs in the population is a parameter which varies with differences in the perception of the risks involved in introducing the innovation. This depends on many factors – the expected profitability of the innovation, the socio-economic structure of the community and other influences affecting the chances of obtaining support for the innovation, and the psychological drive of the innovator. All these characteristics may vary with city size.

Integrating these elements of the model we obtain the following summary conclusion. An urban centre with the population size P_i will adopt an innovation at the time t_i with the probability

$$S_i = 1 - e^{-P_i q} \tag{4.13}$$

where q = frequency of potential innovators in the population when it has received a flow of information about the innovation from earlier adopters not less than the critical flow F_i, i.e. when

$$I_i = \sum_{j=1}^{i-1} [K x_i P_i x_j P_j d_{ij}^{-b}](t_i - t_j) \geqslant F_i \tag{4.14}$$

subject to the constraint $P_i \geqslant \bar{P}$ (4.15)

There are certain obvious conclusions to be derived from this model:

(*i*) The stronger is distance decay (the higher is b), the closer will diffusion follow physical distance and approximate to the spatial diffusion model; the lower is b, the more likely that diffusion will be hierarchical diffusion. Since transport innovations reduce distance decay in the course of economic development, this helps to explain the relevance of the spatial diffusion model to the early phases of economic development and of hierarchical diffusion models to mature, developed economies.

(*ii*) The lower is b, the more rapid the diffusion process. Hence, diffusion time should fall as the level of economic development rises.

(*iii*) The higher the threshold level ($\bar{P}$), the earlier will the diffusion process end. If high-order innovations have become more frequent, this helps to explain the reduction in diffusion time that has been observed empirically.

(*iv*) If the rate of participation in diffusing information declines with decreasing city size, the innovation diffusion process will be retarded and hierarchical diffusion will be reinforced.

(*v*) Because the spatial incidence of entrepreneurs is partly stochastic, this factor will tend to make the diffusion process asymmetrical. It will also slow down the diffusion process especially to smaller towns.

A model of hierarchical diffusion as opposed, say, to a model of innovation waves is clearly much more consistent with our approach to the theory of regional growth with its stress on urban-regional integration. There are, however, many empirically-supported generalisations to back up the hypothesis that in a mature developed economy innovations diffuse spatially down the urban hierarchy, at least in the upper orders of the hierarchy. If this hypothesis is valid, an implication is that it is of critical importance for a backward region to have a large city high in the national urban hierarchy for only by doing this can the region plug itself into the communications network for outside innovations. The facts supporting the hierarchical diffusion model include:

(*i*) The formal communications network, especially for technical innovations, is predominantly an inter-urban network with denser flows between the larger cities.

(*ii*) The social structure and psychological attitudes found in large urban communities are more favourable to the adoption of new ideas, fashions and innovations.

(*iii*) The national innovation-adopting élite (technologists, research and development specialists, managers) is distributed according to the urban hierarchy.

(*iv*) Hierarchical diffusion is promoted by the hierarchical spatial structure of large multiplant business corporations. Many modern forms of business organisation (in commerce, finance and industry) are themselves hierarchical with head offices and centres of decision making in the metropolitan centres and their decision trees spread out spatially down the urban hierarchy.

(*v*) To the extent that technical progress is embodied, the spatial innovation diffusion network will tend to follow the inter-regional flow matrix of mobile capital. This latter matrix is likely to be predominantly inter-urban in form and to be channelled hierarchically.

(*vi*) In cases where innovations are diffused through distributors, hierarchical diffusion will be reinforced since the distribution network for innovations is controlled by the urban hierarchy. This is especially true of innovations the market for which is functionally related to population size.

(*vii*) Agglomeration economies are important for innovation diffusion since agglomeration economies for people attract the innovating elite while agglomeration economies for businesses attract the firms, research and development institutions and other corporations that may increase a region's capacity to absorb innovations. Since agglomeration economies are invariably urban in character and are a direct function of urban population size, they too will promote hierarchical diffusion.

Chapter 5

Towards a General Theory of Spatial Development

INTRODUCTION

I have already stressed the significance of space as a dimension in regional growth. Space is relevant at the inter-regional level since distance between regions affects the regional growth paths. It is even more important at the intra-regional level because a region's spatial structure largely determines its capacity to attract resources from outside and its internal growth potential. Since units of measurement of the costs of overcoming space (transport costs, travel time, etc.) remain the same regardless of whether the focus is inter-regional or intraregional, there is no reason on this ground why we should differentiate between an inter-regional, regional or urban model. Similarly, the case for integrating regional and urban economics suggests the desirability of a *spatial growth theory*.

There are several objections to this line of reasoning – but they are answerable. First, some people might argue that such an approach prevents analysis of the economic inter-relationship between politically bounded regions which is necessary because such 'planning regions' have a unity given to them by regional policy instruments. But the space economy is composed of a great many overlapping government units and public or semi-public agencies at the multi-regional, regional, subregional and city levels, and a satisfactory model would need to treat the existence of all these authorities as constraints on the free movement of factors, goods and persons.

Second, critics might point to the poor results obtained from spatial models developed hitherto. These have usually been metropolitan land-use allocation models which simulate location behaviour in too mechanistic a fashion, or highly mathematical optimisation models that abstract too much from reality (I would classify the entropy maximising models of the mathematical geographers in this category). More seriously, these models have not been able to explain growth; normally, they assume a given increment of growth and then proceed to allocate this spatially. The obvious answer to this criticism is that past failures should not constrain future research. Of course the integration of growth and spatial allocation is difficult; that is the challenge.

Third, there is a body of opinion that believes that regional economics and urban economics are two entirely separate fields with little in common. This argument may take many forms, but a typical line is to suggest that urban problems are in some way unique and cannot be solved by economists either because the problems are social in origin and/or because economic analysis is irrelevant. While I accept that urban problems are multi-dimensional and not solvable by economics alone, this general attitude reflects a philosophy of despair. Of course, much of the corpus of traditional economic theory is not very useful for analysis of the urban economy; this is implicit in many of the arguments in this book. But it is a giant leap from this view to a total rejection of the usefulness of economics for urban analysis. What is needed is more work on urban economics, not less.[1] Although there is obviously a distinction between regional and urban problems, we will do better if we recognise that this is one field, not two.

What are the essential features of development in the space economy that a satisfactory theory of spatial (regional and urban) growth must explain?

(*i*) National economic development is initially polarised (i.e. gets under way in one or a few regions), but the secular growth path is associated with dispersion of economic expansion into other regions. This amplification eventually leads to integration of the national economy spatially.

(*ii*) Within each region, on the other hand, sustained growth is

---

[1] In the urban field, too, the poverty of research into spatial aspects is striking. For example, when we consider the stress in the urban literature on poverty and income inequities, it is surprising that no serious work has been undertaken on *intra*-metropolitan spatial income distribution (apart from a few central city versus suburbs generalisations) despite the fact that data are available from the United States Census.

associated with increasing concentration of activities into a
limited number of urban areas. Regional growth is closely
linked to urbanisation, and national economic integration
reflects, above all, the interdependent links between metropolitan and regional cities.

(*iii*) Within each metropolitan area, economic growth (at least
in this century) has been accompanied by decentralisation of
economic activities and population from the central city. This
trend reflects the successful adaptation of the metropolitan
structure to changing economic, technical and social conditions.

Linking (*i*), (*ii*) and (*iii*) together, we may describe the process of economic growth in the space economy as (if you will
excuse an ugly term) *decentralised concentrated dispersion*. This is
the phenomenon which an acceptable regional growth model
ought to explain, and this must not be at the expense of weaken-
ing analysis of the determinants of the non-spatial aspects of
growth, i.e. the rate of growth in factor inputs and the rate of
technical progress.

THE INTEGRATION OF REGIONAL AND
URBAN ECONOMICS

It is beyond argument that the theory of regional growth has
paid insufficient attention to urbanisation and urban structure
as an influence on regional growth performance. For instance,
if we were asked to assess the growth potential of a region it
would be impossible to do this without looking at its cities and
urban centres. In these circumstances it is hard to justify
theoretical models of regions and of inter-regional growth that
as a result of spaceless assumptions abstract from urban agglomerations. There might be some excuse if we were so ignorant
about the nature of urban economics that we were unable to
make any concrete statements about the relationships between
cities and regions. But this is not the case. Although urban
economics is still a very under-developed field, there is nevertheless an adequate corpus of knowledge about the structure and
growth of cities. An early important step in the improvement
of regional growth analysis is to integrate regional and urban
economics. The failure to achieve this integration hitherto can
probably be explained by the restricted outlook of the field's

practitioners. Too many regional economists borrowing heavily from international trade theory, macro-economics and neo-classical resource allocation models have ignored the importance of intra-regional spatial differentiation. Similarly, urban economists are frequently guilty of treating the city as an isolated organism with a life of its own independent of the regional economy. While there are often sound reasons (e.g. analytical convenience) for this approach, it can lead to neglect of the urban-regional relationship that is critical to understand how regions grow.

An integration of regional and urban economics would increase understanding of the process of regional growth in several respects. First, the phenomenon of inter-regional migration is easier to analyse if the migration streams are decomposed into rural-urban and inter-urban flows; in addition, the spatial distribution of regional growth, and possibly its overall rate, will be influenced by *intra*-regional migration flows which can also be broken down into rural urban and inter-urban components. So much of the research, particularly on inter-regional migration, examines the links between migration flows and unemployment, wage differentials and other aggregate indicators. These studies have limited predictive value, they are incomplete in their explanation of how migration affects regional growth, and they lead to an interpretation of the effects of migration on relative regional *per capita* income differentials that may not be generally valid. If it is accepted that both intra-regional labour mobility and labour inflows into a region play a role in determining its rate of growth, it becomes important to be able to offer satisfactory explanations of these movements. The argument here is merely that such explanations need to take account of the scale and absorptive capacity of urban labour markets, agglomeration economies as an attractive force to migrants and to firms (and the latter helps to determine the rate of growth in job opportunities), distance and mobility costs, relative housing conditions at origin and destination, the leisure and cultural facilities of urban areas, and other factors that can only be allowed for in an urban migration model.[1]

[1] See Chapter 4, pp. 89–103. However, the analysis in that chapter goes only part of the way towards integrating urban centres into inter-regional migration theory.

Second, if the 'residual' is an important component of growth relative to increases in factor inputs, then the rate of growth of a region will depend not only on internal capital accumulation, natural increase and on factor inflows but also on its rate of innovation and its capacity to adopt innovations that have been introduced elsewhere. A region's cities will largely determine how fast the region grows due to the latter effects. The larger and more outward-looking a city, the more likely it will be a centre of innovation. Similarly, whether it offers the agglomeration and other external economies, the quality of life and the amenities to attract the scientists, technologists, research and development institutions and other potential innovators is also relevant. Most important of all, there is reasonably strong evidence that in a developed economy the route for the spatial transmission for new technical knowledge is down the urban hierarchy, so that the presence in a region of large cities with close interconnections with cities in other regions should increase that region's probability of absorbing innovations made elsewhere.[1]

Thirdly, it is arguable that agglomeration and external economies (widely intrepreted) will attract labour, capital and managerial talent to regions over and above their effects in cost reductions in production. The role of agglomeration economies in regional development can be examined only if the urban dimension is introduced. Indeed, many of these economies are urbanisation economies. The attractive force of urban centres of substantial size to factors of production is much greater than would be expected by reference to factor price differentials alone. Analysis of spaceless regions tends to underestimate the polarisation of factor flows towards the more development regions simply because it ignores the agglomeration pull of large, diversified and amenity-abundant cities.[2]

Finally, a common feature of regional development policy in

[1] This paragraph summarises the arguments made at length in Chapter 4, pp. 113–32.

[2] The argument of possible external diseconomies of scale in present-day metropolises does not refute the points made in this paragraph. If such diseconomies slow down the rate of factor inflows (and there is considerable doubt as to whether this is the case), their impact can still be analysed within the general framework. The role of agglomeration economies (and their measurement) is discussed in Chapter 7, pp. 175–96.

many countries over the last decade has been a shift towards a growth centre strategy. The underlying hypothesis is that the spatial concentration of economic activities in a region is much more efficient and has more growth potential than a more dispersed pattern. Yet even a cursory examination of the growth pole/centre literature reveals a great deal of confusion as to how these centres are supposed to operate, why spatial concentration is more efficient (apart from generalisations about lower unit costs of urban infrastructure and the gains from economising on transport costs), and even about the criteria on which centres should be selected. This confusion reflects, above all, the inadequacy of the regional growth theory that growth centre protagonists have had at their disposal.[1] The integration of regional and urban economics is essential to clarification of the issues surrounding the usefulness and feasibility of a growth centre strategy.

THE REGIONAL DISPERSION OF NATIONAL GROWTH AND INTRA-REGIONAL CONCENTRATION

The industrialisation of an economy is always geographically unbalanced. The national economy consequently develops a dualistic character, which has been described in various, though similar, ways: the 'centre' and the 'periphery' (Friedmann, 1966), the 'core' and the 'fringe' (Ullman, 1958) or the 'hinterland' and the 'heartland' (Perloff and Wingo, 1961). If the national economy develops by way of spatial polarisation, this must imply that regional problems are an inevitable by-product of the growth process regardless of whether they receive attention from economic policymakers or not. The relationship between regional and national development can be summarised by three distinct hypotheses: (i) the onset of industrialisation in a national economy is based upon economic expansion in one, two or a few limited regions, leaving the rest of the economy relatively backward; (ii) subsequent national economic development is associated *at some stage* with dispersion into other regions, a process which tends to integrate and unify

---

[1] This point was discussed in more detail in Chapter 3, pp. 78–86.

the national economy; (*iii*) independent of the polarisation and subsequent dispersion tendencies inter-regionally, growth within regions always tends to be spatially concentrated, in the sense of a close degree of interdependence between industrial development and urbanisation and a focus of growth potential upon the limited set of large urban centres.

A fourth hypothesis refers to decentralisation tendencies within metropolitan centres. This latter phenomenon is discussed separately.[1] It is, in any event, not central to an analysis of the relationships between national and regional development but instead reflects the ability of metropolitan cities to adapt their structures to changes in social, economic and technical conditions.

To the extent that these hypotheses are descriptive generalisations, they could be subject to empirical verification on a cross-cultural basis. Secular time series on the geographical distribution of economic activity are scarce in most countries, so the verification procedure would not be an easy matter. Nevertheless, it is a task which would fall within the competence of someone preparing a postgraduate thesis with time available to search and dig for available and fugitive data. In this context, however, the more important task is to explain these hypotheses and their rationale. Treating the problem in this way, it is soon apparent that the second hypothesis is the most difficult to justify theoretically. There are strong reasons why economic growth should be spatially polarised both in the sense of concentration in certain regions of the national economy (Hypothesis (*i*)) and in cities and other limited areas within regions (Hypothesis (*iii*)). It is not self-evident why the imbalance within the national economy should be corrected by the subsequent economic development of other regions. However, in discussing this possibility we should be careful not to mix up the spatial question of 'polarisation-dispersion' with the inter-regional macro-economic problem of 'divergence-convergence'. Although polarisation may be associated with widening, and dispersion with narrowing, regional *per capita* income differentials, this co-variation is by no means inevitable. Thus, for example, we might observe within a country a marked

[1] See pp. 146–50.

tendency for secondary and tertiary industries to become more geographically dispersed even in a period of *per capita* income divergence. This could be explained by inter-regional productivity differentials (especially where due to inter-industry mix) or to marked differences in inter-regional fertility rates. Conversely, continued polarisation is not incompatible with regional income convergence in periods of heavy migration from low to high wage regions or when inter-regional government transfers towards backward regions are on a substantial scale.

Before commenting on each of the critical hypotheses, it may be useful to look at the spatial patterns associated with each national growth sequence as outlined in Friedmann's centre-periphery model. This deserves pride of place as the best formulated construct in a haphazard and rather fuzzy literature. Its drawback is that it harnesses the path of development to a series of stages, the type of historical straitjacket that I deeply distrust. Nevertheless, even this device may be useful for pedagogic purposes if interpreted loosely. Friedmann argues that the national growth process can be viewed as a sequence of four stages, each of which marks a major step towards progressive integration of the space economy. In the first stage, characteristic of pre-industrial societies, the space economy consists of a number of independent local centres that have little or no interconnection with each other and are certainly not structured as a national urban hierarchy such as binds large population centres in a developed economy. Whereas this first stage is stable, the second stage is clearly unstable. The shock of industrialisation is associated with a striking disturbance of the economy's spatial structure, namely the development of the centre-periphery relationship. Growth is spatially concentrated in a single strong centre. There are contacts with other regions (the periphery), but these are imperfect and primarily unidirectional, i.e., take the form of polarisation flows towards the centre. As Friedmann points out, the centre-periphery relationship is, in effect, a 'colonial' relationship in which labour, capital, managerial talent and raw materials flow from the periphery to the centre. The peripheral regions remain economically backward, function largely as primary producers, tend to suffer from unfavourable inter-regional terms of trade, and fail to compete in manufacturing industry with the centre in the open (i.e. free trade) national economy.

However, in the course of time (and partly if not largely due to political pressures and the emergence of offsetting policies) the pure centre-periphery dichotomy gives way to a third, transitional stage in which the central regions remain dominant but some counter-weight is provided by the emergence of viable peripheral sub-centres. The national economy is in the process of integration, but the process is incomplete. The centre and the peripheral sub-centres show some signs of inter-dependence, but other areas in the periphery remain isolated and untouched by development. In the final, fourth stage the space economy can be conceived as a functionally inter-dependent system of cities, or rather as a system of inter-dependent regions structured upon a national urban hierarchy. The integration of all regions into the national economy takes place through what Friedmann calls 'the matrix of urban regions', largely because of the force of agglomeration and urban-isation economies in regional development. In this stage of post-industrial maturity, the space economy has developed a struc-ture capable of sustaining economic growth at an acceptable cost in terms of regional inequities. The national economy is fully integrated, and a system of efficient inter-regional com-modity and factor markets exists.

It is apparent that this sequence of stages is quite consist-ent with the three central hypotheses. The decomposable system of isolated regions characteristic of the preindustrial economy is broken down by industrialisation which connects some of the regions together, though only in a strongly polarised structure (the centre-periphery model associated with Hypothesis (i)). At later levels of development when *per capita* incomes are higher, growth is dispersed in other regions and urban centres develop at the periphery (Hypothesis (ii)) Throughout the course of development industrial growth is predominantly urban growth, and the spatial incidence of growth *within* each region is itself heavily polarised in favour of the larger cities and towns (Hypothesis (iii)).

The arguments for Hypothesis (i) are straightforward and obvious. Because of the scarcity of investment resources during the phase of early industrialisation it is impossible to exploit all profitable investment opportunities simultaneously. Hence industrial development starts out in one or two regions which have specific advantages over the rest of the economy. These may be a favourable natural resource endowment (Perloff and Wingo, 1961) and/or market advantages such as a more densely populated hinterland or, perhaps more likely in view of the fact that industrialisation has frequently been externally induced, closer access to export markets. This greater market potential enables economies of scale to be exploited much earlier at the centre than at the periphery. Once the initial polarisation has occurred, it is not difficult to explain its cumulative reinforcement; as production expands agglomeration and external economies of scale are reaped. Kaldor (1970) refers to Verdoorn's Law as an explanation of the continued build-up in more industrial regions – that their productivity performance is an increasing function of their rate of growth of output. Also, as we have seen, the economic links between the core regions and the rest of the economy at this stage strongly reinforce polarisation because 'backwash' (polarisation) effects dominate over 'spread' ('trickling-down') effects. Resources flow towards the centre, the national economy becomes dualistic, and terms of trade movements favour the centre. The fringe regions find it difficult to adjust to this outflow of resources because of high fertility rates so that out-migrants are easily replaced in terms of numbers, the disruptive effects of the high average quality of out-migrants, and their acute shortage of capital.

Third, and perhaps most important of all, the increasing concentration of population at the core, consequent upon the initial industrialisation, strengthens the advantages of these regions in subsequent development (Ullman, 1958). The concentration of population at the centre reinforces its dominance even if the original locational advantages have been dissipated. It helps to explain the failure of diminishing returns to set in at the core. It accounts for the development of key services (finance, education, research and political control) at the centre which act as a magnet for attracting new industry. The centre becomes, in effect, the national market, and links are strengthened with foreign export markets. With the increase in its size, the population becomes culturally heterogeneous; this favours innovation and risk-taking. Moreover, because of the centre's cultural dominance and the diversification of its economic structure, private investors tend to overestimate the profitability of investment in the core relative to the fringe regions, even in cases where real peripheral investment opportunities exist (Hirschman, 1958, p. 184; Friedmann, 1966, p. 15). Already, in the initial polarisation phase of development locational preferences begin to have an influence on spatial patterns.

Given these cumulative advantages of the initially developed regions, it is not easy to explain the subsequent dispersion of growth into other areas (Hypothesis (*ii*)). However, there are some economic forces which begin to assert themselves at later phases of national economic development and offer the peripheral regions some opportunities for growth; moreover, at some time the relatively puny advantages of the lagging regions will probably be reinforced by political pressures. Nevertheless, it is usually impossible to predict if and when polarisation will be set in reverse.[1] The first factor in favour of the backward regions is that simply because of their remoteness from the centre they do have a protected local market. The problem then becomes how to develop sufficient economies of scale, a problem that can eventually be solved by time itself assuming that both population and *per capita* incomes increase over time. Of course, it remains true that competition from the centre will still be dominant in many industries, but there are sectors where transport costs confer a significant advantage on local producers.

Secondly, the relative impact of 'trickling down' and polarisation effects may alter over time. The 'backwash' effects of resource movements may be offset by rising demand for complementary products made in the lagging regions or by the diffusion of technical knowledge, managerial know-how and social advances over the space economy. In many cases, this may take the form of businesses in the core regions setting up

---

[1] It is of some relevance to refer to Williamson's (1965) mixed results on the hypothesis that divergence and convergence tendencies are functionally related to the level of development. However, apart from his inconclusive findings his analysis was carried out in terms of differentials in per capita incomes rather than with spatial measures of polarisation and dispersion.

branch plants in the lagging regions when demand levels justify more than one plant (Perloff and Wingo, 1961). The possibilities for decentralisation of industrial plants have been reinforced by technological changes such as the reduced reliance on natural resources, the ubiquity of cheap power and energy, the mobility of external economies and improvements in inter-regional transportation and by relative price effects such as lower wages in less developed regions.

Thirdly, and much more nebulous, in some countries the original core regions may develop senescent characteristics and begin to suffer from diseconomies of agglomeration. It is very difficult to quantify these phenomena or even to estimate whether they have any influence at all. Such factors might include: technical obsolescence of industrial plants, decline in the calibre of managers and innovators at the core connected, for instance, with the substitution of social for profitability goals, environmental pollution and other agglomeration dis-economies. However, forces of this kind are probably the exception rather than the rule.

A more important consideration is that political pressure for the introduction of equity criteria into regional policy may be reinforced by economic advantage. For instance, especially in a period of deceleration in foreign export demand, expansion of industry in the core regions may be held back by the insufficient size of the home market and by low income levels in the lagging regions. The failure to exploit the resources of these regions to the full may be the greatest obstacle to faster national growth. Thus, an economic case can be used to bolster the political fact that people in the lagging regions do have votes. The political pressure for government intervention will itself be strengthened by the widening regional disparities that are frequently associated with the preceding polarisation of national development. How-ever, there is an acute problem of timing here since implementa-tion of a regional policy may well retard national growth if introduced too early. The policy impact is likely to be more justi-fiable and more effective when economic forces have already started to shift a little in favour of the lagging regions. Thus, even in a market economy a threshold level of national econo-mic development exists when a turning point is reached and polarisation gives way to a diffusion process in which economic growth spreads out from the core into other regions. In some countries, however, this turning point may occur only at a very late phase of national economic development. Dispersion tendencies are, therefore, much easier to explain in a centrally planned or mixed economy than in a market economy.

Hypothesis (*iii*), that growth *within* regions is spatially concentrated, underlies much of the argument of this book and needs little emphasis here. A large and increasing proportion of total population is urban, almost all economic activities (apart from agriculture[1] and extractive industry) are carried out in or near urban centres, and in a real sense economic growth is urban growth. Agglomeration economies (interpreted widely, that is, including social amenities as well as business services) have become a more powerful locational attractor than natural resources, energy sources or low wages. Economies of scale in many industrial sectors have made concentration of production in or near cities more efficient, even if these economies of concentration have been partially offset by higher transport costs. The patterns of migration during the course of industrialisation have reinforced agglomeration because the rural-urban stream has been supported by inter-urban flows towards larger population centres. Cities have been the prime source of innovations because they have been communication nodes for the transmission of scientific and technical knowledge and have attracted the potential innovators, the research and development and educational infrastructure that are necessary prerequisites for a high rate of innovation. This critical role of cities in the evolution and development of the space economy has been treated extensively by Pred (1966). Moreover, in this century the predominance of urban growth in regional development has been reinforced by changes in the sectoral composition of national growth. The main leaders in national employment growth have been service industries such as commerce, banking and finance, education and health, the government sector, miscellaneous and personal services – all industries that are

---

[1] Nicholls (1961) showed that the influence of urban institutions even results in more efficient agricultural production near urban centres, and outlined a spatial structure characterised by highly developed and interdependent metropolitan-agricultural regions interspersed with bands of stagnating rural regions.

overwhelmingly located in metropolitan areas (see Friedmann and Alonso, 1964, especially p. 211).

Finally, Hansen (1970a, p. 83), taking up a comment by Hoover (1967), has linked Hypotheses (ii) and (iii) together by suggesting that changes in key locational determinants have facilitated regional dispersion within the national economy but have reinforced polarisation within each region: 'the location of economic activity is more free with respect to major regions but less so with respect to size of community'.

URBAN DECENTRALISATION

The forces behind decentralisation and suburbanisation in modern cities are complex. However, it would seem reasonable to express this phenomenon as the outcome of four main factors; urbanisation itself as measured by the rate of urban population growth; rising incomes; changes in urban transport costs (and other measures of the efficiency of the urban transport system); and changes in space preferences. The latter may be treated as primarily a function of income. It is not easy to devise a suitable measure for decentralisation itself. Mills (1970) suggests that the density gradient makes an appropriate measure. I prefer the simpler if cruder index of the area of the S.M.S.A.

If we make some simplifying assumptions, it is relatively easy to show the inter-relationships between the above factors and decentralisation, as measured by the crude surrogate of the size of the urban area. Let us assume a circular city with centralised workplaces and uniform residential densities. This enables us to express changes in the urban area in terms of average behaviour, where the average trip length is determined as half the radius of the city. Let us further assume that transport cost changes affect only the length of trips, not their number.[1]

The main variables are interrelated as a matter of definition. This is because

$$A = NS \qquad (5.1)$$

[1] In a real world application it is difficult to predict the impact of transport cost changes on decentralisation (see Mills, 1970, p. 15).

where A = area of S.M.S.A., N = population, S = average amount of urban space consumed per inhabitant, and

$$A = \pi(2L)^2 \tag{5.2a}$$

where L = average trip length.

Thus,

$$L = \tfrac{1}{2}\sqrt{\frac{NS}{\pi}} \tag{5.2b}$$

$$N = \frac{\pi}{S}(2L)^2 \tag{5.2c}$$

$$S = \frac{\pi}{N}(2L)^2 \tag{5.2d}$$

As suggested above, we may also write

$$S = f(Y) \tag{5.3}$$

where Y = income, and

$$L = f(C) \tag{5.4}$$

where C = average unit transport cost.

Possible formulations of these functions might be

$$S = v + Y^\lambda \tag{5.5}$$

where v = constant, λ = income elasticity of demand for space, and

$$L = qC^{-\beta} \tag{5.6}$$

where q = constant and β = elasticity of trip length in response to changes in transport costs.

Substituting equations (5.5) and (5.6) into equation (5.2c), we obtain

$$N = \frac{4\,\pi q^2 C^{-2\beta}}{v + Y^\lambda} \tag{5.7}$$

Although this expression shows how the main variables influencing decentralisation are inter-related, it is merely an identity with no predictive value. For predictive purposes we need to examine determinants of changes in the urban area (i.e. our surrogate for the decentralisation process itself). Thus, a more useful formulation is

$$a = n + \lambda y + [(1 + \beta c)^2 - 1] \qquad (5.8)$$

where a = rate of change in area of S.M.S.A., n = rate of population growth, y = rate of growth in income, c = rate of change in transport costs, λ = income elasticity of demand for space (λ frequently has a value > 1), β = elasticity of average trip length in response to change in transport costs ($\beta < 0$). This elasticity coefficient reflects the response in terms of locational shifts to transport cost changes. If relocation costs are very heavy, the value of β will be very low.

The values of λ and β may be determined empirically by regression analysis. Although equation (5.8) is a useful way of predicting the extent of decentralisation as a result of changes in population, income and transport costs, its limitations should be kept in mind. The linear aggregation form of the equation assumes independence between, say, population changes and space preferences. Another aspect of the same problem is that, because of strong locational inertia and high relocation costs, the income elasticity of demand for space affects only the plot sizes chosen by residents in the course of moving from one part of the city to another; an immobile resident is unable to enlarge his plot as income rises. Thus, λ makes sense only as an *average* elasticity coefficient in response to *total* urban income change where the actual changes in demand for urban space are made effective merely by a small segment of the urban population (i.e. the mobile element). However, the elasticity coefficient will then have stable values only if the income distribution of the urban population as a whole, the income distribution of mobile households and the proportion of total households moving all remain constant. It is difficult for these conditions to hold when the size and composition of the urban population as a whole is changing, i.e. if $n \neq 0$. The measurement of transport costs presents a problem, primarily because transport costs must contain an estimate of the value of travel time; it has proved notoriously difficult, as any perusal of the urban transportation literature shows, to develop consistent and universally acceptable estimates of travel time. Finally, the assumption of uniform residential densities which is so crucial to the specification of the last term in equation (5.8) needs to be relaxed.[1] However, although this would complicate the mathematics of the urban decentralisation function, it would affect neither its basic structure nor its interpretation.

Some evidence for this conclusion has been presented in a recent urban simulation model by Mills (1972). It is, of course, quite easy to express a population density function that relaxes the uniform density assumption whether in a general form such as

$$\int_{r_m}^{r_1} \mathcal{N}(r)dr = \mathcal{N} \tag{5.9}$$

where r = distance, r_1 = the city centre and r_m = city boundary or in the more specific negative exponential form

$$\mathcal{N}(r) = \mathcal{N}_1 e^{-br} \tag{5.10}$$

where $\mathcal{N}_1$ = population at the city centre and b = parameter measuring the rate at which density declines with distance.

However, to explore the impacts of population growth, income expansion and changes in transport technology it is necessary to incorporate such a gradient into a general urban model. Since the development, or even the description, of such a model would be too much of a digression from our main theme, it is sufficient to present some of the results of the Mills' model.[2] These are shown below.

TABLE 5.1

Percentage changes in:

20 *per cent increase in:*	Urban area	Population Density	Rent at edge of C.B.D.
Transport Technology	+ 7	− 7	−44
Income	+52	−34	−30
Population	+ 2	+22	+158

[1] Apart from Mills, Clark (1951 and 1967) and Muth (1961 and 1969) have stressed the importance of the density gradient as a measure of urban structure.

[2] For the details of this model see Mills (1972, pp. 96–108). It is hardly necessary to say that the magnitude of the changes depends on the particular structure of the model. The directions of the changes would be the same, however, for almost any plausible model.

These findings support those of our simple model. Improvements in transportation technology, income increases and population growth all foster technical progress. The effects on population density and on C.B.D. rents are also predictable, with the possible exception of the impact of income on central rents (in this model the suburbanisation stimulus of rising incomes overcomes the income effect on rising rents). This particular model suggests that increases in income are a more powerful stimulus to urban decentralisation than population growth and technical progress.

The implication of the analysis presented here is quite clear. The rate of decentralisation is determined by the basic forces of economic growth, and hence is a by-product of the growth process itself. This follows if income growth, population expansion and technical progress (in this particular instance, as reflected in changes in transportation technology) can be regarded as major manifestations of economic growth. From another point of view, however, metropolitan decentralisation can be interpreted as an adaptation of the structure of cities to changing social, economic and technical conditions. In this sense, it may have favourable feedback effects on growth by improving intrametropolitan resource allocation and on welfare to the extent that suburbanisation increases households' utility.

Chapter 6

Investment

DETERMINANTS OF REGIONAL INVESTMENT

The determinants of regional investment and the interdependence between regional investment and regional growth have not received much attention from regional economists except in the contexts of inter-regional mobility of capital and regional business cycle analysis.[1] The former has been dominated by neoclassic dogma and the latter by adapting neo-Keynesian macro-economic investment analysis to an inter-regional system. The approach to regional growth analysed in this book is clearly inconsistent with both these lines of thinking. In particular, we would wish to stress the durability of capital, the sequential and interdependent nature of spatial investment decisions, the importance of indivisibilities in the space economy, the distinction between private sector capital and public and social capital, and spatial frictions on inter-regional capital flows.

The purist view of the nature of regional investment and the determinants of inter-regional capital movements relies heavily on the work of Borts and Stein (1964) and Romans (1965). The rate of investment in a region is treated as a function of its marginal efficiency of investment,[2] and an efficient programme of capital accumulation occurs if firms invest in such a way that

[1] See Airov (1963 and 1967), Hartman and Seckler (1967), Borts and Stein (1964) and Romans (1965). See also Richardson (1969a, Chapter 11 and Chapter 12.3, and 1969b, pp. 37–44).

[2] How is the marginal efficiency of investment measured? To quote Borts and Stein (1964, p. 173): 'Ideally, we seek to calculate the marginal rate of return on new investment by comparing the increment of a flow of proprietary income to the purchase price of additional assets. The marginal efficiency of investment is then the discount rate, r, which equates the discounted stream of returns with the purchase price of the additional assets, P'.

the marginal efficiency of investment in all directions (i.e. between regions, within regions, between sectors) is equal. At the individual firm level this implies that firms maximise expected profits, and to the extent that investment is undertaken by new (or relocating) firms it implies a profit-maximising theory of location. At a more macro-level it implies, of course, a neo-classical regional growth model. The arguments against both profit-maximising models of location and neo-classical growth models need not be repeated.[1] Even on the theory's own terms there are difficulties: the need to assume omniscient perfect knowledge on the part of investors; the importance of public investment with its propensity to create external economies that are difficult to include in the marginal efficiency of investment calculus; the existence in space of large-scale indivisible investment projects (e.g. new towns) on which it is virtually impossible to evaluate a rate of return.

The neoclassical explanations rely heavily on the hypothesis that capital is perfectly mobile between regions. As the following statement by Romans (1965, p. 7) makes clear, this assumes that the inter-regional capital market is a perfectly competitive market for a homogeneous good:

> The capital market is analogous to the wheat market. There is a supply of capital offered to all regions by (predominantly) national financial and commercial institutions and markets (equal to national gross saving). There are continuously varying regional demands for capital. Capital, like wheat, flows towards those regions offering the highest price, away from regions offering the lowest price, maintaining at all times an equilibrium of price equality after transport costs (which in the case of capital are negligible between regions). As with wheat, the price of capital is determined by supply and demand. The supply in a region continually adjusts via imports and exports to changes in regional demand so as to maintain inter-regional price equality.

The weaknesses in this fantasyland view of how inter-regional capital markets operate have already been analysed.[2] Some of the obvious arguments against such a view include: the importance of risk-aversion and reducing uncertainty in spatial

[1] See pp. 22–9, 54–7.   [2] See Chapter 4, pp. 103–13.

investment decisions which increase the relative advantages of known, established locations;[1] the embodiment of inter-regional capital flows in locational shifts where decisions are based on 'satisficing' rather than profit-maximising criteria; neglect of the quantitative importance of public capital in total capital.

Multiplier-accelerator models, the most characteristic type of analysis found in the inter-regional business cycle literature, have the advantage that they do not necessarily, or even usually, predict an equilibrium solution. Given certain parameter values, they can simulate an explosive growth path for a region which is compatible, say, with cumulative causation (see Hartman and Seckler, 1967), but they are inadequate in many other respects. They abstract from space relying on a simple amalgam of macro-economics and inter-regional trade theory, and take as the main framework of analysis an inter-regional system that is merely a set of spaceless points.[2] They are much more applicable to short- or, at best, medium-term analysis because of the need to assume stable parameters whereas the critical problems in regional investment theory are the explanation of long-run trends, discontinuities and shifts in investment functions. The induced investment relationship familiar in the acceleration principle approach based on a response of investment to changes in the rate of output is less appropriate in the space economy than other kinds of induced investment links, particularly how changes in the scale and location of public investment (infrastructure) may induce changes in the rate of private sector investment. Similarly, the relevant multiplier relationship is not the one characteristic of these models, not even the 'super-multiplier', but what might be described as a dynamic development multiplier that includes in the evaluation of the effects of a given quantum of investment all the subsequent regional development decisions that may

[1] This may mean that distance counts. For example, the 'cost of transferring confidence may be high enough to give us a capital-supply function which has distance as an important independent variable'. (Chinitz, 1961, p. 285.)

[2] This point is stated explicitly by Airov (1963, p. 16): 'From the regional standpoint, the models of general economics do not reflect – particularly in the treatment of induced and autonomous investment – any determinants which are uniquely regional or geographical or spatial.'

follow from it, some of which may occur only after a substantial time lag.

Another line of analysis that has been given some attention in the last decade (Rahman, 1963; Sakashita, 1967; Ohtsuki, 1971) is the development of an optimisation model for interregional investment within a programming framework. The models developed have been very simplistic using a crude minimum capital-output ratio criterion as an allocative device. In effect, this provides a spatial analogy to the Tinbergen development planning approach discussed earlier[1] since here the optimal solution involves concentration of investment in one region (or at most a limited number of regions) just as the sectoral planning programme involved concentration in the optimum sector. This polarisation of investment in certain regions may superficially represent an observable tendency in real-world multi-regional systems, but the analysis is subject to many qualifications. Some of these have been discussed by Vietorisz (1967). Optimal solutions for spatial investment decisions may require a much longer planning perspective than is consistent with assumptions of stability in capital-output ratios. The durability of fixed capital (particularly transport and urban infrastructure), high relocation costs and sequential interdependence between all spatial investment decisions mean that the regional investment process can be treated as a very long-run, gradual and frequently grossly sub-optimal sequence of locational adaptations where the spatial structure of the economy and the spatial distribution of the capital stock change very slowly. The Rahman model is a one-sector model and introducing several industries increases dispersal tendencies since relative capital productivities may vary widely between industries. Given that most productive factors are in joint demand, the spatial concentration of investment may be ruled out by inelasticities in the supply of other factors. Introducing equity constraints into the optimisation programme may either reduce spatial concentration of capital or lead to switching from one region to another. The existence of upper bounds on levels of particular industries could promote regional dispersal in sectoral investment. Finally, Vietorisz suggests the possibility of what he calls a 'savings incentive hypothesis': that there are

[1] See Chapter 2, pp. 44–50.

incentive effects bringing about a positive correlation between current rates of savings in a region and its past rate of investment. This means that it may well be optimal to invest simultaneously in several regions, and that there will be strong self-financing tendencies built into the savings-investment process in each region. It should be pointed out, however, that this hypothesis has not been subjected to any testing, and there is little direct empirical evidence in its support.

The main characteristic of regional investment decisions is that in space these decisions must be regarded as closely interdependent. The repercussions that follow from this are implicit in much of the argument in this book. In the regional capital stock growth function suggested in the model of Chapter 8 we take account of interdependence in several crude ways: the impact of agglomeration economies on regional investment, the influence of the size of the regional capital stock, and perhaps more important some attempt to measure the influence of its spatial distribution.[1] Here it may be useful to concentrate on a rather different problem – the interdependence between public sector investment and private sector investment.[2] Much of the subsequent analysis is inspired by Leven, Legler and Shapiro (1970).

It is obvious that a large and important share of the regional capital stock consists of social and public capital: transport infrastructure, the urban fabric, health, education and social welfare facilities, and so on. It is also clear that the scale and spatial distribution of public capital may have a big impact on subsequent private investment decisions and on the location decisions made by firms and households.[3] Since the initial size

[1] See equation (8.2), p. 213. The other independent variables are more common: the growth rate in income (to measure the induced investment effects) and the relative rate of return to capital compared with other regions.

[2] In the next section we return to agglomeration effects by examining inter-regional savings – investment flows in a system of regions with built-in agglomeration and polarisation tendencies. This model provides a striking contrast to the 'capital flows embodied in locational shifts' approach discussed in Chapter 4, pp. 103–13.

[3] Boudeville (1966, pp. 85–6) suggests a distinction between *regionally pre-determined* and *location-free* investment which cuts across the public–private investment classification.

and distribution of the public capital stock is, in part at least, pre-determined by the prior spatial distribution of people and economic activities in the region we have an interdependent system of the kind summarised in the diagram below. Once growth in such a system gets under way it is easy for the process to become self-sustained and cumulative.

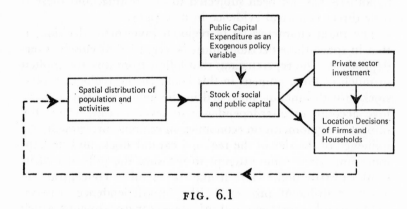

FIG. 6.1

However, if the initial population and level of activity are small and their spatial distribution costly and inefficient a region may remain in a low-level equilibrium trap. In such a case, attempts to promote regional growth may need the exogenous injection of public and social capital expenditure as a generator of expansion rather than merely as a response to changes in the level and spatial distribution of population and economic activity. The difficulty with this approach is that our understanding of the inter-relationships between public and private investment decisions is so limited that we are unable to specify a model of this kind.

Leven argues (following V. L. Smith, 1964) that capital should be considered as a stock rather than a flow of services, and that the production function should be of the following type:

$$Y = f(K, X)$$

where K = capital stock and X = vector of all other inputs. This approach has many advantages when we consider the importance of non-flow elements in regional development and the heterogeneity of capital that is so crucial from a regional growth point of view. It is easier to implement a production function of this type if the capital stock is measured in *physical* terms. Indeed, for public capital this is the only meaningful approach. In a pure public capital case the services of the stock are available to all at a zero price, yet it is also clear that total use of the stock cannot exceed its physical capacity. Moreover, the number of categories of capital in the public sector may be manageable enough for empirical analysis (transportation infrastructure, educational institutions, hospitals, public utilities, etc.) so that each category could enter the regional production function as a separate variable. It is also unnecessary to adjust the physical capital measure for variations in quality since (according to Leven) it is the stock of capital which determines the number of people who can be served, while *the value of the variable inputs* is the prime determinant of the quality of the service. Finally, public capital measured in physical capacity units is more useful to regional planners than its monetary value.

Treating public capital in this way offers some possibility of operationalising the 'population and economic activity → public capital → private investment and location →' loop suggested above, but empirical testing raises many unsettled problems. The links between changes in population and income and the public capital stock may be relatively easy to specify since many components of public capital (especially if measured in physical terms) bear a direct relationship to the number and characteristics of the regional population while the induced effects of changes in income on the demand for public capital may be dealt with by estimation of income elasticity coefficients for public services of different kinds. A more hazy question is whether urban densities and regional population distribution have any marked impacts on public capital needs. Much more serious, however, is our ignorance about the generative impact of public capital stocks and infrastructure on private investment (and location) decisions. Investigating the possibility and scale of such impacts is a question for detailed research much beyond the scope of this book; the answers to such a question would, of course, be of great value in assessing the value of a regional development strategy based on the use of infrastructure as the chief policy instrument. An interesting side consideration of such an empirical analysis would be whether or not there are any constraints built into the cumulative investment growth sequence of the loop. In particular, if public capital is measured in physical capacity terms we might hypothesise a situation where the social rate of return to private investment falls when congestion (i.e. demand greater than 'capacity') develops in the use of public capital. However, we know even less about the relationships between capacity utilisation in public services and infrastructure and rates of growth in regional investment and output than about the overall impact of public capital on location decisions.

A MARKOV CHAIN MODEL OF INTER-REGIONAL SAVINGS AND CAPITAL GROWTH

A model of the investment process both within regions and in the inter-regional system as a whole must take account of certain key characteristics of regional investment. These include: the sequential and interdependent nature of investment decisions in the space economy (the fact that an investment decision in regard to urban and transport infrastructure or an industrial plant must take account of all previous investments and will influence subsequent investments); the durability and fixed location of investment which means that the spatial structure can change but very slowly; the role of spatial agglomeration economies as a locational attractor for new investments; the implications of regions as open economies and of the potentially high mobility of capital (savings). This latter characteristic is of supreme importance in differentiating the theory of regional investment from investment models of the national economy. Because regions are more 'open' than nations and because savings may flow in and out freely in response to relative investment opportunities, the regional location of investments is independent of regional savings rates (Vietorisz, 1967). The supply of savings in a region is endogenous, regions may become net debtors or creditors for long periods, and 'the whole question of a savings-determined "equilibrium" rate of growth becomes hazy' (Hartman and Seckler, 1967, p. 168).

Ideally, we require a model that simultaneously fulfils two objectives: (*i*) offers a satisfactory simulation of inter-regional and intra-regional capital flows which necessitates breaking the deterministic direct link between savings and investment; (*ii*) goes some way towards reflecting the cumulative, sequential, durable and interdependent nature of spatial investment decisions and, in particular, takes account of agglomeration as an influence on regional investment.

A model of this kind is unlikely to be developed with the aid of conventional economic analysis. However, by using an absorbing Markov chain model[1] we may simulate the regional investment process reasonably well. This approach has numerous advantages:

(*i*) Markov processes are ideal for emphasising the sequential character of investment decisions, since the essence of such processes is that the outcome of an event is dependent on the immediately preceding events.

(*ii*) Since the spatial distribution of investment is not primarily determined by where savings are generated but by the interaction between objective conditions (relative investment opportunities at different locations) and how these are subjectively perceived (the behaviour of savers and investors), it is better analysed within a probabilistic (such as a Markov chain) than a deterministic framework.

(*iii*) The transitional probability matrix of the Markov chain model can be used as an inter-area savings flow matrix. We can adapt such a matrix to deal with both inter-regional and intra-regional relationships. In the simple model analysed here we assume a system of two regions (the study region and the rest of the world) and we disaggregate the study region into four hierarchically structured nodal sub-regions. Because this matrix refers to transient states, it allows us to introduce considerable realism into the model since savings do not necessarily have to be invested in the region into which they are first transferred. In other words, the model implicitly recognises the existence of

[1] For an elementary introduction to Markov chains see Springer *et al.* (1968). For more formal mathematical studies see Kemeny and Snell (1960) and Bharucha-Reid (1966). Applications in regional analysis can be found in L. A. Brown (1970), Harvey (1967), Morley and Thornes (1972) and A. Rogers (1966 and 1967).

financial institutions that act as intermediaries between savings and investment. The cells of the matrix may therefore be interpreted as expressing the probabilities of savings being placed in local (regional or sub-regional) and external financial institutions (the diagonal and off-diagonal entries respectively).

(*iv*) The durability of investments can be dealt with by treating investment as an absorbing state, i.e. as irreversible. The equilibrium solution (the *fixed point*) is achieved when all the inputs into the process end up in the absorbing state and when the values for the transient states are zero. In the simplified example described below we assume only one absorbing state representing the act of investment. It would be conceivable, however, to postulate several such states for particular types of investment (transport infrastructure, urban overhead capital, industrial plant, etc.) and another state to represent investment failures.[1]

(*v*) Locational interdependence and agglomeration effects may be reflected to some extent in the structure of the matrix, i.e. in the values assigned to the probability coefficients. In other words, we may build polarisation tendencies into the system. In particular: (*a*) the relative values of the inter-area probability flow coefficients may favour the larger regions (sub-regions); (*b*) the propensity for savings to be channelled into local savings institutions may be a function of regional size; (*c*) if strong agglomeration effects imply profitable investment opportunities, the coefficients in the absorbing state (which reflect 'immediate' and direct transfers from the transient states) may also be positively correlated with the size of the regions; (*d*) the long-run reinforcement of agglomeration tendencies (cumulative causation) may be simulated by substituting a new transitional probability matrix at some stage in the process with adjusted coefficients that reinforce (*a*), (*b*) and (*c*).

(*vi*) A general advantage of the Markov chain approach is that it may help to reconcile two apparently contradictory aspects of the regional growth process – cumulative tendencies in spatial concentration and agglomeration on the one hand, and the notion of a spatial equilibrium in capital flows on the other.

[1] We might also assign a state for depreciation and maintenance expenses but whether this should be transient or absorbing depends upon whether such expenses are regarded as sacrosanct or not.

A NON-ABSORBING MARKOV CHAIN MODEL FOR FLOWS OF SHORT-TERM FUNDS

The basic characteristics of a non-absorbing Markov chain model can be explained by the use of a model of inter-regional 'hot money' flows in which savings are transferred between regions but are never absorbed into fixed investment. In other words, each *state* of the process is *transient* and reversible. Let us assume an inter-regional system of m regions. Associated with each region $(i = 1, \ldots, m)$ there is a volume of savings, s_i. During each time interval a certain proportion of the savings of region i is transferred to region j, and these observations can be summed up in an inter-regional flow matrix which shows the volume of savings which is transferred between each pair of regions during a specified time period

$$(S = \sum_i \sum_j s_{ij})$$

This flow matrix can be transformed into a transition matrix by dividing each element s_{ij} by its corresponding row sum. We thereby obtain a transition matrix P with elements $p_{ij} = s_{ij}/s_i$. Each of these elements can be thought of as probabilities (since $0 \leqslant p_{ij} \leqslant 1$), and hence the P matrix can be treated as the transitional probability matrix of a Markov chain.

Each state of a Markov process is dependent upon the immediately preceding state in the following way:

$$s^{t+1} = s^t P \tag{6.1}$$

where s^t = vector of savings in each region at period t. If we wish to estimate how this volume of savings will be distributed within the inter-regional system after n periods we simply apply the formula

$$s^{t+n} = s^t P^n \tag{6.2}$$

Despite the transient nature of each state, s^{t+n} will be a steady state solution *if* the number of time intervals, n, is large enough. This equilibrium solution is independent of the original state of the system.

For example, in a five-region system if the inter-regional transitional probability matrix could be described as follows:

$$P = \begin{bmatrix} \cdot9 & \cdot05 & \cdot03 & \cdot02 & \cdot00 \\ \cdot3 & \cdot6 & \cdot05 & \cdot04 & \cdot01 \\ \cdot25 & \cdot15 & \cdot5 & \cdot07 & \cdot03 \\ \cdot22 & \cdot20 & \cdot12 & \cdot4 & \cdot06 \\ \cdot20 & \cdot18 & \cdot15 & \cdot12 & \cdot35 \end{bmatrix}$$

the equilibrium distribution of savings between regions, s^{t+n}, is

$$s_1 = \cdot72977; s_2 = \cdot14459; s_3 = \cdot07175; s_4 = \cdot04426; s_5 = \cdot00962$$

Once this 'steady state' of the system is reached it persists. A model of this kind may offer useful insights into the workings of international (or inter-regional) flow mechanisms for short-term funds. In particular, in the absence of further exogenous disturbances, international short-term capital movements will tend to settle down in a stable equilibrium. The equilibrium distribution of funds between financial centres could be predicted if we were able to specify the transitional probability matrix P. Of course, such equilibria may be attained only rarely because of new disturbances or changes in behaviour reflected in variations in the P matrix.

AN ABSORBING MARKOV CHAIN MODEL OF THE SAVINGS-INVESTMENT PROCESS

The preceding model may be of some value for the analysis of inter-regional flows of funds, but since savings are never locked into fixed capital it is inadequate for describing savings-investment relationships. Given that fixed capital is durable once savings are absorbed into investment they disappear from the system; the act of investment has to be treated as irreversible. However, this feature can still be handled by a Markov chain approach by treating investment as an absorbing state. This requires us to partition the probability matrix P into four submatrices:

$$P = \left(\begin{array}{c|c} Q & R \\ \hline O & I \end{array} \right)$$

where Q is the matrix for transient states and R is the matrix for absorbing states. It follows that there is a matrix T with the same dimensions as R such that

$$T = (I-Q)^{-1}R \qquad (6.3)$$

The matrix T contains the probabilities of inputs to the system getting from each transient state to each absorbing state after circulating through the transient states as indicated by the matrix Q.[1] The inverse matrix $(I-Q)^{-1}$ is frequently referred to as the *fundamental matrix* of an absorbing Markov chain.

For regional investment analysis the Q matrix can be represented as showing the probabilistic inter-regional savings flows to and from financial institutions and other intermediaries located in each region. A given rate of savings will flow within the inter-regional system until all the savings are invested, i.e. until all savings are transferred out of the transient states (financial institutions) into the absorbing states (regional fixed capital stocks). When this process is exhausted (and assuming no interference in the process through the introduction of new inputs into the non-absorbing states) an equilibrium is reached with the investment being divided between the absorbing states and between regions in the form of increments to the capital stocks. If the capital stock is disaggregated by type and by region the equilibrium solution is obtained from

$$\Delta K^e = s^0(I-Q)^{-1}R \qquad (6.4)$$

where ΔK^e = matrix of incremental capital stocks by region and type and s^0 = an initial vector of savings where the element s_i represents the savings generated in region i in each time interval. In the model described below we simplify still further by assuming only one absorbing state, i.e. an aggregate capital stock. Let Δk^e = a vector of regional capital stock increments where the element Δk_i^e represents the increase in the capital stock of region i when all savings have been absorbed into investment. Consequently, Δk^e is the new equilibrium distribution vector. Thus

$$\Delta k^e = s^0(I-Q)^{-1}\hat{R} \qquad (6.5)$$

[1] At the limit the P matrix can be written as

$$\lim_{n \to \infty} P^n = \left(\begin{array}{c|c} O & T \\ \hline O & I \end{array} \right)$$

where $\Sigma\Delta k_i^e = \Sigma s_i^0$ and $\hat{R}$ = a diagonal matrix of *intra*-regional absorption coefficients.

Now it is possible to close the system so that it grows endogenously by introducing a savings-income and an output-capital stock relation. Let us do this in the simplest possible manner:[1]

$$s = \hat{A}y \tag{6.6}$$

and $$y = \hat{V}^{-1}k \tag{6.7}$$

where $\hat{A}$ = diagonal matrix of regional propensities to save, y = vector of regional incomes, $\hat{V}^{-1}$ = inverse of the diagonal matrix $(\hat{V})$ of regional capital-output ratios. Linking the two functions together we obtain

$$s = \hat{A}\hat{V}^{-1}k \tag{6.8}$$

Substituting $\hat{A}\hat{V}^{-1}k^0$ for s^0 and Δk^1 for Δk^e in equation (6.5) we obtain

$$\Delta k^1 = \hat{A}\hat{V}^{-1}k^0(I-Q)^{-1}\hat{R} \tag{6.9}$$

The virtue of the endogenous variant of the model is that it allows regional capital stock growth to be expressed as a function of the initial regional distribution of the system's capital stock. It also permits the conditions of inter-regional capital market equilibrium (i.e. total investment at the end of each period equals the sum of inter-regional savings flows during the period) to be satisfied within a framework that describes continuous growth (capital $\rightarrow$ income $\rightarrow$ savings $\rightarrow$ additions to capital). We may write

$$k^1 = k^0 + \Delta k^1 \tag{6.10}$$

$$= k^0 + \hat{A}\hat{V}^{-1}k^0(I-Q)^{-1}\hat{R} \tag{6.11}$$

By matrix multiplication, let

$$Z = \hat{A}^{-}\hat{V}^{1}(I-Q)^{-1}\hat{R} \tag{6.12}$$

$$\therefore \qquad k^1 = k^0 + k^0 Z \tag{6.13}$$

Thus

$$k^1 = k^0(I+Z) \tag{6.14}$$

[1] In particular, we abstract from constant terms, assume no savings-income and output-capital stock lags, and treat the functions as linear.

This equation may be expanded to extend the growth process into the future, i.e.

$$k^n = k^0(I+\mathcal{Z})^n \qquad (6.15)$$

The time periods of the model (and in particular the synchronisation between the Markov process and the growth sequence) are implicit in the way in which the model has been constructed. We assume the absence of time lags in equations (6.6) and (6.7) – the savings-income relationship and the output-capital function respectively, but the $\hat{V}^{-1}$ matrix requires that the ratio of the flow of output to the stock of capital should be measured over a defined time period. If this time is assumed to be one year (so that we are speaking about annual growth rates), then the model as constructed implies that savings-investment equilibrium is also brought about one year after the initial flow of savings was generated. This means that the n rounds of each Markov process are assumed to add up to one year. Similarly, the expanding capital stock does not create income continuously as savings are absorbed but only at the end of each year.

An Illustrative Example

Let us assume that the matrix $P = \begin{pmatrix} Q & R \\ \hline 0 & I \end{pmatrix}$ takes the following form:[1]

	A	B_1	B_2	B_3	B_4	R
A	·50	·05	·03	·02	·00	·40
B_1	·30	·40	·05	·04	·01	·20
B_2	·25	·15	·35	·07	·03	·15
B_3	·22	·20	·12	·30	·06	·10
B_4	·20	·18	·15	·12	·28	·07
R	0	0	0	0	0	1

We have two regions A (the rest of the world) and B, and region B is disaggregated into four hierarchical and nodal sub-regions

[1] The observant reader will notice similarities between this matrix and the one used in the non-absorbing model described above. The difference is that the intraregional coefficient has now been split into local savings and direct absorption into investment.

(where $B_1 > B_2 > B_3 > B_4$). Certain economic characteristics of the system are built into the structure of the probability matrix. The propensities to place savings in local financial institutions (the diagonal entries of Q) and for savings to be absorbed directly into (local) investment (the $\hat{R}$ entries) are both functions of regional size.[1] Also, the relative probable magnitude of savings flows into financial institutions in other regions is a function of relative regional size. Thus, the P matrix is constructed in such a way as to reflect aglomeration effects and polarisation.

Let us further assume that the initial savings sector $s^0 = [800, 80, 60, 40, 20]$. We can now solve for the equilibrium regional distribution of capital stock increments, Δk^e, by applying the formula of equation (6.5) $\Delta k^e = s^0(I-Q)^{-1}\hat{R}$. The solution[2] is

$$\Delta k^e = [845 \cdot 6, 91 \cdot 2, 40 \cdot 8, 18 \cdot 1, 4 \cdot 3]$$

To illustrate some of the properties of the model let us adopt the endogenous version. This implies that we do not treat the initial savings vector, s^0, as exogenous but instead regard it as being generated from income which, in turn, is created by capital. These relationships are shown in Table 6.1 on the basis of assumed regional propensities to save $(\hat{A})$ and capital-output ratios $(\hat{V})$. Using the same parameters we can derive the new rates of savings (s^1) associated with the expanded regional capital stocks (k^1)[3] – see Table 6.2.

Table 6.1

INITIAL SAVINGS, INCOME AND CAPITAL AND PARAMETER VALUES

	s^0	$\hat{A}$	y^0	$\hat{V}$	k^0	$\hat{A}\hat{V}^{-1}$
A	800	·25	3200	2·0	6400	·1250
B	200	·174	1150	2·26	2600	·0769
B_1	80	·20	400	2·1	840	·0952
B_2	60	·20	300	2·2	660	·0909
B_3	40	·16	250	2·4	600	·0667
B_4	20	·10	200	2·5	500	·0400

[1] It should be noted that the structure of the model rules out direct investment in other regions. Absorption into investment always takes place locally.

[2] The figures are subject to rounding.

[3] Of course, $k^1 = k^0 + \Delta k^1$ where $\Delta k^1 = \Delta k^e$ as derived above.

Table 6.2

SAVINGS, CAPITAL STOCK VALUES AND
GROWTH RATES

	Δk^1	k^1	s^1	k^{10}	Growth Rates (%) Closed Economy $(\hat{A}\hat{V}^{-1})$	Growth Rates (%) Open Economy
A	845·6	7245·6	905·7	21,448·1	12·5	12·85
B	154·4	2754·4	213·8	5097·6	7·69	6·93
B_1	91·2	931·2	88·7	2354·8	9·52	10·85
B_2	40·8	700·8	63·7	1300·6	9·09	7·02
B_3	18·1	618·1	41·2	873·0	6·67	3·82
B_4	4·3	504·3	20·2	551·2	4·00	0·98

An apparent limitation of the model is that it abstracts from inter-regional dividend and interest payments by assuming that income is received in the region where it is created. This is a consequence of the structure of the model which makes all investment in effect local, since it is financed either directly out of local savings or by local financial institutions (whose assets, of course, include savings from other regions). Accordingly, all dividend and interest payments are paid locally in the first instance. However, this does not matter. To the extent that these payments are a source of new savings, we can treat them as local savings and as a function of regional income. It can then be implicitly assumed that the first round inter-regional savings flows of the next process cover dividend and interest payments to outside investors as well as transfers from local savers (provided that the former are saved rather than spent on consumption).

Interpretation and Conclusions
Apart from its obvious use as a simulation model of savings-investment lags in an inter-regional system where capital flows take place between financial institutions, this model has two major purposes: to analyse the nature of inter-regional investment and growth relationships and to explore the impact on spatial investment and capital stocks of the agglomeration tendencies that were built into the structure of the probability

matrix. To explore these effects the model was run over a ten-year period using equation (6.15). Some light is shed on the results in the last three columns of Table 6.2 and in Table 6.3.

Table 6.3
REGIONAL AND SUB-REGIONAL SHARES IN THE CAPITAL STOCK
(%)

	k^0	k^{10}
A	71·1	80·8
B	28·9	19·2
B_1 (B_1/B)	9·3 (32·3)	8·9 (46·4)
B_2 (B_2/B)	7·3 (25·4)	4·9 (25·6)
B_3 (B_3/B)	6·7 (23·1)	3·3 (17·2)
B_4 (B_4/B)	5·6 (19·2)	2·1 (10·8)

First, opening up each regional and sub-regional economy to savings in-flows and out-flows alters the growth rates of each unit in the system (Table 6.2). How these growth rates are altered depends, of course, on the structure of the inter-regional savings flow matrix. Given the polarisation tendencies assumed in this case, the growth rate of Region A rises while that of Region B falls, but within Region B the largest sub-region (B_1) gains considerably from polarisation and agglomeration relative to the other parts of the region. Second, these variations in areal growth rates from their closed economy paths have direct and cumulative effects on the future distribution of the capital stock among the different units of the system (see Table 6.3). Since the size of the capital stock at any moment of time is in this model the main determinant of each area's future capacity for growth, the data in Table 6.3 illustrate how growth potential varies over the ten-year period. Sub-region B_1's share of the region's capital stock increases markedly at the expense of the low-order sub-regions, but even so its own growth rate compared with that of Region A is insufficient to prevent a fall in B_1's share of the system's capital stock. The general significance of these results is that this model shows how intra-regional spatial concentration of capital (and growth) may be cumulative in the long run (i.e. through a series of Markov processes) and yet is consistent with the movement of the inter-regional system as a whole from one comparative statics equilibrium state ($\Sigma s = \Sigma \Delta k$) to another. Even in the limiting case where each region and sub-region grow at the same rate when each is considered as a closed economy (in terms of the model this happens if $\hat{A}\hat{V}^{-1}$ is collapsed into a scalar), it is evident that Region A still grows faster than Region B, and B_1 grows faster than the other sub-regions, once we open up the system to inter-regional capital flows. Thus, steady state growth in an inter-regional system is very much a special case requiring the coincidence of most unlikely assumptions.[1] These findings have far-reaching implications for understanding the processes of regional and inter-regional investment and growth.

Some Qualifications

Since it would be possible to obtain similar results using a deterministic model,[2] the question arises: Why bother with a Markov chain at all? The first obvious answer is that the absorbing Markov process offers a strikingly direct analogy to the savings-investment process itself with savings being transferred from one intermediary to another (the transient states)[3] before being converted into fixed investment (the absorbing state). The second and more important reason is that savers (both personal and institutional) do not behave in a deterministic fashion especially in an environment (such as was assumed here) where agglomeration economies are important. The argument is that inflows of savings into a region are determined less by objectively measured and known relative regional rates of return to capital than by agglomeration economies (that are difficult to quantify), subjective preferences for investing in large regions and sub-regions – explained by risk aversion and

---

[1] Namely, that regional variations within $\hat{A}\hat{V}^{-1}$ should be exactly offset by regional variations within the $(I-Q)^{-1}\hat{R}$ matrix.

[2] For instance, a deterministic model similar in structure to an inter-regional input–output model might be used in which it was assumed (reading down the columns of the matrix) that each region took a fixed proportion of its investment resources from other regions of the system.

[3] Since writing this chapter I have discovered an inter-urban money flows model developed many years ago by the Markov chain specialists, Kemeny and Snell. See Kemeny and Snell (1962, pp. 66–77).

attempts to reduce uncertainty,[1] and by the herd instinct. The impact of these considerations depends so much on behavioural factors that a probabilistic framework is obligatory if we wish to build agglomeration and polarisation tendencies into the structure of the inter-regional savings flow matrix.

An admitted limitation of the model is that it takes account of the sequential and interdependent nature of investment decisions only in a very superficial way: first, in the trivial sense that the growth process *per se* must involve sequential investment; second, that sequential decisions in regard to investment are implied indirectly and subsumed within the very obvious sequential and interdependent character of savings decisions as described by the Markov chain; and third, that capital stock growth both between and within regions depends not on the initial capital stock of the area concerned but on the initial *distribution* of the capital stock among the different parts of the system. To achieve more than this would require a much more complex model with an explicit spatial content. In our model space is only treated implicitly, i.e. in the delimitation of the regions and sub-regions and in the agglomeration and polarisation tendencies built into its structure. It would, however, be quite feasible to expand the model to remedy some of these deficiencies. For instance, it would be possible to introduce periodically new adjusted probability matrices (Q', Q'', etc.) to reflect intensified agglomeration effects (or other structural changes). A more radical extension is to disaggregate the capital stock into different categories (urban infrastructure, transport, amenities, e.g. health and education, manufacturing plant, etc.) and to structure the model so that certain key types of capital, e.g. transport facilities and high-order urban amenities, exert a gravitational pull on other investment. A further refinement on similar lines would be to introduce additional sub-partitions in the transition probability matrix in the form of 'semi-absorbing states' to reflect the fact that firms can exercise some locational choice in where to undertake their investment, and that influences on this choice may include the agglomeration pull of the results of previous investments (in infrastructure, transport networks, etc.). Since this allows

[1] Cf. Hirschman's argument (1958, pp. 184–6) that investors tend to exaggerate prospective returns at the centre relative to the periphery.

investment to be inter-regionally mobile, it would mean a relaxation of the earlier assumption that absorption into investment always takes place locally. An additional advantage of this approach is that it would make the model more realistic by making it possible to recognise the existence of multi-plant firms.

Finally, a possible objection to the results obtained here is that they have been 'cooked' by assuming hypothetical values for the matrix cells and growth parameters that gave the model certain properties. Is this charge justified? There is no doubt that it would be possible to construct a matrix and specify growth parameters that would lead to equilibrating tendencies in inter-regional system growth. Whether this would be preferable to the conclusions derived from the assumptions made here is a matter for empirical testing. However, the rationale behind the type of assumptions adopted in our example is different. So many of the regional growth models in current use are equilibrium models; the disequilibrium models that are available, such as the cumulative causation approach, are loosely specified and difficult to formalise. Moreover, there is a widespread tendency in regional economics to extrapolate from a short-run equilibrium to a long-run equilibrium. This model has the pedagogic virtue that it illustrates the possible compatibility between the prevalence of a comparative statics equilibrium in inter-regional capital markets and the dynamics of an inter-regional system in which regional incomes diverge over time. At the same time, it is believed that the model simulates reasonably well how a system of regions *might* operate. These advantages transcend, though do not diminish, the issue of empirical verification.

Chapter 7

Elements in a Spatial Growth Theory

LOCATIONAL CONSTANTS

A serious weakness of general equilibrium models of the space economy that build up the spatial structure from nothing (of which the Löschian model is perhaps the best example) is that they result in a pattern of urban centres and a spatial distribution that bear little relation to reality. The task is too difficult, and is in any event unnecessary. The assumption of a homogeneous plain inhabited by the occupants of evenly dispersed farm households is inconsistent with any spatial pattern found in the real world, either now or in the distant past. If we were attempting to explain the evolution of the space economy in a developed country, the appropriate starting point would not be the homogeneous plain but the spatial structure of the economy immediately preceding the age of industrialisation. Such an economy already contains a substantial number of nodal points, such as pre-industrial cities or concentrations of resource-oriented industrial installations (usually in the extractive industries), which influence the subsequent development of the spatial structure. It is true that in the course of time some of these pre-industrial nodal points will cease to exert much influence (either by agglomeration pull or radial diffusion) and may degenerate into minor settlements. However, by that time their indelible impact on the evolutionary pattern will already have been made and the consequent 'distortions' will persist long after the initial force fields have died away.

These nodal points come within the category of what I call *locational constants*. These constants are fixed locations that act as a focus for the agglomeration of population. In effect, they provide a few reference points in the space economy that mould, perhaps even predetermine, the economy's spatial structure. Although locational constants may be earlier established cities, they may also be natural resource concentrations, though as soon as these are developed they almost always generate some local urban development. Of course, Lösch himself drew attention to non-economic factors determining the location of early cities (e.g. administrative centres, or military towns) but he did not integrate these observations with his general theory, and failed to realise their significance and usefulness. As a consequence, the market area model and the Löschian hierarchy deduced from it have to bear too much weight. This has serious repercussions on the spatial distribution of centres largely because there is no universal tendency for the leading metropolis to be located near the centre of gravity of the economy.[1]

Locational constants fall into (at least) three main categories: (*i*) an immobile natural resource (e.g. an area of mineral deposits, a deep water harbour); (*ii*) a long-established city (its foundation may have been based on a now obsolete locational advantage, pure chance or explained by historical factors); (*iii*) particular sites that have special advantages due to (*a*) the heterogeneity of land or (*b*) being potentially nodal locations from the point of view of future transportation developments, and that are developed earlier than other sites. Although (*i*) and (*iii*) do not immediately involve the creation

---

[1] In fact 'the existing distribution of cities in a developed economy reflects historical patterns of growth, and the initial location of many cities may have been due to factors (raw material orientation, access to strategic transport routes, random elements) other than market area influences. For instance, arguing *ab initio* in a uniform plain model, the main centre should be located so as to minimise transport costs to and from all parts of the economy, i.e. at the centre of the plain. Yet in many countries, particularly outside Europe, the largest metropolis is often found on or near the coast reflecting the fact that the countries were originally opened up for development by colonisation from overseas. The international and entrepôt functions of these leading cities may persist almost indefinitely. Thus, the historically evolved pattern of urban settlement constrains subsequent development. For the purposes of analysis, the fact that the location of some cities is predetermined (due to spatial irregularities and good natural sites as well as to historical factors) makes it much simpler to assign locations to the others, but it does distort the actual from the theoretically predicted spatial distribution' (Richardson, 1972*a*, p. 39).

of a city, this is bound to happen. The sole exception is where the output of an immobile resource (e.g. petroleum) can be transported at low cost to markets and does not require, because of highly capital intensive methods of extraction, much labour at the source.

Locational constants have several important functions in urban and regional analysis. First, as already pointed out, they simplify the task of constructing a general model of spatial development by fixing some key locational co-ordinates. This has the additional advantage of predicting spatial patterns of economic activity that are much closer to observed reality than those derived from *ab initio* assumptions. Incidentally, the locations of the locational constants tend to be arbitrary since they are determined to a large extent by random or physical factors. Consequently, the spatial structure of the economy can be irregular and distorted compared, say, to the regular lattice networks of the Löschian model. Second, they affect the number (and the relative size and spacing) of urban centres in a region which in turn influence the *intra*-regional spatial distribution of industry and population and, more critically, may alter the total agglomeration pull of the region.

Third, a major difficulty in any theory of regional development that emphasises agglomeration economies is to explain why people and industries do not crowd together into one giant centre. Although locational preferences are one element in such an explanation, it is probable that locational constants are the key factor.[1] Since, by definition, these constants are immobile they impose constraints on agglomeration, and are fundamental, particularly in the context of the spatial development of the national economy, for understanding the dispersion process. Moreover, the existence of transport costs on goods,

[1] Of course, some mention should also be made of the role of agriculture as a dispersion factor. Arable farming (the growth of factory farms makes it much less certain in the case of livestock farming) is essentially a space-consuming activity that has led over time to sparsely populated rural areas and widely dispersed small agricultural service centres. Bos (1965) assigns prime importance to agriculture along with transport costs and economies of scale in explaining the relative impact of concentration and dispersion forces on the space economy. This explanation is quite consistent with the arguments in the text. The emphasis on locational constants is merely an additional, though in my view a very important, ingredient.

services and the movement of people explains why these fixed locations attract other activities (e.g. urban services) rather than these being supplied at the original centres of agglomeration. It is useful in this context to refer once again to the concept of a commodity (and service) hierarchy. More light can be shed on the spatial pattern of production of different goods when these goods are classified hierarchically according to the size of the market areas over which the goods and services are traded. Lower order goods restrict the scope for agglomeration since these must be produced locally. Hence many goods and services have to be supplied in all centres regardless of size.

MEASUREMENT OF AGGLOMERATION ECONOMIES

The *a priori* arguments for the importance of agglomeration economies in regional growth are easily understood, are plausible and are consistent with rough observation. Similarly, there are few difficulties involved in defining agglomeration economies, though an all-inclusive definition has to be wide in scope covering external economies of scale, indivisibilities and urbanisation economies. The main problems arise when we attempt to measure these economies precisely enough for use in an operational model. The failure to break this bottleneck satisfactorily remains possibly the most serious obstacle to progress in applied regional economics. There is no pretence that the following analysis provides an effective solution to this problem. At best, it merely points to some approaches that may prove feasible.

Some writers have been pessimistic about the possibilities for measuring agglomeration economies. Darwent (1969, p. 23), for example, argues that 'there is almost no agreement on how external economies are defined' and therefore 'little hope of quantification'. This view is unnecessarily defeatist.

One approach is to devise simple aggregate measures of agglomeration economies. An early though unsatisfactory measure was suggested by Marcus (1965). His argument assumed that agglomeration economies can be measured industry by industry. If the urban growth rate[1] in a given industry is higher than the national growth rate weighted by the *relative* growth of population in the area, he attributes this 'extra' growth to agglomeration economies, i.e.

$$A = g_U - g_N n_U / n_N \tag{7.1}$$

where A = agglomeration economies, g = growth rate in output, n = growth rate of population, U, N = subscripts for urban area and nation respectively. However, this method does little more than provide an alternative variant of 'differential shift'. At best, it is a measure of localisation economies not of the more crucial urbanisation and agglomeration economies.

A similar, but possibly more useful, approach stems from a rather obvious idea suggested by Hansen (1970a). He drew attention to the fact that growth in national employment is mainly concentrated on expanding tertiary industries, and these are primarily located in metropolitan areas. He further argues that their growth in cities is in large measure due to external agglomeration economies. However, the argument can be taken a stage further. Growth in certain service industries (certainly business services, banking and finance) may be almost synonymous with the creation of urban agglomeration economies, while expansion in other services (e.g. sports, leisure, entertainment and cultural activities) may also be relevant if location decisionmakers are utility rather than profit maximisers. If entrepreneurs are attracted to or near metropolitan locations by agglomeration economies, and if these economies encompass tertiary industries in the widest sense (i.e. including social amenities as well as business services), this raises the interesting possibility of whether or not we can use growth in service industries (either as a whole or of selected industrial categories) as an index of agglomeration economies. At least two practical tests suggest themselves. The first would be to compare growth performance in all or selected service industries with changes in city size (using cross-sectional data, of course). The second test would be to look at the interactions

---

[1] Most of the analysis that follows assumes that agglomeration economies are urban, and that regional agglomeration economies depend largely on the size and spatial distribution of its urban centres. The justification for this assumption is given below.

between changes in service and non-service industries to investigate whether agglomeration economies (as reflected in the surrogate of services expansion) stimulate growth in other industries or not. Such a study raises serious methodological problems, e.g. identification of the lags, definition of mobile industries that may be attracted by the presence of particular services and facilities. It will not escape the notice of observant readers that such an inquiry would be almost the very opposite of an export base exercise.[1] Although investigations on these lines would be useful, they obviously would not represent a comprehensive analysis of agglomeration economies since many important aspects (labour market economies, public service efficiency, technological externalities associated with locational agglomeration, etc.) fall outside their scope.

A quite different line of attack on the agglomeration economies measurement problem reflects the fact that many of these economies are directly related to the spatial concentration of people in urban centres. Thus, it seems reasonable to treat agglomeration economies as a function of population. The population variable may be measured in terms of potential, density or size. The latter is the more common though not necessarily the soundest since the size of an urban centre is an ambiguous concept, depending upon how the urban area is defined. Baumol (1967) suggested the following simple agglomeration function:

$$A = KN^2 \qquad (7.2)$$

where A = external economies (or diseconomies), K = a constant, and N = city population. The rationale behind this hypothesis is that if each citizen imposes external benefits (or costs) on every other, and if the scale of benefits gained (or costs borne) by each individual is roughly proportional to population size,[2] then because the benefits (costs) apply to each individual, the total external benefits (costs) will vary in proportion to N^2. Ingenious though this argument is, it has serious flaws. Since there are no means suggested of how to measure the

[1] Although an inquiry of this kind has never been carried out in detail, it is clearly anticipated in the critique of base theory by Blumenfeld (1955).

[2] Baumol accepts that in some cases density rather than size is the more appropriate measure, e.g. in regard to traffic congestion.

dependent variable A, it is untestable. The inference from the theoretical justification of the hypothesis is that A is proportional to N^2, therefore the latter can be used as a surrogate for agglomeration economies. Given the arbitrariness of the assumption that external benefits (costs) are proportional to population size, the use of such a surrogate can hardly be justified. Furthermore, if the agglomeration function is supposed to reflect external economies and diseconomies then, unless we are dealing with a specific case which is either a clear-cut economy or diseconomy (say, traffic congestion), the assumption of proportionality between A and N^2 cannot be maintained. Instead, the *a priori* hypothesis would be that total *net* external economies tend to be positive up to some critical city size (which may or may not have been reached in the real world) and then become negative. Consequently, if the agglomeration function is to be capable of measuring both economies and diseconomies it must be non-linear. There are many possibilities, but an inverted U or a quadratic function are two of the most straightforward cases. A final defect is that to assume that it is the square of the population that determines external economies is unnecessarily restrictive. Relaxations of both the proportionality and the 'exponent = 2' assumptions are considered below.

My alternative suggestion (Richardson, 1969*b*; 1971) is to generalise the Baumol approach and to treat the exponent as a parameter which is itself a function of N, changing in value as city size increases. In other words, a more appropriate agglomeration function is

$$A = f(N^a) \qquad (7.3)$$

where

$$a = f(N) \qquad (7.4)$$

For net external economies to become negative at some high level of city size, then the slope of the second function, da/dN, must eventually become negative. While this modification represents a substantial improvement to Baumol's hypothesis from a conceptual point of view, the end result is as difficult, perhaps more difficult, to operationalise. The exponent merely reflects the presence of external economies and diseconomies rather than measures them. Once again, we encounter the obstacle of how to estimate the parametric path of the exponent when we have no satisfactory measure of agglomeration econo-mies as the dependent variable. There is only one solution to these difficulties, and this is very imperfect. It involves decom-posing the dependent variable to examine how relevant but very partial measures of agglomeration economies (such as the *per capita* cost of urban services, traffic congestion or the productivity of retail and business firms) vary with urban population levels. Also, since we need to take account of the co-variation of a with $\mathcal{N}$, the simplest if approximate solution is to use a large cross-section of urban centres to fit the relation-ship $a \log \mathcal{N}$ against the individual components of A for different size-classes of cities.

Another limitation of this approach from the viewpoint of our focus on the theory of regional growth is that to the extent that it produces meaningful results at all, these refer to the agglomeration economies of cities rather than regions. How-ever, is this a serious problem in view of the fact that so many agglomeration economies are urbanisation economies? One specific exception to this generalisation is the technological spatial spillovers from an integrated industrial complex, but this example is very specific indeed. Apart from this exception, it is reasonable to identify a region's agglomeration economies by those of its leading city or cities. In the model described in Chapter 8 regional agglomeration economies are assumed to depend upon (*i*) the number of urban centres (above a thres-hold size), (*ii*) their relative size with more weight given to the larger centres, and (*iii*) the distances between them. One form of the agglomeration function might be

$$A = a_1 \left(\sum_i^z \mathcal{N}_i{}^{a_i}/z \right) + a_2 z + a_3 \left(\sum_i^z \sum_j^z d_{ij} \Big/ \frac{z!}{2!(z-2)!} \right) \tag{7.5}$$

$$(d_{ii}, d_{jj} = 0)$$

where a_1 and a_i are positive, a_3 is negative, $z =$ the number of urban centres in the region and $d =$ distance. Thus, the larger the number of cities, the greater the relative size of the leading cities and the smaller is average inter-urban distance, the greater are regional agglomeration economies. In other words, a region's agglomeration economies are assumed to be a function of the size distribution and the spatial distribution of its urban population centres. Once again, the basic defects of the crude Baumol hypothesis remain: namely, the lack of an appropriate measure of agglomeration economies *per se* in order to estimate this function, and the incompleteness of the assumption that agglomeration economies are a function of population alone.

In an interesting paper Lave (1970) has suggested that the economies of agglomeration can be equated with the losses of transport cost savings that would have been reaped with a decentralised system of centres. He constructs a model from which transport cost savings can be measured as a large urban centre is progressively broken down into centres of smaller size. For instance, if the city were divided into an equal-sized area with two city centres transportation expenditures would fall by thirty per cent; dividing the city into four centres would lead to a fifty per cent fall in transport costs. By this approach it is possible to offset agglomeration economies against the reduced transport costs associated with decentralisation. Lave suggests the possibility of operationalising this idea to obtain an indirect measure of agglomeration economies. The method is simple. Suppose that there are x commodity groups, each of which is produced under substantial economies of scale. In dividing a city into several sub-centres, it is assumed that each will produce all the output of a particular commodity group. Thus with two centres, each produces one-half of the commodity groups and ships fifty per cent of its production to the other. The offsetting economy of agglomeration is the cost of shipping goods to the other centre. The analysis can be generalised to the case of $z > 2$ centres.

This idea is ingenious rather than helpful. Its main defect is that it attempts to measure not so much agglomeration economies in the broadest sense as economies of scale (including internal economies) in individual industries. The model appears in fact to be little more than the adaptation for metropolitan analysis of Weberian agglomeration theory.[1] Moreover, since the assumption of complete specialisation in each centre is clearly unrealistic, the method can be made operational only

[1] For a brief discussion of Weber's theory of locational agglomeration see Richardson (1969*b*), pp. 73–7.

if sufficient data on costs relative to scale are available to simulate this assumption. But economy of scale data are often very crude and discontinuous. Even more serious is the scarcity of information on the distribution costs of commodities at least in an *intra*-regional context, which is obviously the relevant context for this type of study.

The complementarity between transport expenditures and agglomeration economies in the Lave approach is reminiscent of a much older idea in urban economics – the complementarity between transport costs and urban rent that has characterised many models of urban spatial structure from Haig (1926) on. Is this merely a coincidental analogy or is there a logical link between the two relationships? A case can be made for the latter. Consider, for example, a retailer faced with the choice of one store in the C.B.D. or two or more stores in sub-centres and assume that the retailer bears all the distribution costs to its customers. The suburban locations will hold down these distribution costs but at the expense of sacrificing economies of scale and the external benefits of locating near to other large shops, workplaces, etc. (i.e. agglomeration economies). The central location, on the other hand, will mean higher distribution costs but will offer maximum opportunities for exploitation of agglomeration economies. The choice between one central location and several suburban locations is not necessarily a neutral choice but will depend upon individual circumstances. In other words, there is no special reason for symmetry between the gain in agglomeration economies and the higher transportation expenditures associated with choosing the central site rather than the suburban locations, or vice versa. Similarly, the rent paid at the central site may exceed, be equal to, or be less than the combined rents at the sub-centre sites. Savings in transport costs may be outweighed by agglomeration advantages, and if this is the case the firm will be willing to pay more in rent for the central location. It is possible, therefore, that adoption of the overall value of urban rents as a surrogate for agglomeration economies may not be too outrageous. This is also consistent with the view of W. F. Smith (1969) and others that urban rent should be treated as an index of urban productivity.

However, this proposal is subject to similar criticisms to those levied against all the surrogate measures suggested above. Movements in urban rent may reflect forces which have only the most tenuous relationship to agglomeration economies such as relative changes in the demand for and supply of urban land. This relationship is valid only if it is reasonable to assume a completely inelastic supply curve and if all increases in the demand for land can be traced to either the entry of new consumers of land (whether firms or households) or the expansion of existing consumers in response to agglomeration economies.[1] It is unlikely that these conditions generally hold.

All the suggestions hitherto are similar in the sense that they use a single surrogate (a population measure, an industry growth rate, rent, transport cost savings, etc.) to represent the complex multiple phenomena which fall within the broad concept of agglomeration economies. Such approaches are obviously crude and imperfect. Perhaps the search for a single measure is a chimera, and real progress in measurement may have to be based on breaking down agglomeration economies into many components.

The argument in favour of this is very strong. In our model of regional growth agglomeration economies have several functions: (i) to boost the rate of technical progress and productivity, (ii) to attract industry and capital into a region or metropolitan area; (iii) to influence the decisions of households whether or not to migrate (either by attracting migrants to large cities or by affecting the locational preference function); (iv) to improve the efficiency of the *intra*-regional spatial structure. These multiple roles make it impossible to treat agglomeration economies effectively as a single variable. As a generalisation, agglomeration economies refer to the economies of size and concentration. Since the benefits of size and concentration vary for different sections of the urban community, it is useful for operational purposes and as a first step in disaggregation to draw a distinction between agglomeration economies for society at large,[2] for households and for firms. Thus we have at least three categories:

---

[1] For a recent, more extended argument, that agglomeration economies are capitalised in land values see Edel (1972).

[2] This is somewhat vague since it could mean the metropolitan community as a whole, the urban government sector including the planners, or the national interest, according to circumstances.

(i) Social agglomeration economies

These affect all groups in society, though with differential impacts. Efficiency in public services is the pre-eminent factor.

(ii) Household agglomeration economies

These refer to the benefits and costs of life in large cities for households, especially in-migrants. These benefits may vary significantly according to the income, occupation and social class of the household (e.g. a major league football club versus a symphony concert hall).

(iii) Business agglomeration economies

A metropolitan location offers many advantages to business firms, some of which are greater the larger the city. The difficulty is that the relevant 'mix' of agglomeration economies may vary considerably from one firm to another, especially from industry to industry and by size of firm.

One, perhaps a naïve, possibility is to construct a long list of agglomeration economies of all kinds and then to apply some multivariate correlation technique to them (e.g. factor, cluster or principal components analysis). This requires us to devise quantifiable measures for each economy at each level of city population, and it is also necessary to correlate all the economies with population size. There are several objectives in such a study. First, it may be feasible from the results to reduce the list and obtain a selected small number of key agglomeration economies, *key* not necessarily in the sense that they are quantitatively the most influential but in the sense that they can be treated as surrogates for a larger bundle of economies. Second, in view of the proposed disaggregation into social, business and household agglomeration economies it would be desirable to investigate whether the reduced list contains at least one variable to reflect each of the three main types of agglomeration economy, thereby providing an *ex post* rationalisation for the subdivisions. Third, if the compact set of variables happens to be highly correlated with specific population measures, this might constitute a prima facie case for using population size, concentration and distribution measures as the agglomeration function. The advantage of this would be that it might avoid drawing upon a large number of separate independent variables to measure agglomeration economies or facing the complex and arbitrary weighting problems that construction of a single index of agglomeration economies might require.

In the probable event that the results of such a study would be inconclusive, there would be no alternative other than to deal with each broad group of agglomeration economies (social, business and household) separately, to attempt to identify the main variables and to hope to solve the acute measurement problems. Some of the difficulties may be illustrated by considering each category in turn. It is simplest to leave the social agglomeration economy group until last, since this may be treated in part as a residual.

HOUSEHOLD AGGLOMERATION ECONOMIES

The critical question here is: what advantages (and disadvantages) accrue to individuals from living in large cities (or more generally, in cities of different size), and how can these advantages be measured? One possibility is to attempt to construct an index of agglomeration economies/diseconomies for households which represent the benefits/costs of city life. The index might distinguish between large cities of the same size as well as between cities of different size. The economies taken into account might include leisure and cultural facilities, environmental amenities such as climate and access to open space and countryside, the quality of educational, health and welfare services, access to further educational facilities, and so on, but would also include factors affecting jobs and income, e.g. the availability of job opportunities (including those for members of the family other than head of the household), the possibility of higher incomes per head, differentials in the metropolitan cost of living, and greater security of employment. Some of the first items are, at first sight, non-measurable intangibles, while the quality of urban public services may be treated more satisfactorily within the social agglomeration economies category. The job and real income variables, on the other hand, are more easily quantified and perhaps should be treated separately from the overall agglomeration economy index. It will also be necessary to accommodate diseconomies of agglomeration. The most obvious of these may be higher pollution levels, which pose serious problems of quantification in view of the wide differences *within* each metropolitan area. More nebulous may be such factors as a higher probability of being a victim of crime of mental illness as a result of living in a large city.

There are clearly major problems to be solved before an index of the less easily measured agglomeration economies could be constructed. For instance, what is to be done about facilities that are provided *only* in a large metropolis, e.g. the major league sports club, the opera house, the symphony concert hall, the night clubs, the large museum? These should obviously be taken into account in an index but since they appear only at specific threshold city sizes, there is no satisfactory methods if imputing a cost to *not* having the facility in smaller cities.[1]

Second, even if we suppose that we can select the elements that make up the agglomeration index, how can we assign weights to each component? This is a tricky problem, but not intractable. As a first step, three methods could be tried: equal weights for each factor; subjective weights reflecting the analyst's own value judgements; 'objective' weights reflecting the results of a survey of household preferences. The question may be less critical than appears at first sight, since tests on the sensitivity of the index to choice of weights could reveal that the function relating the index of agglomeration to city size may be smooth and of similar shape regardless of the weighting system selected. Third, there are severe data problems in obtaining information about some of the leisure and cultural

[1] One possible procedure, though inadequate, might be to impute a minimum value to the facility on the basis of the transport and time cost involved in travelling to enjoy it from the most distant areas within feasible travel limits (and to compute an annual value according to the average number of trips per year). For the non-city household using the facility its benefits must, on *ceteris paribus* assumptions, exceed the costs incurred to enjoy it. A defect with this method is that the costs of using the facility may be disproportionately high but that the outlying household still uses it not only because it is important in its scale of preferences but also because the high travel costs are offset against other non-pecuniary benefits of living outside the city. In other words, the travel costs the household is willing to pay reflect many other factors besides the benefits derived from enjoying the facility. Nevertheless, the travel costs give some indication of the value of the service.

facilities that might be included. These arise not because the data do not exist but because they are difficult and time-consuming to obtain. For example, is the measurement of such items as the number and quality of restaurants in different cities worth the effort, even though it might be a significant agglomeration economy?

Finally, and most critical of all, the 'mix' of relevant household agglomeration economies differs according to social class (income, occupation and other status variables). Clearly, this is true of job, income and employment opportunities, but it is equally true of the more intangible economies of agglomeration. For example, lower income and non-college educated households may attach more importance to job and income considerations, shopping, sporting events and some types of leisure facilities; middle class households, on the other hand, may be more concerned with arts and cultural activities, higher educational opportunities, fashion and speciality shops, good quality restaurants, etc. There is no way in which this gap can be bridged with a common index, and if household agglomeration economies are an important variable in the urban migration function it could lead to poor predictions if we rely on a common measure. The implication of this point is that there should be a different index (either with different components or with varying weights for each common factor) for separate social classes; disaggregation into at least two or three social status groups is necessary.

As for the easier to measure agglomeration economies, there are several major empirical questions at stake which have received but little investigation. For instance, how do the following items vary with city size: cost of living, housing costs, average incomes, the probability and risks of being unemployed, the availability of job opportunities (e.g. as reflected in the vacancy/unemployed ratio). Despite the greater ease of quantification, measuring these relationships is not without its problems. For example, devising an urban cost of living index again raises severe 'mix' and weighting decisions. The research results hitherto are rather scanty. Neutze (1965) uses some out-of-data statistics to suggest that medium-sized cities have lower living costs than either the largest metropolises or the small isolated towns. Studies in the United States (e.g. The President's Commission on Income Maintenance Programs, 1970, pp. 87–93; Brackett and Lamale, 1967; Alonso and Fajans, 1970; Ruiz, 1972) using the Bureau of Labor Statistics City Worker's Family Budget index have thrown more light on inter-metropolitan living differentials, though they have certainly not pointed to a clear relationship between living costs and city size. Although housing costs are an important component in any cost of living index, they may be so crucial to migration decisions that it is worth separating them out to examine variations in the quality and price of housing with city size. Moreover, tastes and preferences in housing are so strongly correlated with income and class that this is another instance where an index disaggregated by household groups is necessary.

BUSINESS AGGLOMERATION ECONOMIES

The theoretical analysis of agglomeration economies for firms relies heavily on von Böventer (1970). His model is based on very abstract assumptions and is difficult to make operational. However, its one major thesis – that agglomeration economies vary for different firms, and that because of this the optimal location in the sense of varying city sizes also differs from one firm to another – is very relevant to this discussion. It also raises an acute measurement problem. Since the overall strength of agglomeration economies and their relative weight vary so much from firm to firm, the question arises whether there is a regular enough pattern to permit measurement. It is clear that agglomeration economies vary among industries and according to size of firm. For instance, there is evidence available (e.g. Vernon, 1960) that most agglomeration economies are more important for small than for large firms, especially since the latter can internalise many of them. However, there is insufficient knowledge to permit an evaluation of how far the 'mix' and weights of individual economies should be altered to reflect variations between firms and industries. Yet the question is an important one since agglomeration economies may be a prime determinant of a city's (region's) attractive power for mobile capital.

A first step in an analysis for business agglomeration economies is to classify them. One type of agglomeration economy is different from the rest in that it has very little to do with urbanisation. This is where firms in the same industry derive advantages from locating next to each other. Locational agglomeration was analysed in some detail by Weber (see Friedrich, 1929, and Isard and Smith, 1967). However, adjacent locations may result in competitive pressures as well as potential agglomeration economies, and it is unclear which outweighs the other. Probably the answer varies according to industry. A related phenomenon is the spatial externalities (usually technological linkages) arising from the proximity of related industries.

Important though these economies may be, they are not particularly relevant in explaining regional differentials in the strength of the agglomeration function. This is because they may be created anywhere or, alternatively, occur randomly according to the spatial incidence of the required raw materials (materials orientation).

An exception to this generalisation may be where the planning of a new industrial complex is linked to the development of a growth pole or associated with improving incomes and welfare in an existing city. In this case, the labour supply of the urban area may be the main factor making the industrial complex feasible, and an optimal programme for the complex may be concerned with allocating this labour efficiently among alternative subsets of complexes out of a total set of industries with potential for development.[1] Clearly, the simpler forms of optimising technique (such as linear programming) are inadequate for dealing with external economies. Selection of a complex will also need to take into account the non-linearities inherent in the existence of internal economies of scale in production. Both internal economies of scale (allowing the sum of the elasticities of the capital stock and labour supply functions to exceed unity) and external economies (assumed to be reflected in decreasing intermediate input prices) can be handled if we use a geometric programming method, where the objective function contains power rather than merely linear

[1] Alternatively, the programme may relate to the efficient use of investment or, in a dynamic model, maximising the discounted stream of regional incomes from a given investment.

elements. A major difficulty in implementation arises from the fact that if the set of possible industries for the complex is sizeable, the number of alternative complexes is very large indeed.[1] However, this is not as serious as appears at first sight. First, the number of practical subsets may be predetermined by technical linkages, and the information on these may be obtained extraneously. Second, the number of industries in the complex will tend to be fairly small (e.g. if the original set contains 100 industries it is most unlikely that the optimal solution will contain all, or even fifty or twenty-five of these industries). The reason is that internal economies of scale (and minimum threshold scales of production, i.e. indivisibilities) mean that the programme discriminates heavily in favour of complexes containing a few industries. On the other hand, external economies imply that the optimal complex is unlikely to consist merely of one industry. The optimal complex (and the number of industries it embraces) will, in fact, be determined by a trading-off of these external economies (arising from spatial linkages) against internal economies of scale in production. The end result could well be an industrial complex consisting of more than two but less than, say, six or seven sectors.[2]

Most of the other business agglomeration economies vary with city size. They include labour market pools, the local availability of capital, financial and banking services, the presence of local business consultancy and ancillary services (e.g. computer consultancies, advertising agencies, accounting and legal facilities), the proximity of supplying industries, market potential economies for consumer industries (arising from spatial concentration of population), and efficiency in public services (both in regard to the level of property taxes and charges for public utilities such as electricity and water). Although business agglomeration economies are relatively easy to measure, it is doubtful whether it is necessary to include all of them in an agglomeration function. The critical question is

---

[1] In fact, all possible subsets total $2^n - 1$ where n = the number of industries in the set.

[2] Klaassen's locational attraction model is also useful for identifying industrial complexes. See above, Chapter 3, pp. 81–2. See also the paper by J. Paelinck in Hansen (1972, pp. 139–59).

which are the most important economies for the crucial role of attracting mobile industry into a region. This is a matter for empirical resolution, and may require a detailed statistical analysis of inter-regional moves by firms and of the characteristics of the metropolitan cities with the greatest attractive power. However, it may be possible, on *a priori* grounds, to select certain key business agglomeration economies that can represent the locational attraction of a city for industry. For instance, the following four variables might serve this purpose: a measure of the size of the labour market; an index of market potential (e.g. an income potential measure for the S.M.S.A.); employment in selected ancillary service industries catering for industry; and a measure of relative tax-urban service efficiency (this presents difficult problems). Whether or not these are the key business agglomeration economies, however, requires detailed empirical testing. Moreover, whether these aggregate measures work effectively enough to justify glossing over inter-industry and size of firm differences can again only be resolved empirically.

A major project on agglomeration economies for industries is being undertaken at the Urban Institute, Washington (see Bergsman, Greenston and Healy, 1972). Their work focusses on three basic questions: (*i*) methods of identifying industrial complexes, or 'activity clusters'; (*ii*) the relation of economic structure to the growth rate and to other characteristics of cities; (*iii*) the role of non-manufacturing industries in producing agglomerations. The first stages of the research involve defining the activity clusters, and testing hypotheses about their structure, location and interaction among themselves and with other characteristics of cities. Although an ultimate aim is to look at growth in specific industries and clusters in relation to overall growth of the city, the initial results refer to cross-sectional analysis. The basic information consists of employment data at the three-digit S.I.C. level in manufacturing and the two-digit level in service industries (186 industries) for 203 S.M.S.A.s for 1963.[1] Employment was converted to a *per capita* basis to correct for correlation of absolute levels of employment with city size. A correlation matrix was set up to

[1] Later work will deal with three- and four-digit categories for 1965 and 1970 with the sample enlarged to include selected non-S.M.S.A. counties.

measure the association across S.M.S.A.s between employment in each industry with employment in every other industry; since industries frequently locate in clusters greater than two, factor analysis was used to identify clusters. Out of 17,205 correlations in the matrix, 1003 pairs were significantly correlated at the 0·001 level. Of these only thirty correlations were negative. The positive links reflected familiar patterns of association: association of an industry producing a material costly to transport with another industry using that material as an input (e.g. petroleum refining/chemicals; logging/sawmills; iron foundries/engines and turbines); industries using low wage labour (leather footwear/woollen fabrics; millinery/electronic components); industries using highly skilled workers (e.g. mechanical measuring instruments/photographic equipment); and industries seeking to locate in the same size or kind of city (e.g. non-profit organisations/commodity brokers; banking/advertising). Applying factor analysis enabled forty-two industry clusters to be defined. Some of these were self-evident, e.g. metal products, precision instruments, electronics, machinery, chemicals, petrochemicals, rubber products, glass products, etc.; others were difficult to rationalise, especially clusters in miscellaneous categories. Certain clusters were much more useful analytically: labour intensive; low wage; market centre/business services; market centre/consumer services; resorts/rapid growth; transport and repair. The cities where each cluster was highly concentrated were also shown as an indicator of the types of cities to which particular sets of industries are attracted.

As yet, the results of this study are firmer in regard to describing clusters than in explaining their existence and why they may tend to concentrate in particular kinds of city. One difficulty is that linear correlation could mask many different kinds of relationships. For example, pair correlations could reflect the fact that one industry produces externalities or that both gravitate towards a third industry or that (for independent reasons) both industries tend to locate in cities of a type.

In the 1972 paper the authors merely discussed a few case studies: market centre/business services, metal products and low wage industries. In view of the emphasis on business services in the literature on agglomeration economies it may be useful to consider this cluster.[1] It is disproportionately concentrated in very large metropolitan areas such as New York, Chicago, Boston and San Francicso and in smaller cities with extensive hinterlands (Des Moines, Iowa; Lincoln, Nebraska; Fargo, North Dakota). Although not all of the cities which rank high on this cluster are large, none of the very largest S.M.S.A.s rank low. Specialisation in business services increases significantly, if slowly, with city size with the largest S.M.S.A.s having twice the *per capita* employment of the smallest.

There are several alternative explanations for this variation with city size. It could be due to a hierarchical urban system in which larger cities export services to small ones (but the evidence did not support the hypothesis that employment in business services in other S.M.S.A.s varies directly with distance from the twenty-one largest S.M.S.A.s). Firms in large cities may purchase services which they would otherwise have to provide themselves. Large cities may specialise in other industries, such as administrative offices, which have a substantial demand for business services. Perhaps a more plausible explanation is that business services are attracted to centres with good communications and high accessibility to information resources. These characteristics are not easy to measure, but there was some correlation between business service employment and indicators such as the frequency of domestic airline connections, the number of universities offering graduate degrees and the presence of an international airport. On the other hand, there was no evidence that business service specialisation was any higher in cities experiencing rapid population growth. A final point worthy of notice is that business services may exert a gravitational pull on other industrial clusters. Although the causation may run either way, there was a high spatial correspondence with consumer services, transport and repair, administration, local government and a miscellaneous cluster, i.e. with mainly service industries or light market-oriented manufactures. All these sectors increased in incidence with a growth in city size.

[1] The cluster's constituent industries were commercial printing, communications, banking, security and commodity brokers and exchanges, insurance carriers, advertising, miscellaneous business services, legal services, nonprofit membership organisations and miscellaneous services.

SOCIAL AGGLOMERATION ECONOMIES

These are of two main kinds: first, the frequently analysed problem of whether or not there are scale economies in urban services, and the rather broader question of public service efficiency; second, the impact that urban agglomerations have on both national growth and intra-regional efficiency. The benefits of the former accrue largely to individuals and groups within the metropolitan area itself, but the latter refer to a much wider concept of social benefits in the sense of economic gains to the national and regional communities.

There has been considerable research into the question of efficient city sizes from the point of view of urban service provision.[1] These studies have been inconclusive, partly because of unavoidable theoretical shortcomings, partly because the results have pointed to an amazingly wide range of efficient city sizes (30,000 to 1,000,000) with some tendency, but not a clear-cut one, to settle around the 250,000 mark. However, since these results have been derived from many countries at different levels of development and for different time periods, it is doubtful whether they mean very much from the point of view of measuring agglomeration economies for a regional growth model. Moreover, the studies have referred either to unrepresentative bundles of public services, or to individual urban services, or to urban development and infrastructure costs, and all of these fall far short of a measure of overall urban public sector efficiency.

The main problems are well known, and need little discussion. It is not feasible to aggregate separate services together, particularly because the efficiency of one may be inter-dependent with that of another (Isard, 1960, pp. 527–33). If all cities of all sizes supplied an identical mix of services and if demand was inelastic everywhere for all income groups, then expenditures on public services *per capita* (the most common measure) would be a reasonable index. Unfortunately, these assumptions do not hold; there is a great variety in the number and levels of service between cities, and indeed the division between public and private services may vary between cities. Some big cities

[1] For a brief review see Cameron (1970), pp. 39–44.

have public services (specialist hospitals, ghetto welfare services, specialist crime squads, etc.) that are not found at all in many smaller urban areas. The mix of services provided will reflect the income distribution of the city's residents and, since the demand for a particular type of service will not be constant at all levels of income, variations in the rate and structure of city income growth will influence the demand for services. In the search for a more effective measure, the main trouble is that there is no acceptable index of output for public services (reflecting the absence of a proper market). If we knew how to measure urban service output satisfactorily the obvious procedure would be to examine how the costs of producing a homogeneous unit of output varied with city size. Failing this, we are forced to fall back on inadequate physical or input standards.[1]

A proper evaluation of this type of agglomeration economy or diseconomy must take into account not only the level and quality of services but also the tax levies required to finance them. What is needed is a measure of overall tax-service efficiency, yet the considerations discussed above make it almost impossible to obtain this. Also, it is doubtful whether an aggregate measure is sufficient, since different groups in the metropolitan community (firms, households, commuters) not only enjoy different types of service in varying degrees but, more important, the incidence of taxation varies dramatically from one group to another (and, of course, within groups). As a first step, perhaps the closest we can get is to abstract from these inter-group differentials and to attempt to *rank* cities according to 'value for money' criteria in supplying urban services and then to see how far the rank order is hierarchical. This in itself would be a substantial research task, requiring the use of all available statistical data, expert opinion and possibly even household and business surveys. Although such a limited

---

[1] Size of classes, pupil–teacher ratios, expenditures per pupil, etc., in education; patient–doctor rolls, hospital beds/population ratios, numbers of medical and auxiliary staff per 1000 population, etc., in health; numbers of police per 1000 population, detected crimes/police rate in crime prevention; costs of fire damage relative to expenditures on fire services (or better still, costs of fire damage *prevented* relative to expenditure): all these are examples of the types of measure used.

inquiry falls far short of providing a measure of this particular urbanisation economy suitable for operational analysis, it might reveal whether or not such economies exist (i.e. if there was no correlation between public service efficiency and hierarchical ranks) and hence clarify the need for further research.

The other main form of social agglomeration economy is even more nebulous. This is the question of whether large cities within regions improve regional efficiency and, in an even wider context, influence the level and rate of national economic performance. The problem has several aspects: the degree of concentration of potential innovators in metropolitan cities; whether or not there are substantial agglomeration economies in research and development, and how far research and development institutes are tied to large cities; the position of a region's leading city in the national urban hierarchy (used as a surrogate for its ability to absorb information from the rest of the economy); and the strength of inter-regional communication channels. Many of these considerations refer primarily to a region's capacity to innovate and to adopt innovations first introduced elsewhere.[1] Of course, it is also possible that intra-regional agglomeration into large cities creates net social costs (in addition to those directly affecting the city's firms and households), and that a spatial structure with many large cities is inimical to national growth and welfare. Although it might be desirable to leave this complex and difficult issue aside, it is probably necessary to make some attempt to measure the importance of large metropolitan centres for regional growth in order to specify the technical progress function. Also, the spatial concentration and distribution of the capital stock (which itself will reflect in part the region's inter-urban structure) may influence a region's rate of investment. For instance, it may be useful to include a variable reflecting the rank of the regional metropolis in the national urban hierarchy as well as a measure of the strength of inter-regional communication channels between the region and the rest of the economy in the technical progress function.[2] Whether a dispersion measure of the regional capital stock and urban infrastructure would be a

[1] The problem of the spatial diffusion of innovations is discussed in Chapter 4, pp. 113–32.
[2] See the model described in Chapter 8, pp. 209–16.

significant variable in the regional investment function is more doubtful. These suggestions cannot be treated as a comprehensive appraisal of the role of agglomeration economies in regional and national welfare. However, such an appraisal would be an outcome of the implementation of the regional growth model as a whole.

LOCATIONAL PREFERENCES

Locational preferences are important for understanding the process of growth in the space economy and particularly its spatial distribution. They are a prime factor in explaining why profit-maximising models of industrial location and income-maximising models of regional choice for households predict badly. Thus, inter-regional migration does not take place at the rate predicted by inter-regional wage differentials. Similarly, where capital mobility involves plant and executive re-location it cannot be explained by differences in regional rates of return to capital. This point is important for understanding why investment subsidies to attract firms to backward regions by bridging the gap between rates of return are frequently unsuccessful or, at best, only partially effective. However, it is probable that locational preferences for households are more significant in the sense of having a large impact on the spatial distribution of population and, hence, of economic activity. The reason for this is that in the absence of locational preferences we would expect households to crowd into the centres of agglomeration at least until the effects of in-migration equalised incomes between areas. Yet because of locational preferences substantial numbers of people choose to live away from the centres of agglomeration (both in the sense of the prosperous regions of the economy and the major cities within their domiciliary regions) even when this involves sacrifices in income. Moreover, since preferences of this kind are not the peculiar perversions of one or two eccentric individuals but, on the contrary, are an attribute general to large segments of the population, there are clusters of such people in lagging regions as opposed to prosperous regions and within these regions in smaller cities and towns. Political considerations lead to a reinforcement of these preferences and the continued existence of these population centres by ensuring that urban infrastructure and other government resources are channelled into such areas. Accordingly, these factors are necessary elements (along with locational constants and transport costs) in an explanation of patterns of dispersion within the national economy and of constraints upon agglomeration within each region.

It is obvious that locational preferences are non-economic factors. However, this does not mean that they are irrational, merely that the psychic income attached to living in a particular place is not reflected in monetary valuations. I would argue that it is impossible to understand the dispersion of regional growth rates, and beyond that the pressures for a regional development policy strategy, without taking locational preferences into account. Although some economists might regard it as rather messy to have to include non-economic components in their models, in this case it makes all the difference to the model's predictive power. Thus, the theory of regional growth must contain a locational preference function. It will be essential to include such a function in the sub-model that determines regional rates of growth in population and labour supply, and it may be desirable to include a variant of a locational preference function in the model that determines the rate of growth of capital in each region.

It is worth noting that the locational preference effect on spatial patterns generally works in opposite directions for labour and capital. As pointed out above, locational preferences for households tend to foster dispersion by maintaining population in lagging regions at higher levels than justified by income differentials. Locational preferences for firms, on the other hand, tend to perpetuate concentration and agglomeration since many firms refuse to relocate away from centres of agglomeration even in cases when more profitable sites are available elsewhere. Naturally, if returns to capital are always higher in centres of agglomeration for all industries then it becomes less urgent to allow for locational preferences in regard to capital. However, though the theory of regional growth outlined here predicts that the rate of return to capital is usually higher in rich than in poor regions, it is quite possible that within the former the rate of return is lower in the metropolitan cores than in the suburbs. Thus, locational preferences for firms may still be important in explaining a tendency for decentralisation trends for industry within rich regions to be lower than might be predicted by profit maximisation criteria.[1]

In the context of developing an operational model of regional growth, there are two major problems created by the need to allow for locational preferences. First, how do we specify the locational preference function? Second, because of the importance of subjective factors it is much easier to formalise locational preferences for an individual yet for the purposes of regional analysis we need to measure the net impact of preferences on labour (and capital) immobility. How, then, should we aggregate individual preferences together? A preference function for an individual might take the following form:

$$P_r^i = f(A_r^N;\ d_{i_r N1_r};\ L_r^i;\ Y_s - Y_r;\ TC_{rs}) \qquad (7.6)$$

where P_r^i = locational preference of individual i for living in r;

$\quad A_r^N$ = agglomeration economies for people;

$\quad d_{i_r N1_r}$ = distance of i's residence from the region's largest city;

$\quad L_r^i$ = length of residence in region r;

$\quad (Y_s - Y_r)$ = per capita income differential between second best favoured region s and r;

$\quad TC_{rs}$ = a measure of mobility costs between r and s.

The first three terms in the function attempt to represent the pull of the region on its own residents, while the last two terms measure the benefits and costs of mobility. As can be seen, the fact that locational preferences are essentially non-economic does not preclude economic variables from the preference function. One problem is that the concept of the 'second best favoured region' is subjective, and might vary from individual to individual in a way which prevents us from making it operational. In this case, particularly in view of the subsequent aggregation of individual preferences, it may be acceptable to use either the highest income region in the system or, alter-

---

[1] Firms in backward regions may also exercise locational preferences by not moving to the prosperous regions.

natively, the closest higher income region as a surrogate.[1] Another difficulty, although one that would be resolved by empirical testing, is the ambiguity attached to the sign of the distance coefficient. The case for a negative sign is that access to metropolitan life within the home region and the agglomeration economies created there may reinforce locational preferences. Thus, the predominant migration streams may be from rural areas in some regions to urban areas in other regions. On the other hand, if rural-urban flows predominate in intra-regional migration and inter-urban flows are the main inter-regional migration stream, the distance variable may have a positive sign.

The question of aggregation is not insoluble. Averages can be used for the income differential and mobility costs. Agglomeration economies are in general terms common to the whole population though there might be a case for stratification by social status, income and/or occupation.[2] For instance, the presence of a major sports stadium in a city accessible to a large proportion of the region's residents may appeal to a different sector of the population from that interested in a symphony concert hall or an opera house. The distance effect can easily be aggregated by adaptation of the reciprocal of population potential, density or other measures. An average length of residence is easy to handle conceptually, though data problems may make this difficult to compute precisely. An indirect measure derived from past migration rates may have to be used as a surrogate. However, this raises a severe problem. The implementation of a locational preference function requires us to measure locational preferences, and an obvious way of doing this would be by the gap between actual and 'expected'

---

[1] An additional modification might be to collapse the potential income gains and the mobility costs into a single term where locational preferences are expressed as a function of the potential *net* income gain, i.e. the discounted stream of additional income *minus* the mobility costs. However, since 'pull' factors such as income gains might influence locational preferences in a different manner from negative forces such as spatial frictions, it is desirable to keep the two variables separate both conceptually and for empirical implementation.

[2] We might draw up 'agglomeration economy' demand functions for individuals and groups analogous to the agglomeration economies iso-profit functions for business firms developed by von Böventer (1970).

out-migration rates, in which the latter are forecasted or 'back-casted' from an economic or deterministic migration model.[1] If this were adopted, the locational preferences and the length of residence variables would be defined in very similar fashion. Although meaningful for the individual in the sense that the longer a person lives in an area the more attached he is likely to become to it, aggregation makes the relationship virtually a truism. One solution would be to drop the length of residence term and substitute a strength of kinship or similar variable. The alternative is to work harder on an alternative measure of locational preferences. One possibility is to measure the locational preferences of region i by aggregating the number of people living in other regions who were born in i.[2] This total is a surrogate for cumulative past out-migration, and it could be assumed that locational preferences for living in i are inversely related to this total deflated by the size of i's population.

SOCIAL AND POLITICAL FACTORS IN REGIONAL GROWTH

The inclusion of locational preferences in our theory makes it quite clear that a model of regional growth cannot concern itself solely with the attainment of economic efficiency. Non-economic variables may inhibit the migration of capital and labour and may affect the attitudes to growth of individuals

[1] The simplest type of model would be where inter-regional migration was treated as a function of either relative employment opportunities or relative unemployment rates, since in this case it is easy to derive the equilibrating (i.e. the 'expected') migration rate directly from the labour flows needed to equalise employment opportunities or unemployment. However, a more appropriate model might be one which related migration flows to income or wage differentials between regions. For the purposes of measuring locational preferences, we cannot use regression analysis on past time series data to derive 'expected' flows since the regression co-efficients would be derived from the actual flows. We would be forced instead to specify the relationships between in-migration or out-migration and wage levels in each region. This needs a sub-model to derive the marginal product of labour function.

[2] This measure bears some relation to the migration stock variable discussed in Chapter 4, pp. 96–7. It is similar to the reverse of that variable aggregated over all regions.

and communities in different parts of the country, and in both cases they influence the spatial distribution of activities and relative growth rates between areas. In addition, once regional policies are introduced into the economy we are almost invariably involved in issues much wider than the pursuit of efficiency. Equity goals figure prominently among regional policy objectives, and preoccupation with attaining a satisfactory distribution of welfare among members of society is a social rather than strictly economic concern. Moreover, although regional policy deals primarily with 'place prosperity' (Winnick, 1966) this concept is largely a surrogate for 'people prosperity', that is, measures to change spatial distribution of industry are chiefly intended as a device to redistribute income in favour of people living in poorer areas at the expense of those living in wealthier regions.[1]

Similarly, political factors are inevitable in regional policy decisions. This is not merely because all policy decisions have a political content, but particularly reflects the fact that in all countries voting for national legislative assemblies is organised on a regional or geographical basis. In a two- or multi-party system, the degree of concern with strategies for backward regions may bear some relationship to how many votes these areas can deliver. Furthermore, the national space economy is usually divided into regions on the basis of historical political and administrative territorial boundaries rather than according to functional economic criteria. This fact has major impacts on regional economic performance because the volume of national public investment is frequently divided up by reference to those political units and its spatial distribution within these areas decided, in part, on political grounds. Also, political regions differ in their policies, tax rates, etc. which has some influence on the amount of industry they attract.

If social, political and other non-economic factors are accepted as relevant to a discussion of regional growth differentials, then, inevitably, we will be less satisfied with the content and orientation of our models of regional growth. These are

[1] This is not to say that income redistribution is always achieved. Very often, those who gain from subsidies to lagging regions are the well off, such as industrialists and property owners, rather than the target population, such as the unemployed or the lowly paid

concerned with measuring the levels and rates of growth in G.R.P., regional output and personal income *per capita*. The introduction of social objectives into the analysis, however, makes monetary incomes too narrow an index of human welfare Accordingly, the dimensions of our regional growth models are inadequate and incomplete. Part of the problem lies in the fact that some elements affecting individual and social welfare fall under the heading of public goods that are not registered in G.R.P. statistics because they have no market price; clean air, beautiful surroundings, and a sunny climate are obvious examples. Other aspects reflect irreconcilable value judgements, such as the question of whether it is desirable to pump Federal resources into infrastructure and providing job opportunities on the Indian reservations of South-West America at the risk of destroying the cultural values and traditions of Indian civilisation. Or to consider another problem, under what conditions do regional policymakers take locational preferences into account? Has every individual a right to work and to enjoy an acceptable standard of life at any location he chooses? Is the Hansen strategy (Hansen, 1970*b*) of encouraging people to migrate from Appalachia and other lagging industrial and rural regions combined with a welfare payments strategy for those who choose to remain socially justifiable as well as economically viable? These few examples illustrate the complications that enter into the analysis of regional growth and change once doubt is cast on the all-embracing character of a monetary calculus.

As an economist it is difficult for me to do more than recognise the existence and significance of non-economic variables except for the cases where they have a clear-cut and measurable impact on regional growth differentials and on the structure and efficiency of the space economy. For a detailed analysis of these variables and for a socio-political theory of regional growth I must look to my fellow social scientists. Here, comments will be restricted to a few brief random reflections on some relevant aspects.

As a first observation, it is not out of place to refer to the importance of non-economic variables in the argument of this book. The approach to regional growth elaborated here is a direct attack on regional growth models based on assumptions about strict economic rationality, profit maximisation and automatic tendencies to equilibrium of factor prices and regional *per capita* incomes. Instead, great emphasis is placed on the frictions of the space economy, the incomplete linkages of information networks, and the impact of uncertainty on decision-makers' behaviour. In particular, stress is laid on the psychic costs of migration, the critical role played by information flows, the structure of inter-regional communications channels and the national urban hierarchy as an influence on innovation diffusion, and the impact of locational preferences as a constraint on agglomeration and on factor mobility. The implication of modifications of this kind is that models of economic determinism have to be replaced by stochastic and probabilistic models. The crucial point is that the existence of space limits the spread of knowledge, and once we accept that decision-makers lack perfect knowledge the case for crude deterministic models falls to the ground. Relaxation of the dogma of profit-maximising behaviour also implies that the analyst is much less clear about the outcome of actions and decisions in the space economy (Olsson and Gale, 1968, p. 232). Although there has been some discussion of probabilistic models in this book, particularly in the context of the mobility of capital and spatial diffusion of innovations, it is arguable that use of this approach does not go far enough.

It is also clear that many of the concepts of sociology and social psychology are relevant to the analysis of regional growth and the evaluation of its impact on social welfare. The class structure, patterns of social stratification, the life styles and expectations of social groups may all have a more than negligible role in the capacity of regions, especially backward regions, for growth. Some of the more obvious influences were pointed out by Hoselitz many years ago (Hoselitz, 1954–5). First, he referred to the arguments of Kolb (1954–5) that emergence of what he called a universalist-achievement-oriented value structure was essential for development of the urban-industrial matrix. Second, he stressed the relevance of the theory of social deviance for understanding the part played by capitalists in the early phases of economic development. By definition, he argued, the capitalist entrepreneur is an innovator, a finder or applier of new combinations and must be a deviant in a society where innovation and change are not respectable. In a more modern context, and in a regional growth setting, this hypothesis may be relevant in cases where it is believed that a tightly-knit social structure and attitudes hostile to growth in a backward region can be transformed only by the entry of outsiders (such as entrepreneurs, managers, innovators and technologists) with a quite different set of values. The long-term aim of such a strategy will be to make the behaviour of these outside 'deviants' the norm. In growth pole literature, it is sometimes argued that this transformation of values may assume a spatial dimension – that values and attitudes favourable to a high rate of economic growth will gradually radiate out from the growth centre and diffuse through the hinterland of the backward region. However, it must be admitted that as yet there is little empirical evidence in support of such a hypothesis. If anything, it is more likely that the growth centre remains an isolated enclave more in touch with metropolitan centres located at great distances than with the surrounding region in its vicinity.

Third, Hoselitz argued that ideology and social structure are important forces behind the regional dispersion of national economic growth especially in those societies, such as the United States, where less-developed regions were opened up by migration from the original metropolitan core centres. The interaction between high rates of internal migration and exploration of the frontier has been particularly important in large countries with a widely dispersed natural resource endowment. Yet the opportunities for national economic integration and the opening up of new regions could not have been realised unless large numbers of households or even whole communities were willing to leave familiar surroundings and assume the high risks of settling in a new area. This willingness requires an ideology that holds out large rewards for the migrant, and this in turn depends upon a social structure which is open and fluid, in which vertical social mobility is relatively unconstrained and which places emphasis upon material possessions. The initial migrants were able to create conditions favourable to sustained growth in the frontier regions by establishing social institutions in these areas that replicated those of the core regions with the same characteristics (channels for upward mobility, stress on equality, materialistic rewards, etc.).

The class structure of society in backward regions may be an important element in determining its capacity for change. For instance, the social structure of rural areas may lack the fluidity found in large cities and this inflexibility may be associated with a resistance to change and open hostility to industrialisation.[1] The power of conservationist pressure groups in rural regions, to take an obvious and fairly topical example, is not unconnected with the social structure of these areas. Similarly, we know that the social structure of a community can affect the number of potential receivers of information flows from outside, and hence the number of potential adopters of innovations that are first introduced elsewhere. The fact that the social structure found in large cities is much more favourable to economic development because of a greater concern with material acquisitions and because metropolitan society contains a greater proportion of what the sociologists have called 'spirallists' supports the stress placed in this book on the leading cities of backwards regions as a funnel through which new ideas, innovations and capacity for industrial transformation is channelled into the region.[2] The more these cities have national and international contacts, the more, to use Webber's terminology (1964), they form part of non-place urban realms, the more likely that they will fulfil this growth-inducing function. Thus, the critical role that large cities play in regional development is not merely associated with their economic characteristics, such as the creation of substantial agglomeration economies, but also with their social structure and their cultural (predominantly cosmopolitan and materialistic) values.

Another group of factors reflects dissatisfaction with the meaning of G.R.P. statistics and doubts about whether G.R.P. can be equated, even approximately, with the welfare of citizens living in the region in question. If this is the case, the analysis of regional growth becomes much more indeterminate and the construction of an operational regional growth model

[1] Somewhat surprisingly, however, farmers are not necessarily slow to adopt revolutionary agricultural innovations.

[2] For a similar argument in the sociological theory of growth poles see di Tella's concept of 'associationist leaders' discussed in Chapter 3, pp. 84–5.

much more difficult. The inadequacy of growth rates measured in G.R.P. or even regional personal income *per capita* terms may be illustrated with just a few out of many possible examples. The growing significance of environmental and 'quality of life' goals means that a widening range of phenomena now generally recognised to be influences on human welfare remains excluded from standard income and output measures. Secondly, an incremental unit of income can have a different value from one place to another not only because of relative price differences, or even because of a simple diminishing marginal utility of income hypothesis, but also because in highly urbanised regions expectations may rise faster than incomes. As Alonso and Fajans (1970) have suggested, it may cost much the same to live in big cities as in small towns but people are less content do so so. In the large city of the prosperous region, the rate of expenditure is higher, there is a much greater variety of goods and services on which to spend money, and the pressure to spend is much greater. Accordingly, people *feel* worse off unless they have much higher incomes than if they lived in a small town or in a poorer region. This is clearly a version of the relative income hypothesis, though the expectations effects are somewhat more complex.

Thirdly, a finding of some importance by Firestone (1973*a*) is that in Canada regional disparities in social indicators such as health indices, educational levels, social welfare facilities, etc., are much narrower than in *per capita* incomes. It is probable that this point could be generalised to experience in many other countries too. Its significance for the interpretation and value of regional income statistics is quite serious. For one thing, higher levels of consumption of social welfare, educational and health services which in many countries are distributed through the public sector may be more relevant to increases in welfare than higher incomes. Furthermore, to the extent that a better performance in levels of social indicators can be stimulated by public expenditures, both current and capital, it is arguable that different components of regional income carry weights that are not adequately reflected in their monetary values. Thus, if ten million dollars spent on a regional hospital have a bigger impact on societal welfare than ten million dollars of increased industrial output in the region, then the case for regional income accounting and use of a common monetary standard is no longer valid. Questions of this kind may send shivers down the economist's spine, but they are being raised with increasing frequency and not without justification. The economist's excuse that G.R.P. is merely a surrogate for regional welfare, to be used simply because we have nothing better, is lame rather than reassuring.

Regional growth analysis is thus incomplete if we leave out sociological and general social influences. It is equally deficient to ignore political factors, particularly in the areas where regional development and regional policy intermesh. In few countries is regional growth left to the free play of market forces. Government activity has both unintended and purposeful impacts on regional growth differentials. In regard to the latter, political factors assume some importance particularly where political gains are clear-cut while economic benefits are nebulous and ill-defined. There are many obvious examples to support this point. For instance, in countries which are federations and where the federation is rather insecure, regional development measures may discriminate heavily in favour of the less committed areas; the flow of Federal funds into Quebec in Canada and into Slovakia in Czechoslovakia are merely two of many instances.

Another more general illustration is that in many countries pressure is building up for regional devolution in economic development policies out of a desire for greater local political participation. Giving way to this pressure may interfere with overall economic efficiency since independent regions may pursue counterproductive competitive policies when the strategy pursued by one region is aborted by offsetting measures implemented by another. Avoidance of 'wasteful' inter-regional competition demands a firm control of and responsibility for regional development policy by the central government. Nevertheless, some forms of inter-regional competition may be a spur to efficiency, and the economic price of local control of a region's development may be worth paying for the political gains that devolution may bring.

Regional policy decisions are inevitably political decisions; that is, they are taken by policy makers, usually with the explicit justification that they are reflecting social preferences, who have to weigh and balance not merely the economic costs and benefits but also social impacts, political gains and losses and, perhaps most important of all, political feasibility. Subsidies to inefficient industries in backward regions, new infrastructure investment in obsolete and badly located cities, the selection of urban centres as growth poles that have relatively little economic potential for growth – actions of this kind are frequently taken and justified on political grounds. However, if we consider the opportunity costs of alternative action, it is clear that such measures have a direct effect on regional growth differentials. Hence, they are relevant components of an explanation of regional economic growth.

This brief discussion of non-economic influences on the path of regional development has been both elementary and unsystematic. Since this book is concerned with *economic* analysis, the preceding arguments stand for little more than a passing lip-service to the need for a broader approach. As an economist, I must plead as an excuse for failure to develop the comprehensive all-embracing theory of politico-socio-economic development of regions that many of the relevant considerations are outside my sphere of competence. Ultimately, however, the partial and opaque theories of the individual social science disciplines must yield to a more comprehensive general theory. Until this becomes practicable, we can only hope that sharpening the specific analytical focus of each discipline now will eventually help to make the required integration, when it comes, easier.

Chapter 8

The Model

DESCRIPTION AND CHARACTERISTICS

It is not difficult to state what the basic requirements of a regional growth model on the lines implied in the preceding chapters might be. The following list of characteristics shows some of the features that a theory of regional growth might contain.

1. Locational constants are important in the analysis of the space economy. These constants represent fixed locations that provide a few reference points in the space economy that will mould and, to some extent, predetermine the economy's spatial structure. Such constants might include: (i) an immobile natural resource; (ii) the existence of a large city established in the long distant past as a result of a now obsolete initial location advantage or chance; (iii) heterogeneity of land means that certain sites have special advantages that lead to earlier development than on other sites.

It should be noted that the presence of (ii) implies that we should not try to explain within the scope of a single theory the historical development of the space economy from the beginning. This would be too ambitious, and is unnecessary.

2. An area's growth potential depends upon (i) its internal immobile resources; (ii) its capacity to attract mobile resources from elsewhere and to retain its internally generated mobile resources.

Although (ii) depends in part upon the prospect of higher returns to factors these are not independent of 3 below.

3. Agglomeration economies, external economies of scale and indivisibilities[1] are crucial elements in regional and urban

[1] Bos (1965) has argued that the distinction between these concepts is blurred and fuzzy.

growth, especially spatial externalities and urbanisation economies. Agglomeration economies are important for two main
reasons: (*i*) they explain spatial concentration in certain
regions within the national economy and in cities within
regions; (*ii*) since they imply increasing returns, they can
explain why factors of production are attracted into an area
(also if we accept 5 below, this accounts for the attraction of
cities to firms, households, executives, etc., even in the absence
of higher monetary returns).

It is relatively easy to accommodate agglomeration economies in a model in a generalised way. What is difficult is that
when we come to operationalise the model we have as yet
made little headway in how to measure, even how to define,
these agglomeration economies.

4. The locational constants impose constraints on agglomeration, and are fundamental for understanding the dispersion
process in national growth. The existence of transport costs
explains why these fixed locations attract other activities (e.g.
urban services) rather than these being supplied at the original
centres of agglomeration. In accounting for the spatial distribution of production of different goods it may be useful to
classify commodities in a hierarchy where the orders in the
hierarchy reflect the size of the market areas over which goods
are traded; lower order goods restrict the scope for agglomeration since these must be produced locally.

Non-economic factors are also important for an explanation
of dispersion. Locational preferences explain why substantial
numbers of people live away from the centres of agglomeration
even when this incurs potential loss in income, and political
considerations bolster these locational preferences (if the population centres concerned are large enough) by ensuring that
infrastructure and other resources are channelled to these areas.

5. These locational preferences that cannot be rationalised
in terms of monetary costs and benefits are important in the
space economy both for households and firms. They are the
main reason why migration flows do not occur at the rate
predicted by wage differentials and they also account for the
limited mobility of capital.

The theory of regional growth must contain a locational
preference function. It should be possible to specify this with

some non-economic sub-model, e.g. relating locational preferences to access to metropolitan living or to regional origin.

6. Reductions in transport costs and increased flexibility of the transportation system have been prime factors making decentralisation within regions possible. These have enabled firms to take advantage of other technical changes (e.g. forces dictating changes in factory layout) and allowed households to exercise much greater choice in new housing and residential site preferences (e.g. desire for a new suburban home). In addition, preferences for more space have been one element in the decentralisation of both firms and households.

7. The space economy is characterised by a high degree of locational intertia, partly due to heavy relocation costs, partly due to locational preferences. In addition, the durability and fixed location of urban infrastructure and the overhead capital of intra-regional and inter-regional transport systems impose severe constraints on the flexibility of the spatial structure over all time horizons except the very long run. For these reasons, the spatial structure of the economy responds very slowly to changes in costs, demand and technical conditions.

8. The durability and fixed location of regional and urban investments make investment decisions (especially infrastructure decisions) critical forces in the development of the space economy. These investment decisions are sequential and interdependent. An investment decision in regard to a plant, urban infrastructure or section of a transport system must take account of previous investments in regional and urban infrastructure and will influence the scale and nature of subsequent investment decisions. Consequently, investment functions, even for an individual plant, must contain an element that takes account of the location and scale of all previous investments.

9. Above all, an acceptable theory of regional growth must be able to deal with the determinants of the rate of technical progress, its spatial incidence and its diffusion over space to other areas in the economy. Unless the rate of technical progress is exogenously determined, both the rate and spatial incidence of technical progress at any location will depend upon agglomeration economies. It is also necessary to include a framework for spatial diffusion of innovations. A high diffusion rate requires a closely connected urban hierarchy of outward-

looking cities and highly developed inter-urban (inter-regional) communication channels. Furthermore, if technical progress is embodied the rate and spatial distribution of technical progress will be bound by the same constraints that limit the mobility of capital; the spatial diffusion network will tend to follow the inter-regional flow matrix of mobile capital.

A REDUCED-FORM VERSION

In this section we describe a reduced form version of a regional growth model of the kind suggested in the previous pages. The advantage of presenting a reduced form model is that it shows the *minimum* data requirements for testing the model. In this particular case, we are still left with eleven independent variables in the growth equation. For simplicity, all the equations of the model are expressed in multiple linear regression form.

THE MODEL

We start from a definitional growth equation:

$$y = [ak + (1-a)l]^{a} + t \qquad a \gtreqless 1 \qquad (8.1)$$

where y = growth rate of regional income, k = growth rate of capital, l = growth rate of labour, t = rate of technical progress, a = capital's share in income, $(1-a)$ = labour's share in income, a = exponent, the value of which reflects increasing, constant or decreasing returns to scale according to whether a is greater than, equal to, or less than unity. The reason for including a in the growth equation is to avoid the restrictions of the constant returns to scale assumptions of the neoclassical model.[1] The familiar neoclassical growth equation is very useful as a *definitional equation* provided we allow for the possibility of increasing returns to scale as implied in our stress on agglomeration economies in regional development. Thus, we would expect a normally to have a value greater than unity.

The model includes a separate equation for capital stock

[1] Strictly speaking, constant returns to scale in the traditional neoclassical model are obtained only where $t = 0$. The formulation here, in effect, splits the 'residual' into two components – agglomeration economies and technical progress.

growth, labour supply growth and technical progress. The capital stock equation[1] might be structured as follows:

$$k = b_1A + b_2y - b_3K - b_4 \overset{z}{C}V(K_i/\pi d_i^2) + b_5(R - \bar{R}) \qquad (8.2)$$

where A = a measure of regional agglomeration economies,[2] K = regional capital stock, $\overset{z}{C}V(K_i/\pi d_i^2)$ = coefficient of variation of the capital stock per unit of area in each city ($i = 1$) of the z urban centres in the region, R = rate of return on capital in the region, $\bar{R}$ = average rate of return in the rest of the inter-regional system. Capital stock growth is boosted by agglomeration economies and a high growth rate. The third and fourth terms are a crude attempt to take account of the size and the spatial distribution of past investments as an influence on the current rate of investment as hypothesised in 8 above (p. 211). The last term retains the relative rate of return as a determinant of the rate of growth of the capital stock.

The labour supply function might take the form

$$l = b_6n + b_7A + b_8\bar{P} + b_{14}(W - \bar{W}) \qquad (8.3)$$

where n = rate of natural increase of population, $\bar{P}$ = a measure of average locational preferences, W = regional wage, $\bar{W}$ = average wage in rest of the system. Agglomeration economies and wage differentials are assumed to determine the rate of in-migration. An index of average locational preferences in favour of the region is included to measure the retentive power of the region for its own residents. A possible formulation of a locational preference function might be

$$\bar{P} = b_9A - b_{10}1/V_{N_1} + b_{11}\bar{L} - b_{12}(\bar{W} - W) + b_{13}TC \qquad (8.4)$$

---

[1] In all the equations that follow constant terms have been ignored.

[2] How to develop an index of regional agglomeration economies is a thorny problem the solution of which requires much more research. A crude agglomeration function might express agglomeration economies as a function of the size distribution and spatial distribution of the region's urban centres, i.e.

$$A = a_1(\overset{z}{\Sigma}N_i{}^{\beta_i}/z) + a_2z - a_3\bar{d}_{ij}$$

where z = number of urban centres (above a threshold size), N_i = population of urban centre i, β = exponent, where $\beta = f(N)$, $\bar{d}_{ij}$ = average distance between each pair of urban centres in the region. See Chapter 7, pp. 175–96.

where $1/V_{N_1}$ = reciprocal of the population potential of the region's leading city (N_1), used on this occasion to measure the average distance of the region's residents from N_1, L = average length of residence in the region, TC = an estimate of mobility costs between the region and the closest higher income region. Locational preferences for not moving are assumed to vary directly with regional agglomeration economies and length of residence in the region, and inversely with distance from the region's leading metropolis. The fourth and fifth terms reflect the influence of sacrificed income gains and the costs of moving.

Finally, a technical progress function might take the form

$$t = b_{15}A + b_{16}k + b_{17}G_{N_1} + b_{18}q\bar{t} \qquad (8.5)$$

where G_{N_1} = rank of region's leading city in the national urban hierarchy, q = a measure of the degree of the region's connectivity with the rest of the economy, $\bar{t}$ = national rate of technical progress. The first two terms represent the importance of agglomeration economies and capital embodiment in determining the rate and spatial incidence of technical progress. The third and fourth terms make some attempt to evaluate the region's ability to adopt innovations introduced elsewhere: the third term measures the position of the region's major metropolis (N_1) in the national urban hierarchy; the $q\bar{t}$ term represents the fraction of national technical progress that might be absorbed into the region as determined by the strength of the region's communication channels with the rest of the economy.

REDUCED FORM OF THE MODEL

The reduced form is obtained by substituting equation (8.4) into equation (8.3), and substituting equations (8.2), (8.3) and (8.5) into equation (8.1).

Let

$$c_1 = (b_{16} + a\log a)$$
$$c_2 = a\log(1-a)$$

we obtain

$$y = \beta_1 A + \beta_2(\overline{W} - W) + \beta_3 K + \beta_4 C\overset{z}{V}(K_i/\pi d_i^2) + \beta_5(R - \bar{R}) + \beta_6 n$$
$$+ \beta_7 1/V_{N_1} + \beta_8 \bar{L} + \beta_9 TC + \beta_{10} G_{N_1} + \beta_{11} q\bar{t} \qquad (8.6)$$

where

$$\beta_1 = \frac{[c_1 b_1 + c_2(b_7 + b_8 b_9) + b_{15}]}{1 - c_1 b_2}$$

$$\beta_2 = \frac{-c_2(b_8 b_{12} + b_{14})}{1 - c_1 b_2}$$

$$\beta_3 = \frac{-c_1 b_3}{1 - c_1 b_2}$$

$$\beta_4 = \frac{-c_1 b_4}{1 - c_1 b_2}$$

$$\beta_5 = \frac{c_1 b_5}{1 - c_1 b_2}$$

$$\beta_6 = \frac{c_2 b_6}{1 - c_1 b_2}$$

$$\beta_7 = \frac{-c_2 b_8 b_{10}}{1 - c_1 b_2}$$

$$\beta_8 = \frac{c_2 b_8 b_{11}}{1 c_1 - b_2}$$

$$\beta_9 = \frac{c_2 b_8 b_{13}}{1 - c_1 b_2}$$

$$\beta_{10} = \frac{b_{17}}{1 - c_1 b_2}$$

$$\beta_{11} = \frac{b_{18}}{1 - c_1 b_2}$$

The characteristics of the model are easily summarised. The growth rate in regional income depends upon: agglomeration economies; locational preferences; the size and spatial distribution of the capital stock; the rate of natural increase; the relative rates of return to capital and to labour; and measures of the

region's capacity to absorb innovations first introduced elsewhere (as indicated by the rank of the region's leading metropolis and the strength of the region's channels of communication
with the outside world). Despite the weaknesses of testing
reduced-form as opposed to structural models, it should at
least be possible to evaluate the relative importance of the key
features of our model (e.g. agglomeration economies, locational
preferences, rank of the region's leading city in the national
urban hierarchy) compared with the capital yield and wage
differential variables that feature so prominently in neoclassical and similar models.

PROBLEMS OF TESTING – AN APOLOGIA

The theory of regional growth developed in this book has been
translated into an operational model, even to the extent of
producing a reduced-form version of one variant. Moreover, it
has been stressed in this volume and elsewhere that the crucial
test for any theory is not its elegance or logical consistency but
its explanatory and predictive power. Yet, after long consideration, much hesitation and with great reluctance, I have pur-
posefully declined to subject the model to direct quantitative
testing. This failure to take the final, some may say the most
important step, requires some explanation.

The decision not to test is based on a mix of reasons – the
unfortunate experience of predecessors, shortage of data and the
conviction that such testing would be premature. It cannot be
traced to any doubts about the necessity of empirical testing for
any economic theory. My belief in the value of operational
models remains unshakeable. This value appreciates in the
particular context of the argument of this book – that the
theory of regional growth must be made more relevant and
useful to the regional policy-maker. Since we cannot expect
policy-makers to base their decisions on hunch and intuition
alone, it is very important indeed that the theoretical propositions about the regional growth process expressed here should
be subject to empirical scrutiny. Thus, the decision taken now
is not to abandon testing, merely to postpone it. The expected
gains from postponement include refinement and more accurate

specification of the regional growth model, an improvement in the quantity and quality of available data, and the hope that more reliable conclusions may be obtained from the tests. It would be unfortunate if the theory had to be rejected prematurely because it failed to pass incomplete, flimsy and poorly designed tests.

The problems arising out of premature testing can be illustrated by referring to a recent study by Olsen (1971). Olsen's book is one of the most interesting studies in regional economics in recent years. He constructed a model to explain regional growth differentials by integrating different strands of international trade theory (particularly the Heckscher–Ohlin model) with the income potential concept drawn from the social physics school of Stewart, Zipf, Warntz and others and with certain elements of Myrdal's cumulative causation theory. These apparently irreconcilable approaches were skilfully blended into a single model. Yet the attention that these ideas deserve has been distracted by Olsen's empirical tests and the hostile critical reception that these have received. The defects of the empirical component of Olsen's work were mainly outside his control. The most insuperable obstacle was the shortage of data. Another difficulty was the poverty of the results, and how to interpret them. Running the overall model yielded results that did not make sense, and several of the coefficients of individual parameters were of the wrong sign. But did this mean that the model was disproved, or merely that the data were imperfect and the estimation methods inappropriate?

Olsen's dilemma was similar to that faced by this author. One possibility was to abandon direct testing altogether until the theory is improved and the data deficiencies remedied. This was the easiest, and perhaps the most sensible, solution. It was courageous of Olsen not to adopt this course, but undoubtedly the main source of the criticisms levied against the study. The second alternative was to build up the data prior to testing. Olsen rejected this line of approach for a number of reasons. His analysis was carried out on United States regions – regional data are less sparse and generally of better quality in the United States – and Olsen, as a Scandinavian, did not feel knowledgeable enough about American data to embark upon data base construction on a large scale. Secondly, he recognised that such a task would require a huge input of resources, far beyond those available to him. Thirdly, he argued that the relevance of his model needed demonstrating before investment was made in tailor-made data. This last argument, in fact, is not very convincing since the data required for testing Olsen's model, such as *series* of regional output, capital stock and rates of return, measures of the level of education prior to 1940 and improved measures of the degree of urbanisation, would also be useful for testing other aspects of regional economic theory, including other theories of regional growth. However, if there are multiple uses for regional data of this kind, this constitutes a case for a large co-ordinated data base research project in the United States and responsibility for neglect of this task cannot be laid at Olsen's door.

Olsen thus chose the third possibility – to take empirical analysis as far as he could with available data. Since it was impossible to subject the model to a formal test with a full set of data, he used the data which he could obtain to give an impression of whether the model made sense, i.e. did it result in plausible time paths for income, and to obtain some idea of the orders of magnitude of the key parameters. He also carried out a sensitivity analysis by assuming different values for some of these parameters. His results were, on the whole, rather unsatisfactory. However, to interpret his efforts as a waste of time would be wrong. He performed a sensitivity analysis on a simple model very different from his own – a Cobb–Douglas Heckscher–Ohlin model. This particular test turned out very well, and showed that a model of this kind was very well-behaved. There is a lot of wisdom in Olsen's comment on this finding: 'Life of the conventional economist is easy. But is it worth living?' (Olsen, 1971, p. 216). It is surely better to try something new and to fail rather than to repeat tests on familiar models that yield, because of excessive over-simplifications that conflict too much with the realities of the space economy, trite and empty results. On the other hand, with Olsen's attempt and failure before us, it is sensible to be cautious and not to go too far in repeating the kind of experiment carried out by Olsen until more and improved data are available.

The justification for such caution may become clearer by commenting on some of the specific problems encountered by

Olsen in his empirical analysis.[1] The centrepiece of his model was a production function, and this meant that he needed regional outputs. Because of lack of data, Easterlin's personal income statistics had to be used and even these were available only for a few selected years of the test period (1880, 1900, 1919–21 and 1949–51). This latter point is illustrative of a more general problem – the fact that full sets of data were available only for three and four years of the seventy-year period (1880–1950), allowing only twenty-seven and thirty-six observations respectively. The model was constructed in the form of sets of equations to which exponential parameters were attached to the independent variables, where these exponents were intended to have positive values. Yet seven out of nineteen exponenst turned out to be negative, and Olsen was able to find some explanation for only three of these cases, and even these attempts were rather implausible. Some of the results were very difficult to explain indeed. For instance, education and urbanisation were found to have a negative effect on productivity growth, while relative income potential had a negative effect on capital stock growth. A C.E.S. production function was hypothesised so that each region might have a different elasticity of substitution, allowing the model to reflect the impact of different industrial structures for each region. Yet, according to Olsen's tests, regional elasticities of substitution were very close to each other in value, and all of them so close to unity that a Cobb–Douglas production function would have served just as well. Finally, the model – though performing badly as a whole – worked much better in the first half compared with the second half of the period. This could have been explained by a tendency for built-in errors to accumulate over time, and could

---

[1] Since we are concerned here with problems of empirical estimation, it is not directly relevant to discuss Olsen's model. However, the model can be summarised in two or three sentences. It contains a complicated interaction between equilibrating and disequilibrating forces. The equilibrating forces are derived from factor substitution possibilities assumed in the production function and from the convergence tendencies of inter-regional factor movements. The main disequilibrating forces are the tendency for capital to accumulate faster in rich regions and for the labour supply to grow faster in the poorer regions. Also, other favourable influences on growth such as high productivity, education and urbanisation may increase most rapidly in the wealthier regions.

be handled either by grafting on sequential error-regulating mechanisms or by starting the runs in the middle of the period and working forward to 1950 and back to 1880. Another possible explanation of the variation in the model's performance over time might have been the estimation method, namely adoption of a series of partial multiple regressions rather than simultaneous estimation of all the model's parameters. However, the latter was tried but the results were even worse.

Of course, the supporters of alternative theoretical approaches to regional growth suffer under the same handicap of data shortages. This is as true of the neoclassicists, such as Borts and Stein (1964) and Romans (1965), as of other growth theorists. Thus, they were forced to make do with indirect and partial tests of their theories. Romans, for instance, carried two tests. The first was to estimate equilibrating secular investment

$$I_s = \frac{R}{r}\left(\frac{dL}{L}+\frac{t}{1-a}\right) \qquad (8.7)$$

where I_s = secular investment, R = net entrepreneurial income, r = the interest rate that makes the sum of secular investment in each region equal to gross U.S.A. investment, $K = R/r$ = capital stock, dL/L = rate of growth of labour force, t = rate of technical progress, $1-a$ = labour income's share. The second was a rank correlation analysis between the equilibrium growth rate

$$y = \frac{I_s r}{R} = \left(\frac{dL}{L}+\frac{t}{1-a}\right)$$

and the actual growth rate; the rank correlation coefficient was 0·929, 1929–59, when growth was measured by personal income and 0·953, 1929–53, when the growth index was regional income produced. It is difficult to evaluate these results in view of the severe deficiencies in the data. The main drawbacks were: t had to be assumed constant between regions; the rates of growth in employment were assumed equal to the rates of growth in the labour force; the time period over which growth rates were measured was arbitrary (in fact, nine years); and the investment data referred to one year only.

In testing the simple neoclassical model, Borts and Stein too had to resort to indirect hypotheses: that capital grows faster in low wage areas; that employment grows faster in high wage areas; that wages grow more slowly in high wage areas. In fact, out of three periods (1919–29, 1929–48 and 1948–53) these hypotheses were supported only in the middle period and were refuted in the other two. Again, the question arises as to whether these findings could be explained in terms of the limitations of the data or whether they were conclusive evidence of the irrelevancy of the neoclassical model. Borts and Stein's explanation was that the crude neoclassical model had to be rejected, but that if the theory were extended to reflect the real world more closely the results could be explained. The crucial modifications were: interstate differences in the rates of growth of employment in a given manufacturing industry could be explained by interstate differences in the rate of growth in the labour-supply function; *in a multi-sector model*, capital may grow faster in high wage regions because of shifts in demand in favour of the products of capital-intensive industries in which these regions will tend to specialise, even though the return to capital in a given industry may be higher in low wage regions. However, it must be recognised that some of these findings, particularly that both capital and wages increased more rapidly in high wage areas in the first and third period, are compatible with views of the regional growth process that are not extensions of but are quite contradictory to the neoclassical approach. In fact, these particular findings are quite compatible with our theory of regional growth, and especially with the emphasis on agglomeration economies as determinants of growth in prosperous regions.

Another reason for caution in addition to the only partially successful and sometimes chastening experience of predecessors is that the data requirements of our model are rather heavy. In the first place, many of the variables that feature in the neoclassical, Olsen's and other models are also common to our model. These include: regional income (or output); capital stock, regional investment and rate of return measures; labour force, employment and regional wage data; and measures of regional productivity and technical progress. As far as the United States is concerned, the country with probably the most plentiful regional data, there are some statistics available for most of these variables, but in most cases only for odd years, or, at best, for short annual runs. These data gaps certainly prevent adequate testing of most regional growth models, except by using unsatisfactory (for the purpose of explaining long-term growth differentials) cross-sectional techniques.

Secondly, as the discussion in earlier chapters suggests, some of the variables peculiar to our model present severe definitional and measurement problems. Pre-eminent among these, both in terms of their role in the theory and the difficulty involved in their measurement, are agglomeration economies and locational preferences. It may be possible, as suggested earlier,[1] to use a regional population distribution that takes into account the relative size and spacing of urban centres in a region as a surrogate for regional agglomeration economies. However, it might be necessary to disaggregate agglomeration economies into those relating to households, business and the public sector. One difficulty is that many agglomeration economies important in generating regional growth are urbanisation economies, and in translating these into a regional context we have an 'adding up' problem, possibly requiring weights to be assigned to the economies arising in each urban centre. In a paper dealing with metropolitan employment forecasting (Richardson, 1972*b*), I suggested six types of agglomeration economy that might be crucial in an urban economy for attracting outside industry: public service efficiency; labour market economies; the availability of business services; leisure and cultural facilities; the availability of sites for industrial and commercial expansion; and an index of market potential. Clearly, a classification of this kind is too disaggregated for use in a regional growth model.

The measurement of locational preferences may be easier to handle, provided that we are satisfied with an index of 'average' locational preferences for the regional community as a whole. To the extent that locational preferences relate to labour, there are two obvious methods of measurement. The first is, assuming that a satisfactory migration model is at the analyst's disposal, to use the shortfall between the actual and the 'expected' out-

---

[1] See Chapter 7, pp. 179–80.

migration rate as an index of locational preferences, where the 'expected' estimates are obtained from implementing the migration model. The alternative is more straightforward. This involves measuring the locational preferences in region i by aggregating the number of people living in other regions of the system who were born in i. This total is a surrogate for cumulative past out-migration from region i, and locational preferences can be assumed to be inversely related to this total. A locational preference index for capital is a more intractable problem. It was suggested above (p. 112) that it would be useful to have a matrix of probability coefficients reflecting the risks, uncertainty and psychic income benefits influencing each bilateral inter-regional capital flow, though it is very difficult to make such a matrix operational except by assuming implicit valuations for these coefficients obtained by the response or non-response of capital flows to inter-regional differentials in the rates of return. Even this possibility is ruled out by shortages of data, since it requires, in effect, a series of inter-regional capital flow matrices.

Some of the other variables in the regional growth model present few difficulties other than data collection and routine calculation, e.g. the population potential of the region's leading city, measures of rank in the national urban hierarchy, average length of residence in the region. Other variables require conceptual clarification and definition and/or much more data than are currently available, e.g. the spatial distribution of the capital stock, household mobility costs between regions, a measure of the degree of connectivity with inter-regional communication channels.[1] These are not data problems that can be resolved overnight. Also, most of the phenomena for which data are required for this model are relevant to many other research problems in regional and urban studies. If this is so, the responsibility for more and improved data falls upon statisticians, compilers and indeed all researchers in this field, not upon one individual.

Given that the construction of complete data sets would take years even if the task were started today by a large research

---

[1] Crude indicators such as the number of airline connections or the density of telephone, telegraph and telex ownership are obviously unsatisfactory.

team, the shortage of data on which to base reliable tests should not be used as an excuse for failing to present ideas and theories about the regional growth process. At the same time, it must be recognised that the worth and value of any theory will ultimately have to be settled by its predictive power as revealed in empirical tests. The argument of this book is presented in a naked state (i.e. without the protection of 'objective' scientific testing) out of both confidence and modesty – confidence in the belief that the ideas on regional growth put forward here are valuable enough to be worth discussing now rather than burying them away until they can be tested conclusively, but modesty because I am quite sure that the structure and consistency of the theory, and the regional growth model derived from it, will be improved by its exposure to the criticisms of my fellow practitioners.

Until such a time when the data requirements are met, it is possible that some support can be found for this or that regional growth model from historical analysis of the growth performance of an individual region or of inter-regional development as a whole. It is true that such support must of necessity be partial and inconclusive, in that it will not be derived from scientific tests of precise hypotheses, but this does not mean that it is without value. For instance, an interesting study of the growth of the New England economy over the period 1870–1964 by Eisenmenger (1967) backs up some of the central hypotheses of our theory. The problem which Eisenmenger posed was: why did the New England economy perform so well in view of its many locational and other disadvantages? New England had few natural resources or other locational advantages, an early asset – its ports – was obsolete by the later nineteenth century, raw material and energy costs were high, living costs and taxes were higher than in most other cases, and it had a hostile climate (compared with other regions of the United States). Yet *per capita* income was about ten per cent higher than the national average, population had continued to increase, and unemployment had been below average, at least in the later years of the study period.

Eisenmenger explained this paradox in terms of two groups of reasons, one that is not part of our model (and indeed may conflict with it), while the other supports its key features – the stress on agglomeration economies and locational preferences. The first favourable factor was a wage rate advantage of up to ten per cent over employers in other regions of the country.[1] This induced specialisation in labour-intensive industries, many of which have in recent decades been high-growth industries (electronics, research and development oriented metal-working industries, non-manufacturing establishments, e.g. universities, research laboratories, insurance and finance houses, hospitals) rather than older labour-intensive manufacturing industries such as clothing, shoes, textiles, jewellery and leather. The second explanation is that New England's continued growth can be explained by the personal locational preferences of owners and executives of New England-based firms and by the growth momentum resulting from external economies, urbanisation economies and the investments of past generations.[2] Two pieces of evidence supporting this hypothesis are that a high proportion of New England firms is in the hands of local managers and that a higher proportion of workers in New England lives in urbanised areas (a fact that is consistent with the 'urbanisation economies induce growth' thesis). This helps to explain relative specialisation in the high-growth metropolitan service industries, while external economies generally are relevant in explaining New England's manufacturing specialisation in such industries as primary and fabricated metals, machinery and transportation equipment. The trouble with this diagnosis and the method of analysis is that in the absence of quantitative empirical tests it is impossible to assess the relative weight of the 'low wage rate effect' compared with the 'locational preferences and external economy effects'. Though quite consistent with each other, nevertheless if one factor was much more important than the other it would imply a radically different view of the determinants of regional growth.

[1] The apparent contradiction between low wage rates and high per capita incomes is explained by higher participation rates and by substantial property income, much of it due to inherited wealth that had originally been created in the nineteenth century.

[2] Pred's study (1966) of the spatial dynamics of urban-industrial growth in the United States in the nineteenth century also gives a similar kind of historical support to our theory of regional growth. In addition, Pred's analysis has theoretical significance as a contribution to the theory of urban growth.

Chapter 9

Policy Implications
of the Theory

Does the theory of regional growth described in this book have any policy implications? The answer must be yes since a dominant factor in the argument to develop new and reject existing models was the desire to make regional growth theory more relevant to policymakers. However, it would be dangerous and misleading to jump directly from theory to policy. Although the theory suggests particular kinds of policy strategy, we must be careful about drawing universal policy prescriptions from components of the model. For example, the stress on the role of urbanisation economies in regional development points to the importance of subsidies for urban infrastructure investment as an instrument of regional policy. But this does not imply that such subsidies are the sole useful policy measure or that they are appropriate in all circumstances and in all countries.

There are at least two reasons for caution in deriving policy implications. First, the theory outlined remains untested. The formal version of the model developed in Chapter 8 provides an operational framework for evaluating the quantitative significance in regional growth of agglomeration economies and locational preferences relative to, say, wage differentials and capital yield differentials. However, in the absence of such tests it is difficult to assert that our theory is the more correct. A preference for one theory rather than another must be based on its predictive ability and on how far it increases our understanding of the regional growth process. The most that can be said for the theory developed here is that a fair volume of casual empirical evidence can be marshalled in its support. But this is thin ice on which to base a particular regional development strategy or to risk the investment of billions of dollars.

Second, even if our theory of regional growth has general validity for developed economies this does not mean to say that regional development problems are the same in all countries. The scale and severity of these problems vary according to the area of the country, its natural resources, degree of industrialisation, level of *per capita* income and many other factors. Moreover, even for two countries with similar regional development characteristics it does not follow that identical regional policy measures are appropriate. The choice of policy instruments and how strong they are applied will be influenced by many considerations: the 'normal' degree of government intervention in economic affairs; the quality of entrepreneurship and the structure of corporate organisations particularly in lagging regions; the value goals and socio-cultural traditions of the society; the size and complexity of the fiscal sector; the nature and extent of economic planning, if any; the degree of geographic mobility of labour and capital; the country's constitution, political structure and scope for public consultation and participation. Consequently, we cannot presume a clear and direct link between the theory and any particular policy strategy. In devising the latter close attention must be paid to the institutional environment of the economy, its traditional public-private sector mix and its spatial structure.

Some light can be shed on the relationships between regional growth theory and policy by looking at the implications to be drawn from the neoclassical models. These models rely to a greater or lesser degree on the basic proposition that the price mechanism is an efficient spatial allocator of resources. In an extreme case, this may imply *laissez-faire*, allowing market forces to bring about an acceptable regional allocation of labour and investible funds. Even in this case, however, the government may need to play some role if only to make welfare payments to immobile unemployed in depressed areas. A more common diagnosis is that market imperfections in the space economy are fairly common so that the price mechanism works inadequately. In this situation, the appropriate neoclassical prescription would be to improve the operation of the market by 'lubrication'. The predictions of the pure neoclassical theory are that the marginal products of capital and labour are inverse and direct functions respectively of the capital-labour ratio, and that disequilibrium between regions will show itself by labour flows from low to high wage regions and flows of capital in the reverse direction. If factor flows are insufficient to eliminate idle resources this may be explained by market imperfections, such as mobility costs for labour and high subjective risk premiums for capital. Subsidies to migrants to cover mobility costs and to firms to cover the higher risks attached to investment in lagging regions are fully consistent, therefore, with neoclassical views of the inter-regional growth process. Incidentally, if the space economy really were a neoclassical world, the predictions of the model suggest that subsidies to capital to move into lagging regions and to migrants to move out reinforce rather than pull against each other, if regional *per capita* income convergence is a dominant policy objective. The compatibility of simultaneous action on both the capital and labour fronts is rarely appreciated.

However, what complicates the problem is that fact that this policy inference, though the most obvious, is not the only kind of policy consistent with neoclassical theory. There are other possibilities. Moes (1962), for instance, argued that local governments in depressed regions might tax immobile resources and use the revenue for local wage subsidies. The idea is that these subsidies would act as a substitute for wage flexibility, the absence of which constitutes another market imperfection. Moreover, neoclassical frameworks can allow for the existence of external economies; thus, for instance, in certain circumstances subsidies for education and retraining or for natural resource development may be justified. However, external economies of this kind can be dealt with by enlarging the unit of control until the economies are internalised, that is, they can be handled by the government rather than by the individual firm. Such external economies are different in kind from the urbanisation and other agglomeration economies that are central to the regional growth process in our model, in the sense that they can be treated by supplemental policies rather than calling for a completely different policy strategy. Finally, in the case where unemployed labour in a lagging region is immobile it may pay the government to invest in that region even if the rate of return to capital is much lower than in prosperous regions. The justification is that the opportunity cost of immobile unemployed labour is zero so that the rate of return to capital in the backward region is the gross marginal product of capital, i.e. the increase in value added, not the net marginal product which applies in prosperous regions (Borts and Stein, 1964, p. 197).

The distinctive characteristic of the main policies prescribed by neoclassical models is that they attempt to influence relative prices leaving private decision-makers free to change their location in response to the adjusted sets of prices. The theory of regional growth suggested here, however, does not lay much stress on the allocation function of prices. Non-economic factors are important determinants of the rate of migration, while locational preferences explain why both capital and labour may remain where they are even in the face of substantially higher returns obtainable elsewhere. The crucial significance assigned to urbanisation and agglomeration economies as generators of regional growth emphasises cumulative non-linearities, interdependence in location decisions, discontinuities and critical minimum thresholds – all forces that fall outside the scope of neoclassical marginalism. The spatial structure of the economy as a whole, the location of urban and transport infrastructure, the distance between metropolitan regions – these become relevant variables in determining the spatial efficiency of the national economy and its constituent regions, but are excluded from neoclassical analysis by its spacelessness assumptions.

Given these major differences in the nature of the theories, it is not surprising that there are equally striking differences in their implications for policy. The role of prices and substitution effects is played down, so price subsidies (to capital and labour) are no longer given major emphasis. Moreover, the switch in attention from locational shifts in response to relative price changes towards the long-run generation of regional growth induced by economies of spatial concentration involves an extension of the time horizon for policy implementation. With the move from short-term to long-term strategies it becomes much more difficult to evaluate the effectiveness of policy in terms of quantifiable criteria. This lack of quantification is exacerbated by the change away from price subsidies to induce relocation, the resource costs of which are relatively easily calculable, towards large-scale investments in urban infrastructure and physical planning programmes. Although it is not impossible to evaluate some of the costs and benefits involved in such a programme (see, for example, the 'planning balance sheet' approach recommended by Lichfield),[1] the scale and repercussions are so far-reaching that we cannot hope to calculate a social rate of return on the capital invested. The longer gestation period, the irreversibility of much of infrastructure investment (capital or wage subsidies can be revised or abandoned almost at will), and the difficulties involved in making an estimate of economic efficiency costs mean that it becomes almost impossible to evaluate the on-going effectiveness of such a policy. Proper evaluation can be made only on an *ex post* basis long after the investments have been made and the policies carried out. In effect, this means that policymakers implementing a strategy based on subsidies for spatially concentrated infrastructure investment proceed much more on faith than rational calculation. This increases the political pressures on regional policymakers since it is difficult to justify the investment of millions on the basis of faith alone.

Our theory of regional growth stresses the spatial aspects of development at all levels: the spatial structure of the national economy, the efficiency of inter-regional transport and communication networks and the organisation of the national urban hierarchy; the internal spatial structure within each region, the relative size and spacing of its urban centres and the location of its industries and infrastructure; and within the region's leading cities and spatial structure of the metropolises, the efficiency of the urban transport system, their adaptation to new technical and social conditions as revealed in the extent and nature of the decentralisation process, their social and cultural amenities and their accessibility to outdoor recreation and leisure. If all these considerations are relevant, regional policy and planning becomes a much more complex and far-reaching operation than simply trying to persuade industries and people to change their locations by subsidising movement.

[1] Lichfield (1966) and Lichfield and Chapman (1970).

What is really required is the interdependence of regional economic planning and physical planning, since decisions on the location and scale of transport and urban infrastructure will have direct repercussions on regional and inter-regional economic performance.

A serious obstacle to the integration of physical planning and regional policy is that in most countries the execution of these functions is separated in different government departments, while within the broad area of physical planning capital spending decisions in relation to transport, housing, hospitals, schools, etc. are also diffused both horizontally (among government departments) and vertically (at different hierarchical levels). In certain situations, such as the development of a new town, the physical planning and the economic policy components may be brought together and co-ordinated under a single agency, but this is not the general rule. The normal procedure is for the capital spending programmes of central, regional and local governments to be fragmented among different groups while their marked repercussions on regional economic performance either go unnoticed or are miscalculated. Accordingly, a major upshot of a spatial approach to regional growth analysis is a plea for more co-ordination between government departments and different levels of government and the integration of all infrastructure decisions into an overall strategy for the regionalisation of national development.

This raises difficult political problems with regard to the reorganisation of government in general and the centralisation versus decentralisation issue in particular. The latter issue is a prickly one, especially in countries with a Federal system of government. It does not inevitably follow that a plea for the integration of regional economic and physical planning implies more centralisation, though that is one practicable, and possibly the easiest, solution. However, it does imply more forward planning, more evaluation of the regional and local side-effects of capital expenditure programmes, more exchange of information between government departments, public agencies and different levels of government, and more co-operation between physical planners and economic policy-makers. These aims can be achieved with many alternative political and administrative structures. To explore this question in further detail would be to stray outside the scope of this book.

If the growth of a region depends, above all, on the creation of agglomeration economies, the question arises as to whether it is possible to stimulate these economies in all types of lagging area. In particular, it may be necessary to draw a distinction between an underdeveloped, primarily agricultural area with a low degree of urbanisation and an old-established depressed industrial area in need of revitalisation. Some economists take the view that government subsidies for infrastructure and the generation of agglomeration economies are inappropriate for declining mature industrial areas.[1]

This does not necessarily follow, though it is indisputable that the problems of underdeveloped areas and declining industrial regions are quite different. In the former case, the main task of infrastructure subsidies will be to generate the minimum critical size of urban centre that is capable of functioning as a core for metropolitan-regional growth and that can link up the under-developed region with the national communications and know-ledge diffusion network, thereby opening the area up to outside expertise, capital and technology. In the case of the mature depressed region, the role of government must be much more selective. Such a region will already have metropolitan centres above the minimum size, but these cities may no longer generate net agglomeration economies, at least in comparison with metropolitan cities of similar size in other regions. Policy objectives must concentrate on improving the relative com-petitive power of these cities. The problem is less one of abso-lute size than of intra-metropolitan and metropolitan-regional efficiency. This may involve action to counteract existing dis-economies as much as to create new economies. For instance, subsidies for an efficient urban transit system, for revitalising the downtown area or renewing dilapidated inner city neigh-bourhoods, expenditures on cleaning up the environment, in-vestment in outdoor recreational facilities, even subsidies for arts, cultural, sports and leisure facilities may all play a part in such a programme, as well as the more obvious type of invest-ments in roads, hospitals, schools, public buildings and housing. Moreover, in relation to both new and old areas public invest-

[1] For example, see Borts and Stein (1964, pp. 195–6).

ment in improving the links between these areas and the rest of the economy may be a useful, if indirect, means of increasing the growth potential of these areas.

In the underdeveloped region case there is a parallel between the policy implications of this theory of growth and a growth centre strategy. A growth centre strategy also stresses the significance of agglomeration economies and of the inter-urban spatial distribution within regions. But it should be noted that the value of our theory of regional growth to policymakers does not stand or fall on the validity of growth centre policy. Growth poles are not usually a suitable policy instrument for depressed already urbanised areas nor do the policy proposals discussed here depend on the viability of a growth centre-hinterland relationship. In other words, while a growth centre strategy is quite compatible with our interpretation and analysis of the regional growth process it is by no means an inevitable policy implication. Improving the efficiency and competitive power of a region's leading metropolis may be the most direct method of maximising the region's growth potential yet may be quite at odds with a growth centre strategy which might suggest diverting new infrastructure resources to a distant secondary centre.

The most obvious policy conclusions to be derived from the theory, if the theory is supported by empirical tests, is that subsidies for infrastructure investment and measures to stimulate urbanisation and other agglomeration economies are more likely to pay off in the long run than investment incentives to firms and other subsidies to private capital. In addition, the structure, efficiency and cosmopolitanism of the region's largest city may be the chief determinant of the region's rate of technical progress. Also, locational preferences have such a strong influence on the spatial distribution of population that they may need to be accommodated in the formulation of regional policy goals. Unfortunately, these observations are very general in character and are hardly specific enough to be of much immediate value for policy implementation. Indeed, they raise many unanswered questions. For example, how do we identify the mechanisms by which infrastructure investment and the creation of agglomeration economies generate regional growth? What types of infrastructure investment are crucial for promoting regional growth? Is investment in essential business services and in roads, public utilities and housing, etc. more or less important than investment in amenities, shopping and leisure facilities? In the context of the earlier discussion on the benefits of 'generative' versus 'competitive' growth,[1] what measures will tend to stimulate the former, thereby improving the growth performance of the national economy?

Many of the important issues revolve around the crucial question of what degree of spatial concentration is appropriate for reducing the costs of infrastructure and maximising the scope for agglomeration economies. Since I am sceptical of the value of the optimal city size concept[2] and given the emphasis in the model on creating favourable conditions for innovation diffusion which implies raising the regional metropolis's rank in the national urban hierarchy, there is a clear presumption in favour of building up agglomeration economies in a region's leading urban centre. Although this is easily justified in underdeveloped sparsely populated regions, it is not necessarily the universal prescription for developed densely populated regions. The possibility of agglomeration diseconomies cannot be dismissed without examination. Furthermore, if locational preferences do figure among regional policy goals these are likely (at least as far as the distribution of population is concerned) to favour infrastructure investment in smaller centres. At what level does dispersion become socially preferable and economically viable relative to concentration? There is no unique answer to this crucial question. It depends on the strength of locational preferences, the social content of regional policy objectives, the size and natural resource distribution of regions and their relationship in space to the rest of the economy. Finding acceptable answers is made more difficult by the failure to measure the social benefits of spatial concentration, the lack of quantification of agglomeration economies and the problems involved in the measurement of psychic income variables such as locational preferences.

Providing all the caveats and qualifications are kept in mind, and on the condition that these conclusions are not interpreted as a universal prescription to be applied in all cases without due regard to the individual economic and social characteristics of each region, it is possible to draw a general policy conclusion

[1] See above, pp. 86–8.   [2] See Richardson (1972a).

from the analysis. This is a strong preference for infrastructure subsidies rather than investment incentives, a preference that is quite consistent with treating regional development as a cumulative process and regional development problems as solvable only in the very long run. The cumulative nature of regional growth implies the generation of development by internal stimuli (such as agglomeration economies) rather than the redistribution of activities from other regions. However, a policy emphasising infrastructure and agglomeration economies can mean many things. Inter-regional communications and transport channels, basic urban infrastructure, social amenities and cultural facilities, educational institutes, all these may be relevant. Which agglomeration economies are critical may vary from one situation to the next. Transportation improvements may be a necessary pre-requisite for faster growth, but are most unlikely to generate development if undertaken in isolation. In some cases it may be crucial to make the leading urban centres attractive to households in other parts of the region (hence housing and social amenities may be important); in other cases integrating these centres with other parts of the national economy may be the top priority. The general prescriptions invariably need much closer specification.

When regional development policy's primary concern is with lagging regions, it is doubtful whether subsidies for infrastructure and agglomeration economies will normally be sufficient. The aim of long-term development must be to attract private capital to backward regions and while infrastructure policies will create attractive conditions for such development they will not necessarily offer an immediate incentive. This suggests that infrastructure subsidies may need to be supplemented by a direct subsidy to private firms. The most usual type of direct subsidy is a capital subsidy. However, this is not very appropriate to this case. First, private firms probably receive some reduction in their capital costs as a consequence of the infrastructure subsidies (e.g. provision of roads, power and water utility services). Second, if regional problems manifest themselves primarily in the form of unemployed immobile labour it is inefficient to choose a subsidy that biases investment in favour of capital-intensive industry. The argument on the other side is that the presence of capital-intensive industry in a region generates further growth. This proposition probably rests on the view that technical progress is embodied and that capital-intensive industry may transmit new technology and ideas to other industrial sectors. There is no firm evidence in favour of this argument. Indeed, far from transforming the rest of the industrial structure there is evidence that in many cases a capital-intensive industry located in a lagging region may function as a 'colonialist enclave' insulated from the other components of the regional economy and with little concern for the long-run welfare of the region, reinforced by the fact that it employs few of its residents. The case for capital-intensive industry is very often made with the stereotypes of a large technologically advanced capital-intensive plant and a small low-productivity, backward, labour-intensive firm in mind. Such stereotypes are hardly typical. For example, relatively labour-intensive service industries have figured among the fastest growing sectors in recent decades. The capital-intensive sector contains stagnating and risky as well as technologically advanced industries.

Since the argument that capital-intensive industry deserves favourable discrimination because of its long-run generating effects is unconvincing, the most efficient supplemental subsidy is a wage subsidy. This also reduces producers' costs and/or raises household incomes depending on whether or not, or to what extent, the subsidy is passed on. Most important of all, a wage subsidy is the most direct attack on the problem of regional unemployment and must tend to raise the level of employment more than capital-biased measures. A practical objection is that many investment incentives take the form of an initial subsidy and are therefore more certain than continuous wage subsidies that could be withdrawn after the location decisions had been made. This argument, too, is not very strong since wage subsidies can be guaranteed for a finite period (say seven to ten years). Thus, the general case for a social, urban and transport infrastructure subsidy policy to generate agglomeration economies supported by a wage subsidy to attract firms to lagging regions remains unimpaired. On the other hand, this general prescription may need to be modified in the light of the value goals and interventionist traditions of each society and the economic and social characteristics of individual regions.

References

ABBREVIATIONS

AER	*American Economic Review*
ASR	*American Sociological Review*
EDCC	*Economic Development and Cultural Change*
GA	*Geographical Analysis*
JPE	*Journal of Political Economy*
JRS	*Journal of Regional Science*
PPRSA	*Papers and Proceedings of the Regional Science Association*
QJE	*Quarterly Journal of Economics*
RE&S	*Review of Economics and Statistics*
US	*Urban Studies*

G. J. Aeyelts Averink, *De gevolgen van de Euromarkt voor de intra-Europese handel* (Rotterdam: Netherlands Economic Institute, 1960, 1961).

J. Airov, 'The Construction of Inter-regional Business Cycles'. *JRS*, 5 (1963), 1–20.

J. Airov, 'Fiscal-policy Theory in an Inter-regional Economy: General Inter-regional Multipliers and Their Application', *PPRSA*, 19 (1967), 83–108.

R. E. Alcala and A. H. Klevorick, 'Food Prices in Relation to Income Levels in New York City', *Journal of Business*, 44 (1971), 380–97.

W. Alonso, 'Industrial Location and Regional Policy in Economic Development' (Berkeley, Calif.: I.U.R.D., U.C.L.A., WP 74, 1968).

W. Alonso and M. Fajans, 'Cost of living and income by urban size' (Berkeley, Calif.: I.U.R.D., U.C.L.A., Berkeley, WP 128, 1970).

W. Alonso, 'The System of Intermetropolitan Population

Flows' (Berkeley, Calif.: I.U.R.D., U.C.L.A., WP 155 1971a).

W. Alonso, 'Problems, Purposes and Implicit Policies for a National Strategy of Urbanisation' (Berkeley, Calif.: I.U.R.D., U.C.L.A., WP 158, 1971b).

R. J. Anderson, Jr, 'A Note on Economic Base Studies and Regional Forecasting Models', *JRS*, 10 (1970), 325–33.

B. Balassa, *The Theory of Economic Integration* (Allen and Unwin, 1962).

J. Bargur, *A Dynamic Inter-regional Input-Output Programming Model of the California and Western States Economy* (Berkeley, Calif.: Water Resources Centre, U.C.L.A., 1969).

W. J. Baumol, 'Macro-economics of unbalanced growth: the anatomy of urban crisis', *AER*, 57 (1967), 415–26.

G. S. Becker, *Human Capital* (N.B.E.R., Princeton U.P., 1964).

W. Beckerman, 'Distance and the Pattern of Intra-European Trade', *RE&S*, 38 (1956), 31–40.

M. J. Beckmann, 'The Analysis of Spatial Diffusion Processes', *PPRSA*, 25 (1970), 109–17.

F. W. Bell, 'An Econometric Forecasting Model for a Region', *JRS*, 7 (1967), 109–27.

J. Bergsman, P. Greenston and R. Healy, 'The Agglomeration Process in Urban Growth', *US*, 9 (1972), 263–88.

E. Berman, 'Spatial and Dynamic Growth Model', *PPRSA*, 5 (1959), 143–50.

B. J. L. Berry, 'Hierarchical Diffusion: The Basis of Developmental Filtering and Spread in a System of Growth Centres', in *Growth Centres in Regional Economic Development*, ed. N. M. Hansen (New York: Free Press, 1972) pp. 108–38.

A. T. Bharucha-Reid, *Elements of the Theory of Markov Processes and Their Applications* (Toronto: McGraw-Hill, 1966).

C. Blanco, 'The Determinants of Interstate Population Movements', *JRS*, 5 (1963), 77–84.

C. Blanco, 'Prospective Unemployment and Interstate Population Movements', *RE&S*, 46 (1964), 221–2.

D. Blondel, 'Transmission des Innovations et développement entraîné', *Revue Économique*, 17 (1966), 434–66.

H. Blumenfeld, 'The Economic Base of the Metropolis', *Journal of American Institute of Planners*, 21 (1955), 114–32.

R. E. Bolton, *Defense Purchases and Regional Growth* (Washington D.C.: Brookings Institution, 1966).

G. H. Borts, 'The Equalisation of Returns and Regional Economic Growth', *AER*, 50 (1960), 319–47.

G. H. Borts and J. L. Stein, *Economic Growth in a Free Market* (New York: Columbia U.P., 1964).

H. C. Bos, *The Spatial Dispersion of Economic Activity* (Amsterdam: North-Holland, 1965).

J. R. Boudeville, *Problems of Regional Economic Planning* (Edinburgh U.P., 1966).

E. G. von Böventer, 'Determinants of Migration into West German Cities, 1956–61, 1961–6', *PPRSA*, 23 (1969), 53–62.

E. G. von Böventer, 'Optimal Spatial Structure and Regional Development', *Kyklos*, 23 (1970), 903–24.

R. V. Bowers, 'The Direction of Inter-Societal Diffusion', *ASR*, 2 (1937), 826–36.

J. C. Brackett and H. H. Lamale, 'Area Differences in Living Costs', *American Statistical Association, Proceedings of Social Statistics Section*, (1967), 144–8.

K. M. Brown, 'Regional Differences in Efficiency: Implications for a Model of Regional Income and Growth', *GA*, 3 (1971), 354–60.

L. A. Brown, *Diffusion of Innovation: A Markov Chain-Type Approach* (Evanston, Ill.: Department of Geography, Northwestern University, DP3, 1963).

L. A. Brown, *Diffusion Dynamics*, (Lund Series in Geography, 1968*a*).

L. A. Brown, *Diffusion Processes and Location* (Regional Science Research Institute, Bibliography Series, No. 4, 1968*b*).

L. A. Brown, 'Diffusion of Innovation: A Macroview', *EDCC*, 17 (1969), 189–211.

L. A. Brown, 'On the Use of Markov Chains in Movement Research', *Economic Geography*, 46 (2), Supplement, (1970), 393–403.

R. Burton and J. Dyckman, *A Quarterly Econometric Forecasting Model for the State of California* (Berkeley, Calif.: Center for Planning and Development, U.C.L.A., 1967).

G. C. Cameron, 'Growth Areas, Growth Centres and Regional Conversion', *Scottish Journal of Political Economy*, 17 (1970), 19–38.

R. Carrillo Arronte, *An Empirical Test on Inter-regional Planning: A Linear Programming Model for Mexico* (Rotterdam U.P., 1969).

E. Casetti, 'Why do Diffusion Processes Conform to Logistic Trends'?, *GA*, 1 (1969), 101–5.

E. Casetti and R. K. Semple, 'Concerning the Testing of Spatial Diffusion Hypotheses', *GA*, 1 (1969), 254–9.

C. Cherry, *On Human Communication* (Cambridge, Mass.: M.I.T. Press and Wiley, 1957).

B. Chinitz, 'Contrasts in Agglomeration: New York and Pittsburgh', *AER*, Papers 51 (1961), 279–89.

M. J. D. Chisholm and P. O. Sullivan, *Freight Flows and the British Space Economy* (Cambridge U.P., 1972).

A. N. Christakis, 'Regional Economic Development Futures: A Methodological Review and Study Design', *Futures*, 4 (1972), 13–23.

W. Christaller (translated by C. W. Baskin), *Central Places in Southern Germany* (Englewood Cliffs, N.J.: Prentice-Hall, 1966; original German ed., 1933).

C. Clark, 'Urban Population Densities', *Journal of the Royal Statistical Society*, 114A (1951), 490–6.

C. Clark, 'Industrial Location and Economic Potential', *Lloyds Bank Review*, no. 82 (1966), 1–17.

C. Clark, *Population Growth and Land Use* (Macmillan, 1967).

C. Clark, F. Wilson and J. Bradley, 'Industrial Location and Economic Potential in Western Europe', *Regional Studies*, 3 (1969), 197–212.

R. L. Crain, 'Fluoridation: The Diffusion of an Innovation among Cities', *Social Forces*, 44 (1966), 467–76.

R. T. Crow, 'An Econometric Model of the Northeast Corridor' (unpublished Ph.D. dissertation, Pennsylvania University, 1969).

S. Czamanski, *An Econometric Model of Nova Scotia* (duplicated monograph) (Nova Scotia: Dalhousie U.P., 1968).

S. Czamanski, 'Regional Econometric Models: A Case Study of Nova Scotia', in *Studies in Regional Science* ed. A. J. Scott (Pion, 1969), 143–80.

D. F. Darwent, 'Growth Poles and Growth Centres in Regional Planning: A Review', *Environment and Planning*, 1 (1969), 5–31.

E. G. Davis and J. A. Swanson, 'On the Distribution of City Growth Rates in a Theory of Regional Economic Growth', *EDCC*, 20 (1972), 495–503.

R. H. Day, 'A Theoretical Note on the Spatial Diffusion of Something New', *GA*, 2 (1970), 68–76.

T. S. Di Tella, 'The Concept of Polarised Development in Regional Planning – A Sociological Interpretation', 145–89, in Hermansen *et al.* (1970).

S. C. Dodd, 'Diffusion is Predictable: Testing Probability Models for Laws of Interaction', *ASR*, 20 (1955), 392–401.

S. C. Dodd, 'Testing Message Diffusion in Harmonic Logistic Curves', *Psychometrika*, 21, (1956), 191–205.

M. Edel, 'Land Values and the Costs of Urban Congestion: Measurement and Distribution', 61–90, in École Pratique des Hautes Études, VIe Section, *Political Economy of Environment: Problems of Method* (The Hague: Mouton, 1972).

S. L. Edwards and I. R. Gordon, 'The Application of Input-Output Methods to Regional Forecasting: The British Experience', in *Regional Forecasting*, ed. M. Chisholm, A. E. Frey and P. Haggett (Butterworth, 1971), pp. 415–30.

R. W. Eisenmenger, *The Dynamics of Growth in New England's Economy, 1870–1964* (Middletown, Connecticut: Wesleyan U.P., 1967).

R. A. Fabricant, 'An Expectational Model of Migration', *JRS*, 10 (1970), 13–24.

O. J. Firestone, 'Regional Economic and Social Disparity', in *Regional Economic Development*, ed. O. J. Firestone (Ottawa U.P., 1973*a*).

O. J. Firestone (ed.), *Regional Economic Development* (Ottawa U.P., 1973*b*).

K. A. Fox and T. K. Kumar, 'The Functional Economic Area: Delineation and Implications for Economic Analysis and Policy', *PPRSA*, 15 (1965), 57–85.

J. Friedmann, *Regional Development Policy: A Case Study of Venezuela* (Cambridge, Mass.: M.I.T. Press, 1966).

J. Friedmann and W. Alonso, *Regional Development and Planning: A Reader* (Cambridge, Mass.: M.I.T. Press, 1964).

C. J. Friedrich, *Alfred Weber's Theory of the Location of Industries* (Chicago U.P., 1929).

G. Fromm (ed.), *Transport Investment and Economic Development* (Washington: Brookings Institution, 1965).

L. E. Gallaway, R. F. Gilbert and P. E. Smith, 'The Economics of Labour Mobility: An Empirical Analysis', *Western Economic Journal*, 5 (1967), 211–23.

N. J. Glickman, 'An Econometric Forecasting Model for the Philadelphia Region', *JRS*, 11 (1971), 15–32.

M. L. Greenhut, *A Theory of the Firm in Economic Space* (New York: Appleton-Century-Crofts, 1970).

M. J. Greenwood, 'An Analysis of the Determinants of Geographic Labour Mobility in the US', *RE&S*, 51 (1969), 189–94.

M. J. Greenwood, 'Lagged Response in the Decision to Migrate', *JRS*, 10 (1970), 375–84.

Z. Griliches, 'Hybrid Corn: An Exploration in the Economics of Technological Change', *Econometrica*, 25 (1957), 501–22.

Z. Griliches, 'Profitability vs. Interaction: Another False Dichotomy', *Rural Sociology*, 27 (1962), 327–30. (Rejoinder by Rogers and Haven, *Ibid.*, 330–2; comment by J. M. Babcock, *Ibid.*, 332–8).

'Der Güterverkehr der Weltschiffahrt', *Vierteljahrshefte zur Statistik des Deutschen Reichs*, Ergänzungsheft zu Heft 1928, I, vom Statistischen Reichsamt (Berlin, 1928).

T. Hägerstrand, *The Propagation of Innovation Waves* (Lund Studies in Geography, Series B., Human Geography, No. 4, 1952).

T. Hägerstrand, 'On the Monte Carlo Simulation of Diffusion', *European Journal of Sociology*, 6 (1965a), 43–67.

T. Hägerstrand, 'Quantitative Techniques for the Analysis of the Spread of Information and Technology', in *Education and Economic Development*, ed. C. A. Anderson and M. J. Bowman (Chicago: Aldine, 1965b), 244–81.

T. Hägerstrand, 'Aspects of the Spatial Structure of Social Communication and the Diffusion of Information', *PPRSA*, 16 (1966), 27–42.

T. Hägerstrand (translated by A. Pred), *Innovation Diffusion as a Spatial Process* (Chicago U.P., 1967).

R. M. Haig, 'Towards an understanding of the metropolis', *QJE*, 40 (1926), 179–208.

N. M. Hansen, 'Development Pole Theory in a Regional Context', *Kyklos*, 20 (1967), 709–25.

N. M. Hansen, 'On Urban Hierarchy Stability and Spatial Polarisation: A Note', *US*, 7 (1970a), 82–3.

N. M. Hansen, *Rural Poverty and the Urban Crisis* (Bloomington: Indiana U.P., 1970b).

N. M. Hansen (ed.), *Growth Centers in Regional Economic Development* (New York: Free Press, 1972).

C. C. Harris, Jr, 'A Multi-regional, Multi-Industry Forecasting Model', *PPRSA*, 25 (1970), 169–80.

L. M. Hartman and D. Seckler, 'Towards the Application of Dynamic Growth Theory to Regions', *JRS*, 7 (1967), 167–73.

D. Harvey, 'Models of the Evolution of Spatial Patterns in Human Geography', 549–608, in *Models in Geography*, ed. R. J. Chorley and P. Haggett (Methuen, 1967).

H. ter Heide, 'Migration Models and their Significance for Population Forecasts', *Milbank Memorial Fund Quarterly*, 41 (1963), 56–76.

T. Hermansen *et al.*, *A Review of the Concepts and Theories of Growth Poles and Growth Centres* (U.N. Research Institute for Social Development, Programme IV – Regional Development) (Geneva, 1970).

J. G. Hilhorst, *Regional Planning: A Systems Approach* (Rotterdam U.P., 1971).

A. O. Hirschman, *The Strategy of Economic Development* (New Haven: Yale U.P., 1958).

G. Hodge, 'Urban Structure and Regional Development', *PPRSA*, 21 (1968), 101–23.

E. M. Hoover, *The Location of Economic Activity* (New York: McGraw-Hill, 1948).

B. F. Hoselitz, 'Generative and Parasitic Cities', *EDCC*, 3 (1954–5), 278–94.

J. C. Hudson, 'Diffusion in a Central Place System', *GA*, 1 (1969), 45–58.

W. Isard and G. Freutel, 'Regional and National Product Projections and their Interrelations', in N.B.E.R., *Long-Range Economic Projections* (Studies in Income and Wealth, vol. 16) (Princeton U.P., 1954).

W. Isard and M. Peck, 'Location Theory and International and Inter-regional Trade', *QJE*, 68 (1954), 97–114.

W. Isard, 'Location Theory and Trade Theory: Short-Run Analysis', QJE, 68 (1954c), 305–20.

W. Isard, E. G. Schooler and T. Vietorisz, *Industrial Complex Analysis and Regional Development: A Case Study of Refinery–Synthetic Fibres Complexes in Puerto Rico* (New York: Wiley, 1959).

W. Isard, *Methods of Regional Analysis* (Cambridge, Mass.: M.I.T. Press, 1960).

W. Isard and T. E. Smith, 'Location games: with applications to classic location problems', *PPRSA*, 19 (1967), 45–80.

E. C. Isbell, 'Internal Migration in Sweden and Intervening Opportunities', *ASR*, 9 (1944), 627–39.

N. Kaldor, 'Marginal Productivity and the Macro-economic Theories of Distribution', *Review of Economic Studies*, 33 (1966), 309–19.

N. Kaldor, 'The Case for Regional Policies', *Scottish Journal of Political Economy*, 17 (1970), 337–47.

G. J. Karaska, 'Manufacturing Linkages in the Philadelphia Economy: Some Evidence of External Agglomeration Forces', *GA*, 1 (1969), 354–69.

E. Katz, M. L. Levin and H. Hamilton, 'Traditions of Research on the Diffusion of Innovation', *ASR*, 28 (1963), 237–52.

J. G. Kemeny and J. L. Snell, *Finite Markov Chains* (Princeton, N.J.: Van Nostrand, 1960).

J. G. Kemeny and J. L. Snell, 'Stabilisation of Money Flows: An Application of Discrete Potential Theory', in Kemeny and Snell, *Mathematical Models in the Social Sciences* (Boston: Ginn, 1962), 66–77.

L. H. Klaassen, *Methods of Selecting Industries for Depressed Areas* (Paris: O.E.C.D., 1967).

L. H. Klaassen, *Social Amenities in Area Economic Growth* (Paris: O.E.C.D., 1968).

L. H. Klaassen, 'Growth Poles in Economic Theory and Policy', 93–144, in Hermansen (1970).

L. H. Klaassen and A. C. van Wickeren, *Inter-industry Relations: An Attraction Model* (Rotterdam: Netherlands Economic Institute, 1971).

L. R. Klein, 'The Specification of Regional Econometric Models', *PPRSA*, 23 (1969), 195–215.

W. L. Kolb, 'The Social Structure and Function of Cities', *EDCC*, 3 (1954-5), 30-46.

S. Kuznets, A. R. Miller and R. A. Easterlin, *Population Redistribution and Economic Growth, United States, 1870-1950* (Philadelphia, Pa.: American Philosophical Society, Philadelphia, 1960).

E. E. Lampard, 'The History of Cities in Economically Advanced Areas', *EDCC*, 3 (1954-5), 81-136.

J. B. Lansing and E. Mueller, *The Geographic Mobility of Labor* (Ann Arbor: Survey Research Center, University of Michigan, 1967).

J. R. Lasuen, 'On Growth Poles', *US*, 6 (1969), 137-61.

L. B. Lave, 'Congestion and Urban Location', *PPRSA*, 25 (1970), 133-49.

L. Lefeber, *Allocation in Space* (Amsterdam: North Holland, 1958).

W. W. Leontief and A. A. Strout, 'Multiregional Input-Output Analysis', in *Structural Interdependence and Economic Development*, ed. T. Barna (Macmillan, 1963), 119-49.

C. L. Leven, J. B. Legler and P. Shapiro, *An Analytical Framework for Regional Development Policy* (Cambridge, Mass.: M.I.T. Press, 1970).

N. Lichfield, 'Cost-benefit Analysis in Town Planning: a Case Study, Swanley', *US*, 3 (1966), 215-49.

N. Lichfield and H. Chapman, 'Cost-benefit Analysis in Urban Expansion: a Case Study, Ipswich', *US*, 7 (1970), 153-88.

H. Linnemann, *An Econometric Study of International Trade Flows* (Amsterdam: North Holland, 1966).

A. Lösch, *Die Raumliche Ordnung der Wirtschaft* (Jena, 1943), translated by W. H. Woglom as *The Economics of Location* (New Haven, Conn.: Yale U.P., 1954).

I. S. Lowry, *Migration and Metropolitan Growth: Two Analytical Models* (San Francisco, Calif.: Chandler, 1966).

E. Mansfield, 'Technical Change and the Rate of Imitation', *Econometrica*, 29 (1961), 741-66.

E. Mansfield, 'Intrafirm Rates of Diffusion of an Innovation', *RE&S*, 45 (1963*a*), 348-59.

E. Mansfield, 'The Speed of Response of Firms to New Techniques', *QJE*, 77 (1963*b*), 290-311.

E. Mansfield, *The Economics of Technical Change* (New York: W. W. Norton, 1968).

D. F. Marble, 'An Approach to the Direct Measurement of Community Mean Information Fields', *PPRSA*, 11 (1963), 99–109.

M. Marcus, 'Agglomeration Economies: a Suggested Approach', *Land Economics*, 41 (1965), 279–84.

P. N. Mathur, 'Economic Implications of Cost Minimisation in a Dynamic Input-Output Framework' (5th International Conference on Input-Output Techniques) (Geneva, 1971).

J. M. Mattila and W. R. Thompson, 'The Measurement of the Economic Base of the Metropolitan Area', *Land Economics*, 31 (1955), 214–28.

J. M. Mattila and W. R. Thompson, 'Towards an Econometric Model of Urban Economic Development', in *Issues in Urban Economics*, ed. H. S. Perloff and L. Wingo (Resources for the Future, Baltimore, Md.: Johns Hopkins Press, 1968), 63–78.

R. L. Meier, *A Communications Theory of Urban Growth* (Cambridge, Mass.: M.I.T. Press, 1962).

L. B. Mennes, J. Tinbergen and J. G. Waardenburg, *The Element of Space in Development Planning* (Amsterdam: North Holland, 1969).

K. Mera, 'Regional Production Functions and Redistribution Studies: The Case of Japan', Harvard University (May 1970).

W. H. Miernyk *et al.*, *Impact of the Space Program on a Local Economy* (West Virginia U.P., 1967).

W. H. Miernyk *et al.*, *Simulating Regional Economic Development: an Inter-industry Analysis of the West Virginia Economy* (Morgantown, W.Va.: Regional Research Institute, 1969).

E. S. Mills, 'Urban Density Functions', *US*, 7 (1970), 5–20.

E. S. Mills, *Studies in the Structure of the Urban Economy* (Resources for the Future, Baltimore, Md.: Johns Hopkins Press, 1972).

R. P. Misra, 'Growth Pole Hypothesis Re-examined', in Hermansen (1970), 233–53.

J. E. Moes, *Local Subsidies for Industry* (Chapel Hill: North Carolina U.P., 1962).

H. Mohring and M. Harwitz, *Highway Benefits: An Analytical Framework* (Evanston, Ill.: Northwestern U.P., 1962).

C. D. Morley and J. B. Thornes, 'A Markov Decision Model for Network Flows', *GA*, 4 (1972), 180–93.

R. L. Morrill, 'The Distribution of Migration Distances', *PPRSA*, 11 (1963), 75–84.

R. L. Morrill, 'Waves of Spatial Diffusion', *JRS*, 8 (1968), 1–18.

L. N. Moses, 'A General Equilibrium Model of Production, Inter-regional Trade, and Location of Industry', *RE&S*, 42 (1960), 373–97.

R. F. Muth, 'The Spatial Structure of the Housing Market', *PPRSA*, 7 (1961), 207–20.

R. F. Muth, *Cities and Housing* (Chicago U.P., 1969).

G. Myrdal, *Economic Theory and Underdeveloped Regions* (Duckworth, 1957).

P. Nelson, 'Migration, Real Income and Information', *JRS*, 1 (1959), 43–74.

G. M. Neutze, *Economic Policy and the Size of Cities* (Canberra: Australia National University, 1965).

W. B. Nicholls, 'Industrialisation, Factor Markets and Agricultural Development', *JPE*, 69 (1961), 319–40.

V. Nichols, 'Growth Poles: An Investigation of their Potential as a Tool for Regional Economic Development' (Regional Science Research Institute, D P No. 30, 1969).

J. H. Niedercorn, *An Econometric Model of Metropolitan Employment and Population Growth* (Santa Monica: RAND, 1963).

D. C. North, 'Location Theory and Regional Economic Growth', *JPE*, 63 (1955), 243–58.

B. Ohlin, *Inter-regional and International Trade* (Cambridge, Mass.: Harvard U.P., 1933).

Y. Ohtsuki, 'Regional Allocation of Public Investment in an *n*-Region Economy', *JRS*, 11 (1971), 225–33.

E. Olsen, *International Trade Theory and Regional Income Differences: United States 1880–1950* (Amsterdam: North-Holland, 1971).

G. Olsson and S. Gale, 'Spatial Theory and Human Behaviour', *PPRSA*, 21, (1968), 229–42.

P. O. Sullivan, 'Forecasting Inter-regional Freight Flows in Great Britain', in *Regional Forecasting*, ed. M. Chisholm, A. E. Frey and P. Haggett (Butterworth, 1971), pp. 443–50.

J. Paelinck, 'La théorie du développement régional polarisé', *Cahiers de l'Institut de Science Économique Appliquée*, série L, no. 15 (1965), 5–48.

J. Paelinck, 'Programming a Viable Minimal Investment Industrial Complex for a Growth Center', 139–59, in N. M. Hansen (ed.), *Growth Centers in Regional Economic Development* (New York: Free Press, 1972).

A. Peaker, 'Regional Growth and Economic Potential: A Dynamic Analysis', *Regional Studies*, 5 (1971), 49–54.

P. O. Pedersen, 'Innovation Diffusion within and between National Urban Systems', *GA*, 2 (1970), 203–54.

H. S. Perloff, E. S. Dunn, Jr, E. E. Lampard and R. F. Muth, *Regions, Resources and Economic Growth* (RFF, Johns Hopkins Press, 1960).

H. Perloff and L. Wingo, Jr, 'Natural Resource Endowment and Regional Economic Growth', in *Natural Resources and Economic Growth* ed. J. J. Spengler (Resources for the Future, Washington, D.C., 1961), pp. 191–212.

F. Perroux, *L'économie due XXme siècle*, pt. 2 (Paris: Presses Universitaires du France, 1964).

F. R. Pitts, 'Problems in Computer Simulation of Diffusion', *PPRSA*, 11 (1963), 111–22.

K. R. Polenske, 'A Case Study of Transportation Models Used in Multi-regional Analysis' (Ph.D. thesis, Harvard, 1966).

K. R. Polenske, 'Empirical Implementation of a Multi-regional Input–Output Gravity Trade Model', in *Contributions to Input–Output Analysis*, ed. A. P. Carter and A. Brody (Amsterdam: North-Holland, 1970), pp. 143–63.

A. Pottier, 'Axes de communication et développement économique', *Revue Économique*, 14 (1963), 58–132.

P. Pöyhönen, 'A Tentative Model for the Volume of Trade between Countries', *Weltwirtschaftliches Archiv*, Band 90, Heft 1 (1963), 93–100.

A. Pred, *The Spatial Dynamics of U.S. Urban-Industrial Growth, 1800–1914* (Cambridge, Mass.: M.I.T.. Press, 1966).

A. Pred, *Behaviour and Location: Foundations for a Geographic and Dynamic Location Theory, Part I* (Lund Studies in Geography, Series B, 27, 1967).

A. Pred, *Behaviour and Location: Foundations for a Geographic and Dynamic Location Theory, Part II* (Lund Studies in Geography, Series B, 28, 1969).

The President's Commission on Income Maintenance Programs,

Background Papers (Washington: U.S. Government Printing Office, 1970).

K. Pulliainen, 'A World Trade Study', *Ekonomiska Samfundets Tidskrift*, 16 (1963), 78–91.

G. F. Pyle, 'The Diffusion of Cholera in the United States in the Nineteenth Century', *GA*, 1 (1969), 59–75.

M. A. Rahman, 'Regional Allocation of Investment', *QJE*, 77 (1963), 26–39.

R. L. Raimon, 'Interstate Migration and Wage Theory', *RE&S*, 44 (1962), 428–38.

A. Rapaport, 'Nets with Distance Bias', *Bulletin of Mathematical Biophysics*, 13 (1951), 107–17.

A. Rapaport, 'The Diffusion Problem in Mass Behaviour', *General Systems*, 1 (1956), 48–55.

F. Redlich, 'Ideas, their Migration in Space and Transmittal over Time', *Kyklos*, 6 (1953), 301–22.

T. A. Reiner, 'Sub-national and National Planning Decision Criteria', *PPRSA*, 14 (1965), 107–36.

H. W. Richardson, *Regional Economics: Location Theory, Urban Structure and Regional Change* (New York: Praeger, 1969a).

H. W. Richardson, *Elements of Regional Economics* (Harmondsworth: Penguin, 1969b).

H. W. Richardson, *Urban Economics* (Harmondsworth: Penguin, 1971).

H. W. Richardson, 'Optimality in City Size, Systems of Cities, and Urban Policy', *US*, 9 (1972a), pp. 29–48.

H. W. Richardson, 'An Approach to Metropolitan Employment Forecasting' (mimeographed, 1972b).

H. W. Richardson, *Input–Output and Regional Economics* (Weidenfeld & Nicolson, 1973).

P. O. Roberts and D. T. Kresge, 'Transport for Economic and Social Development', *AER*, 58 (1968), pp. 340–59.

H. W. Robinson, 'The Response of Labour to Economic Incentives', in *Oxford Studies in the Price Mechanism*, ed. P. W. S. Andrews and T. Wilson (Oxford: Clarendon Press, 1951), 204–72.

A. Rogers, 'A Markovian Policy Model of Inter-regional Migration', *PPRSA*, 17 (1966), pp. 205–24.

A. Rogers, 'Matrix Analysis of Inter-regional Population Growth and Distribution', *PPRSA*, 18 (1967), 177–96.

E. M. Rogers, *The Diffusion of Innovations* (Glencoe, Ill.: Free Press, 1962).

E. M. Rogers and E. Havens, 'Adoption of Hybrid Corn: Profitability and the Interaction Effect', *Rural Sociology*, 26 (1961), 409–14.

J. T. Romans, *Capital Exports and Growth among U.S. Regions* (Middletown, Conn.: Wesleyan U.P. 1965).

E. Ruiz, 'Urban Family Budgets Updated to Autumn 1971', *Monthly Labor Review* (June 1972), 46–50.

J. C. Saigal, *The Choice of Sectors and Regions* (Rotterdam U.P., 1965).

N. Sakashita, 'Regional Allocation of Public Investment', *PPRSA*, 19 (1967), 161–82.

D. Salvatore, 'The Operation of the Market Mechanism and Regional Inequality', *Kyklos*, 25 (1972), 518–36.

W. Schramm, 'Information Theory and Mass Communication', in *Reader in Public Opinion and Communication*, ed. B. Berelson and M. Janowitz (New York: Collier, 1966).

A. Sen (ed.), *Growth Economics* (Harmondsworth: Penguin, 1970).

C. Shannon and W. Weaver, *The Mathematical Theory of Communication* (Urbana, Ill.: Illinois U.P., 1949).

H. Siebert, *Regional Economic Growth: Theory and Policy* (Scranton: International Textbook Co., 1969).

H. A. Simon, 'Theories of Decision Making in Economics' *AER*, 49 (1959) 253–83.

L. A. Sjaastad, 'The Relationship between Migration and Income in the United States' *PPRSA*, 6 (1960), 37–64.

L. A. Sjaastad, 'The Costs and Returns of Human Migration', *JPE*, 70 (1962), Supplement, 80–93.

D. M. Smith, *Industrial Location* (New York: Wiley, 1971).

V. L. Smith, 'The Measurement of Capital', in US Congress, Joint Economic Committee, *Measuring the Nation's Wealth* (Washington, D.C., 1964), 329–46.

W. F. Smith, 'Optimum lot size when site rent is a transfer payment', *Annals of Regional Science*, 3 (1969), 8–15.

W. H. Somermeijer, 'Een analyse van de binnenlandse migratie in Nederland tot 1947 en van 1948–1957', *Statistiche en Econometrische Ondersoekingen* (1961), 115–74.

C. H. Springer, R. E. Herlihy, R. T. Mall and R. I. Beggs,

Probabilistic Models (Mathematics for Management Series, Vol. 4), (Homewood, Ill.: Richard D. Irwin, 1968).

J. Q. Stewart, 'The Development of Social Physics', *American Journal of Physics*, 18 (1950), 239–53.

S. A. Stouffer, 'Intervening Opportunities and Competing Migrants', *JRS*, 2 (1960), 1–26.

F. L. Strodtbeck, 'Equal Opportunity Intervals: A Contribution to the Method of Intervening Opportunity Analysis', *ASR*, 14 (1949), 490–7.

D. B. Suits, *et al.* (Research Seminar in Quantitative Economics), *Econometric Model of Michigan* (Lansing, Michigan: State Resource Planning Division, 1966).

A. Sutherland, 'The Diffusion of an Innovation in Cotton Spinning', *Journal of Industrial Economics*, 7 (1959), 117–35.

H. Thomassen, 'A Growth Model for a State', *Southern Economic Journal* 24 (1957), 123–39.

W. R. Thompson, 'Locational Differences in Inventive Effort and their Determinants', in N.B.E.R., *The Rate and Direction of Inventive Activity* (Princeton U.P., 1961).

B. Thorngren, 'Regional and External Economies' (mimeographed, Stockholm, 1966).

C. M. Tiebout, 'Location Theory, Empirical Evidence and Economic Evolution', *PPRSA*, 3 (1957), 74–86.

C. M. Tiebout, 'An Empirical Regional Input-Output Projection Model: the State of Washington, 1980', *RE&S*, 51 (1969), 334–40.

J. Tinbergen, 'The Spatial Dispersion of Production: a Hypothesis', *Schweizerische Zeitschrift fur Volkwirtschaft und Statistik*, 97 (1961), 412–19.

J. Tinbergen, *Shaping of the World Economy*, Appendix VI, 'An Analysis of World Trade Flows' (New York: Twentieth Century Fund, 1962), 262–93.

J. Tinbergen, 'Sur un Modèle de la Dispersion Géographique de l'Activité Economique', *Revue d'Economie Politique*, 74 (1964), 30–44.

J. Tinbergen, 'The Economic Framework of Regional Planning', in *The Econometric Approach to Development Planning*, ed. E. Malinvaud and H. Wold (Pontificiae Acadamicae Scientarum, Scripta Varia, No. 28) (Amsterdam, 1965).

J. Tinbergen, *Development Planning* (Weidenfeld & Nicolson, 1967).

J. Tinbergen and H. C. Bos, *Mathematical Models of Economic Growth* (New York: McGraw-Hill, 1962).

W. R. Tobler, 'Of Maps and Matrices', *JRS*, 7 (1967), 275–80.

H. Tolosa and T. A. Reiner, 'Economic Programming of a System of Planned Poles', *Economic Geography*, 46 (1970), 449–58.

G. Törnqvist, 'Flows of Information and the Location of Economic Activities', *Geografiska Annaler*, 50 B (1968), 99–107.

B. Tuck, *An Aggregate Income Model of a Semi-Autonomous Economy* (Fairbanks: Federal Field Committee for Development Planning in Alaska, 1967).

E. L. Ullman, 'Regional Development and the Geography of Concentration', *PPRSA*, 4 (1958), 179–98.

J. Vanderkamp, 'Inter-regional Mobility in Canada: A Study of the Time Pattern of Migration', *Canadian Journal of Economics*, 1 (1968), 595–608.

J. Vanderkamp, 'Migration Flows, Their Determinants and the Effects of Return Migration', *JPE*, 79 (1971), 1012–31.

R. Vernon, *Metropolis 1985* (Cambridge, Mass.: Harvard U.P., 1960).

T. Vietorisz, 'Locational Choices in Planning', 39–130, in Universities – N.B.E.R. Conference, *National Economic Planning* (Princeton U.P., 1967).

O. Wärneryd, *Interdependence in Urban Systems* (Gothenburg, 1968).

W. Warntz, *Macrogeography and Income Fronts*, Monograph Series No. 3 (Philadelphia, Pa.: R.S.R.I., 1965).

M. M. Webber, 'The Urban Place and the Nonplace Urban Realm', in *Explorations in Urban Structure*, ed. M. M. Webber (Philadelphia, Pa.: Pennsylvania U.P., 1964), 79–153.

J. G. Williamson, 'Regional Inequalities and the Process of National Development', *EDCC*, 13 (1965), 3–45.

A. G. Wilson, 'Inter-regional Commodity Flows: Entropy Maximising Approaches' (Centre for Environmental Studies, W.P. 19, 1968).

L. Winnick, 'Place Prosperity vs. People Prosperity: Welfare Considerations in the Geographic Redistribution of Economic Activity', in Real Estate Research Program, *Essays in Urban Land Economics in Honor of Leo Grebler* (Los Angeles: U.C.L.A., 1966), 273–83.

J. Wolpert, 'Behavioural Aspects of the Decision to Migrate', *PPRSA*, 15 (1965), 159–69.

M. H. Yeates, 'A Note Concerning the Development of a Geographic Model of Inter-national Trade', *GA*, 1 (1969), 399–404.

G. K. Zipf, 'The P_1P_2/D Hypothesis: On the Inter-city Movement of Persons', *ASR*, 11 (1946), 677–86.

Index of Names

Index of Subjects